UTAH GUN LAW

Third Edition

The FULL TEXT of EVERY UTAH GUN LAW under ONE COVER!

with Interesting, Entertaining, and Easy to Read "PLAIN TALK" Summaries

by Attorney James D. "Mitch" Vilos

Written and published in the United States of America
by James D. Vilos.
ISBN 978-0-9669721-2-2

James D. "Mitch" Vilos, P.C.
PO Box 1148
Centerville, UT 84014
1(800) 530-0222
Mobile and Voice Mail: (801)560-7117
E-Mail: mitchv@firearmslaw.com
Fax: (801)295-3345
Internet Home Pages: www.firearmslaw.com
and utah-injurylaw.com

Pancho's Wisdom

Preserve our Freedom into the next Generation:
Take a Child Shooting!

ABOUT THE COVER: Pancho's pearl-handled 4 & 3/4 inch pistola with both the "Rampant Colt" and Pancho posing menacingly defiant against infringement.

DEDICATION

To my lovely wife Bonnie who has tolerated with good humor my consuming fascination with firearms law and guns ever since I turned forty, chalking it up, I'm sure, to mid-life crises. She astutely recognizes shooting as a relaxing diversion for a trial lawyer who stresses over the rights of the "little guys." You might say she has bought into my excuse of playing cowboy and hunting varmints for medicinal purposes. She even refrains from initiating commitment proceedings when I dawn the garb (sombrero, leather bandoliers, holsters, guns ["gons"] and bullets ["booolets"]) of the notorious pistolero "Pancho Vilos" and shoot it out with the gringos of the Deseret Historical Shootist Society and Wasatch Desperadoes. What a woman, every gun owner's dream!

To my two sons Jason and Evan. Jason completed a mission for the L.D.S. Church in Richmond, Virginia, a fact of which I am very proud. He has a degree in Anthropology and a fascination for the human past as well as an insatiable need to shoot black powder flintlocks. His aspiration is to teach Junior High History. Moving completely to the other end of the political spectrum, my youngest son, Evan, is an accomplished "head-banger" guitarist who began composing rock music at the tender age of 17. He wisely decided to delay superstardom to serve a mission in British Columbia and get his degree in Pre-Law at BYU Hawaii; with a minor in "Surfer Dude!" My sons' pursuit of their passions, almost at the exclusion of everything else, has given me the assurance that it is "O.K." to divert occasionally from the pursuit of earning a living, to "chill out," as the teenagers put it, and do "gun stuff."

To my three exquisitely beautiful daughters, all accomplished dancers, who have leavened my life with music and culture. But back off boys, they know how to shoot! That's why they're known as Pancho's Angels.

Like most Western children outside the "Metro," my kids feel safer and more secure because they have guns and know how to shoot (I wonder if they would fit in the "Eastern Canadian Provinces" of California and New York?)

To my cousins Mike and Randy Rasley who instilled in me the love of shooting and hunting and the courage to speak up for what is right despite the unpopularity of my comments among the politically-correct elite. To my friends and colleagues without whose help this edition could never have been completed Finally, I dedicate this edition of my book to those who have brought to my attention the "unanswered questions" in the first two printings.

And finally, to my children's children for generations to come. May they always be better armed than the multitudes of human predators who respect only the law of the jungle. And may they always live among citizens who are better armed than any tyrant's army.

DISCLAIMER

Every attempt has been made to insure the accuracy of this book but state and federal statutes and regulations are often vague and subject to different interpretations. They are often enacted, amended, replaced and repealed with little notice to the public. Therefore, the author accepts no liability, express or implied, for damages of any kind resulting from reliance on any aspect of this book, including but not limited to, consequential damages. This book should be used as a guide only and not considered as legal advice. Because the gun laws may change from year to year, you may want to ask us to place you on our mailing list (see form in Appendix D) to keep you informed of subsequent editions of this book.

FURTHERMORE, because laws are subject to different interpretations, there is no guarantee that police, wildlife officers, prosecuting attorneys and ultimately the courts will agree with the author's interpretation. Even if the author's interpretation is right, you may still have to pay an attorney to defend you, if charges are brought.

WARNING: Because laws and regulations may change with little or no publicity, the reader is encouraged to access the code section or regulation cited to see if it has been changed since this book was printed. The current Utah Code is located at: http://www.le.utah.gov/~code/code.htm. Although the location on the web of various statutes may change, readers can usually find them by doing a "Google" search for "Utah Code," "Utah Administrative Rules," "United States Code," and "Code of Federal Regulations." Many County and City Ordinances can be accessed through the municipality's web page.

Pancho's Wisdom

Preserve Freedom in (and increase the I.Q. of) our Generation: Take a Soccer Mom Shooting!

"We don't need no stinkin' grammar!"

PREFACE

Pancho's Wisdom

I love God, my family, my country, my guns, my dogs and my truck; oh, and my fellow man, as long as he KEEPS HIS MITS OFF all of the above!

Here it is, the sequel to the sequel! I never imagined I'd be writing Utah's gun law books for this long. **This edition is current through the 2007 Legislative Session.** Its coverage of Utah's gun laws is even more comprehensive than the first two editions.

The most significant event since the last edition was the terrorist attack of September 11, 2001. Life has not been the same for any of us since then. We must not forget, and we must never allow ourselves to be unprepared. Armed citizens are an important part of this preparation, even if politicians, judges and CEO's of large companies don't get it. As the T-shirts say, "the Right to Bear Arms IS homeland security!"

Pancho's Wisdom

Gun confiscation is tyranny; so gun registration is attempted tyranny.

Utah's gun laws are scattered throughout thousands of pages, in dozens of law books that contain countless laws relating to everything from "adoption" to "water rights." Consequently, Utah legislators, county commissioners, city council members, judges, lawyers and police officers (let alone shooters and hunters), have a tough time keeping up with firearms law. To make gun laws easier to find, I boiled off all the "fat," leaving only the gun laws, and then stuck them all under this one cover. Pardon the use of the personal pronouns **"I"** and **"you." I** didn't write this book for the eggheads in academia who would wet their pants before using a gun to defend themselves or their students; **I** wrote it for **you. I** use the word **"you"** to emphasize that it's **your brass that's**

on the line if you either don't **know** the gun laws or don't **obey** them. Me 'n you and Pancho don't need no stinkin' grammar!

This book is the only publication in existence that contains virtually ALL Utah State gun laws in ONE volume. Notice we said "State" gun laws, not "local" ones. Because most city, town and county ordinances are not readily available to the public, it would be impossible for us to compile and comment upon all of them. **To be safe, just assume that all cities and towns prohibit shooting within their boundaries, except at public shooting ranges.** You'll be surprised to learn that the counties have not been given authority by the Utah Legislature to pass gun laws (except relating to spotlighting and night hunting). There are several federal gun laws that impact Utahns. We discuss these in detail in Chapter XIII. In short, this book contains all of the information you need to conduct yourself safely and legally with a firearm anywhere in the state of Utah.

TABLE OF CONTENTS

Pancho's Wisdom

Live by the gun, die by the gun. Sure beats cancer, stroke, emphysema, pneumonia, heart attack, blunt head trauma from a car accident, choking, diabetes, drowning, burning up in a house fire, old age, plane crash, bear attack, black widow bite, snake bite, renal failure, hangin, ... (oh, and REAL cowboys NEVER die of AIDS)!

CHAPTER VI

CHAPTER VII

CHAPTER IX

CHAPTER XII

CHAPTER XIII

Pancho and "Tom" standing guard over our right to keep and bear arms.

CHAPTER I

INTRODUCTION

The Purpose of the Right to Keep and Bear Armss

Pancho's Wisdom

Citizens who quietly watch our freedom eroded, who don't want to rock the "comfort boat" by speaking out (many of whom are couch-potato-sports addicts) are no longer Americans; they are rich, comfortable, over-sexed Romans who foolishly believe Rome could never fall.

The RIGHT to BEAR ARMS is an extremely important right to all free people for at least three reasons: (1) It is a vital "check" on government tyranny, (2) It is an important deterrent to foreign invasion, (3) It allows free citizens to defend themselves from violent criminal attack.

1. A"CHECK" ON GOVERNMENT TYRANNY - The Founding Fathers of our country knew that it is the character of every government to grow and become more powerful - to keep moving on a spectrum from freedom to tyranny. They and their forefathers had witnessed this phenomenon for centuries in Europe culminating with Great Britain's tyranny over the American Colonies.

At the time the Bill of Rights was adopted, several notable citizens commented on the importance of the Right to Bear Arms in protecting the newly formed republic from tyranny:

Whereas civil-rulers, not having their duty to the people duly before them, may attempt to tyrannize, and as military forces, which must be occasionally raised to defend our country, might pervert their power to the injury of their fellow citizens, the people are confirmed by the article in their right to keep and bear their private arms.

Tench Coxe, in Remarks on the First Part of the Amendments to the Federal Constitution.

To preserve liberty it is essential that the whole body of the people always possess arms and be taught alike, especially when young, how to use them.

Richard Henry Lee, Letters from the Federal Farmer to the Republic (1787-1788).

The best we can hope for concerning the people at large is that they be properly armed.

Alexander Hamilton, The Federalist Papers at 184-188.

No freeman shall ever be debarred the use of arms.

Thomas Jefferson, Draft Virginia Constitution, 1776.

Before a standing army can rule, the people must be disarmed; as they are in almost every kingdom in Europe. The supreme power in America cannot enforce unjust laws by the sword; because the whole body of the people are armed, and constitute a force superior to any band of regular troops that can be, on any pretense, raised in the United States. A military force, at the command of Congress, can execute no laws, but such as the people perceive to be just and constitutional; for they will possess the power, and jealousy will instantly inspire the inclination, to resist the execution of a law which appears to them unjust and oppressive.

Noah Webster, An Examination of the Leading Principles of the Federal Constitution (Philadelphia 1787).

Who are the militia? Are they not ourselves? Is it feared, then, that we shall turn our arms each man against his own

> *bosom. Congress have no power to disarm the militia. Their swords, and every other terrible implement of the soldier, are the birthright of an American...[T]he unlimited power of the sword is not in the hands of either the federal or state governments, but, where I trust in God it will ever remain, in the hands of the people.*

Tenche Coxe, The Pennsylvania Gazette, Feb. 20, 1788.

In their Declaration of Independence from Great Britain, the Founding Father's proclaimed when "any Form of Government" begins to destroy its citizens' inalienable rights to "Life, Liberty and Pursuit of Happiness." "It is the Right of the People" to "throw off" [abolish] "Such Government." How do completely disarmed citizens (or even those relegated to archaic, ineffective, sssllllooooowwwww-loading-and-shooting guns) tell a ruthless tyrant, brandishing flesh-consuming weapons that Old Testament prophets saw in their nightmares, "we are abolishing your Hillaryschumerboxerpelosiness because you are trampling on our inalienable rights?" So the Founding Fathers incorporated a number of checks and balances in our Constitution to reduce the chances of the government they founded becoming so powerful that it destroyed the liberty and freedom of it's citizens. One of the most important "checks" on this power was the right to keep and bear arms. The theory was that all of the armed citizens, the "militia," would be better armed than a "standing army" (one assembled by the federal government in times of war). This would prevent tyrants from using the standing army to force a free citizenry to submit to their tyranny. I could reveal my paranoia here and talk about Hillary Clinton and the possibility of a bunch of little Bill Clinton clones running around not knowing yet who their daddy is, but I won't. Let me just say that I have been a witness to some pretty unjustified and brutal (in my humble opinion) tactics of the part of the Bureau of Alcohol, Tobacco and Firearms (BATF or ATF) against ordinary Utah gun owners who posed no threat to the public. One young man had thousands of dollars of his and his brother's property confiscated without a search warrant under the guise of proving that he was "dealing guns without a license." It made me wonder why such a powerful government agency would go after obviously innocent men for such a "rinky dink" crime in a time when there are rumors of terrorists with nuclear weapons within our nation's borders. To make matters worse, prominent members of the United Nations want participating countries (including ours) to completely disarm all of their civilians. Does this kind of stuff upset anyone besides me, myself and Pancho?

So you don't think I pulled these ideas out of Pancho's sombrero, I urge you to buy and read a remarkable book about the political thought that culminated with the drafting of the Second Amendment of the United States Constitution. The book is entitled ***That Every Man Be Armed: the Evolution of a Constitutional Right*** by Stephan Halbrook, Ph.D. It contains a difficult-to-refute analysis of the development of the Second Amendment that persuasively establishes the points I am making in the limited space of this introduction. Dr. Halbrook is a well-respected constitutional scholar. He is the attorney who argued the *Printz* case discussed in Chapter XIII holding part of the "Brady Handgun Violence Prevention Act" unconstitutional. His book was cited with authority in that case in a concurring opinion by Justice Thomas of the United States Supreme Court. Every Utah gun owner should Have Dr. Halbrook's book, my book and John Lott's book, ***More Guns, less Crime*** in their "arsenal." (Yeah, keep 'em in yer gun safe!)

2. A DETERRENT TO FOREIGN INVASION - I spent two years as a missionary in the tiny country of Switzerland which has enjoyed its independence for over two thousand years. Switzerland issues every militia member (every able-bodied man) a machine gun (or some other weapon that's about as much fun to play with) and trains him how to use it. It did this well before the Nazis took control in Germany. Hitler never attacked Switzerland. Golly, I wonder why? Instead he attacked countries all around Switzerland, the citizens of which were not nearly as well armed or prepared for war as the Swiss. Currently Switzerland still issues its citizens FULLY AUTOMATIC weapons and trains them how to use them, while gun-hating urban liberals in Congress are trying to prevent law-abiding U.S. citizens from having SEMI-AUTOMATIC FIREARMS or HIGH CAPACITY MAGAZINES.

It's an awful thought, but suppose someday a powerful enemy "nukes" the U.S. in a few strategic locations and this convinces a whimpy, left-leaning president to surrender (for a "I-won-the-lottery" chunk of money and a bi-sexual "lover" with a hyphenated last name.). With the number of guns we presently own, do you suppose a foreign army could occupy our country maintaining any degree of safety for its troops? Not hardly. Varmint hunting would take on a new meaning! Why attack us if you have to spend so much time dodging bullets you can't enjoy the spoils of war? Comprende how an armed citizenry acts as a deterrent to ambitious foreign despots drooling over our resources?

3. CRIME PREVENTION - An exhaustive analysis of crime statistics compiled by the FBI over an 15 year period involving 3,054 counties in the U.S. proves statistically that gun control does not work. The book containing this research is entitled *More Guns, Less Crime*. The second edition of the book is now available in paper back. Every gun owner should arm himself with this book's findings because it persuasively refutes claims by the uninformed that gun control reduces crime. Briefly, the book convincingly establishes that states and counties that encourage gun ownership and liberally issue concealed weapon permits have significantly less violent crime than states that enact oppressive gun control laws. For example, Vermont, the state with the least restrictive gun laws, in a recent comparison between states, had the nation's lowest rape rate and second lowest murder rate. Additional statistics of interest in Lott's two editions include: States that ban concealed carry have murder rates 127% higher than those with the most liberal concealed-carry laws. (2d ed.p. 47) For each additional year that concealed carry laws were in effect, murders fell by an additional 1.5%, and rape, robbery, and aggravated assault fell by 3% per year. (2d ed.p. 170) After states enacted "must issue" concealed-carry laws, the number of multiple-victim public shootings declined by 84%, deaths declined 90% and injures declined 82%. (2d ed.p. 196) "The very few attacks that still occur in states after enactment of right-to-carry laws tend to occur in particular places where concealed handguns are forbidden, such as schools." (2d ed.p.196) In the first two years after Australia's sweeping gun bans, armed robberies had risen by 73 %, unarmed robberies by 28 %, assaults by 17% and kidnaping by 38%. (2d ed.p. 241) More children died from bicycle accidents than die from all types of firearm accidents. (1st ed., p. 9) Almost twice as many children drown each year in bathtubs as die from all types of firearms accidents. (2nd ed., p. 9) Anyway, you can't expect me to do all your readin' for you, so buy the book and read it yourself.

But Lott's statistics don't tell us red-necked cowpokes what we didn't know all along. . . . bad guys are allergic to lead. Think about it. If you were a "home invader," would you rather break into a home in Washington D.C. where almost nobody has a gun, or Virgin, Utah where every adult is encouraged to own one?

It is extremely important for Utahns, indeed all Americans, to understand the nature of the right to bear arms and the reasons that our Founding Fathers sought to preserve it. Gun control severely restricts the right and erodes our ability to preserve liberty. Many of our nation's gun laws are based upon the false gun control premiss that gun control works. It doesn't.

If Utah would change it's gun laws to a "Vermont type system" our citizens would be much safer. In a nutshell, Vermont allows all non-felon adults, to carry a concealed weapon, even non- residents, unless they are carried with the intent to commit a crime. Until such a system of gun laws is adopted, Utahns need to know and obey this state's gun laws. It is for this purpose that I have written this book.

Pancho's mission is to use his "armor piercing" revolutionary wit to reveal the ridiculous nature of many of the state and most of the federal gun laws. He takes full credit for his controversial opinions. Please do not attribute them to any of the organizations mentioned herein; we do not have authority to speak in their behalf.

Pancho's Wisdom

"Pancho's Wisdom" is PORTERHOUSE STEAK for the SOULS of gun owners (Why settle for Chicken Soup when you can eat RED MEAT!?)

CHAPTER II

HOW THIS BOOK IS ORGANIZED

Pancho's Wisdom

Real Americans Love their Guns 'cause they Cherish their Liberty!

A. OVERVIEW OF ALL THE CHAPTERS

There ain't nothin' more boring than reading code section after code section in a law book. (Actually, there is - knocking over bowling pins with a bowling ball rather than bullets!) So I decided to break up the monotony by throwing in some fun stuff like Pancho's Wisdom. I added so much salsa to this edition that I worried it might get a little confusing, so I put this chapter up front as kind of a road map. Even the most experienced shooters and hunters will be astonished at how little they know about Utah gun law when they take the test in Chapter III called the Gun Owners' Gauntlet. You too may have many misconceptions. So run the Gauntlet if you dare. The answers are in Chapter IV.

No gun owner wants to unintentionally commit a felony and lose his or her right to bear arms. Anyone with a conscience knows it's a crime to murder, rape, or assault another person. In contrast, the acts prohibited by many gun control laws are only crimes BECAUSE THE GOVERNMENT SAYS SO! If you haven't read the law, you might not know that some of the things you do with guns are felonies. In Chapter V, we warn of more than twenty ways gun owners can commit a felony without realizing it.

The "meat" of this book are the parts of the Utah Constitution, Utah Code Annotated and Utah Administrative Code ("Utah

Regulations") comprising what we call "Utah Gun Law." Our analysis begins with Utah's Constitution in Chapter VI and then covers everything from weapons laws to the law of self defense. These chapters appear as follows:

CHAPTER VI: Utah's Constitution
CHAPTER VII: Utah's Weapon Laws
CHAPTER VIII: Concealed Weapon Permits
CHAPTER IX: Hunting Laws and Regulations
CHAPTER X: Civil Liability Arising from Use of Firearms
CHAPTER XI: The Law of Self-Defense (Criminal and Civil)
CHAPTER XII: Miscellaneous Gun Laws
CHAPTER XIII: The Brady Law and other Important Federal Statutes
CHAPTER XIV: Civil Rights Law Suits to Enforce the Right to Bear Arms
CHAPTER XV: Conclusion
CHAPTER XVI: About the Author
CHAPTER XVII: You Just Might be a GUNNUT if…

B. THE BREAKDOWN OF EACH CHAPTER

Each chapter begins with an explosion of wisdom compliments of your pontificating pistolero, Pancho. Then every law reported in the chapter is carefully dissected and explained using the following subtitles:

- Code Section or Regulation Number and Title
- "Plain Talk" Summaries
- The Actual Text of the Law

and, if necessary,

- Our Commentary
- Proposed Changes in the Law

1. Pancho's Wisdom - Today's politicos know that wielding a pen with wisdom is a powerful weapon. Pancho blasts weak-minded-anti-self-defense liberals with clever logic containing more foot pounds of energy than a .50 Cal. BMG. Pancho's hot and spicy bumper-stickers-in-a-book express the sentiments of every true Westerner. Like picante, Pancho's quips burn gun haters from the lips to the hips. His persuasive, yet entertaining blossoms of "blam!" are interspersed throughout the book to activate your axons. Look fer 'em sportin' this design:

Pancho's Wisdom

If, <u>after I die</u>, I qualify for the job of "Destroying Angel"... I want FIRST DUBS ON HOLLYWOOD!!!!!!!!!!

2. <u>Numbered Code Section or Regulation and Title</u> - Utah gun laws appear as either code sections (Utah Code Annotated, abbreviated U.C.A.), or regulations (abbreviated by a capital "R" followed by a number). After the number, both code sections and regulations have a descriptive title. For example, the title of the state spotlighting code section looks like this, **"U.C.A. 23-13-17. Spotlighting of coyote, red fox, striped skunk, and raccoon—County ordinances—permits."** This means Utah Code Annotated, Title 23, Chapter 13, Section 17 contains the state spotlighting statute. When we say, "Utah gun law," we mean only the state law. We are not talking about county or city ordinances. Although many counties have enacted spotlighting ordinances under the authority of and patterned after the state statute, this book does not contain county ordinances. To make the book easier to use as a reference guide, we organized every chapter like this:

a. Code sections (designated by "U.C.A." e.g. U.C.A. 76-3-1) generally appear before regulations (designated by "R" e.g. R724-3-1).
b. Both code sections and regulations appear numerically within any given chapter usually beginning with the smallest numbers first.
c. For some unexplained reason, regulations relating to the same subject matter as code sections often repeat verbatim the text of the code section. When this occurs we will include the code section, but omit the corresponding regulation.
d. Sometimes when a code section is so closely related to a regulation, we break the pattern referred to above and

simply lump the two together. This allows the reader to read the entire law covering the subject matter without having to skip around in the book.

e. When a code section is long and many of the subsections do not contain "gun law," we cut these subsections out to spare you the bother of digging through depleted soil. You know we cut something out when you see the three little dots [. . .] together.

f. Occasionally, we insert a federal law at the end of a discussion of state law when the two are closely related. The penalties for violating the state law may not be as severe as federal law and we wanted to alert you. For example, under state law it's a misdemeanor to carry a concealed weapon into an airport. The same act under the anti-terrorist provisions of federal law triggers severe felony-like penalties. See the Commentary under the discussion of U.C.A. 76-10-529.

g. Sections Omitted - Sections are omitted for several reasons including (1) they have been repealed (2) they are primarily regulatory (eg. describing how a board or committee is set up) and (3) they have noting to do with using a firearm. Omissions get the [. . .] sign.

3. "Plain Talk" Summaries - Unfortunately, most laws are written in "legalese," a language spoken and written only by lawyers. Legalese is similar to English, but boring, complicated, convoluted, lengthy, circumlocutious, redundant, and confusing to boot. In this book we translate legalese into "Plain Talk." This translation follows the title but precedes the actual text of the code section or regulation in a double-bordered box that looks like this:

"PLAIN TALK"

The title appears in large, bold print, and the Plain Talk translation appears in a different font to help you distinguish our translations and commentary from the actual text of the code section or regulation. We have not translated every subsection of every gun law into Plain Talk. Some subsections need no explanation and others are simply too dull and irrelevant to our discussion to include in the Plain Talk summaries.

4. Actual Text of Code Section or Regulation -The actual text of the code sections and regulations is plain, non-bold print like this paragraph preceded by a bold heading indicating "**ACTUAL TEXT**." We have not drawn single or double-bordered boxes around the actual text of the law.

5. Commentary - Sections entitled "Commentary" compliment or ridicule and propose changes to laws and regulations. These comments are enclosed in a single-lined box like this:

COMMENTARY

6. Proposed Amendments - Bad and ugly gun laws should be amended or repealed. When legislators introduce amendments to existing state law they use a specific format. Undesirable language is stricken out by using the ~~strike out~~ key. New statutory language is inserted as <u>underlined</u> text. The changes proposed in this book use the same format. Send a copy of this book to your legislator so he or she can submit the changes during the next legislative session.

7. Appendices -The appendices contain a parental consent form and order forms for books and updates. Parents can use the form in Appendix A to give their minor children permission to possess a firearm for certain purposes such as target practice, farming and ranching activities. It complies with both Utah and federal gun law (see discussion on federal gun law requiring minors to have written permission from their parents to possess a handgun, Chapter XIII). Appendix B contains an order form for additional copies of this edition. You may want to purchase copies for your friends and legislators. Appendix C is an order form for the ***Utah Spotlighting and Night Hunting Manual*** that reveals how and where hunters can use spotlights at night to hunt certain predators and varmints. Use Appendix D to request to be informed when future editions of this book are published (or simply send me an email). Appendix E contains a request to be notified of the publishing of my new book exclusively about Utah's law of self defense.

Appendix F will keep you from frying your brain trying to sort out all of the state and federal laws governing when and how juveniles can possess guns and ammo. Appendix G is a copy of a contour map showing the forest service property in Davis County subject to a federal "No Shooting" order. Appendix H contains the convenient reference guide Quick Draw Gun Law.

CHAPTER III

GUN OWNERS' GAUNTLET

How Well Do You Understand Utah Gun Law?

Pancho's Wisdom

You just might be a GUNNUT if yer girlfriend thinks the smell of Hoppes No. 9 is yer AFTERSHAVE!

Run the Gauntlet by answering the following questions about Utah gun law. The answers are in Chapter IV. Careful, there have been subtle changes made to these questions since the last edition to fully test the degree to which you understand these topics! Remember, unless otherwise stated, these questions and answers relate solely to conduct WITHIN the boundaries of the State of Utah.

1. **QUESTION:** Under the Utah Constitution, the right to bear arms is a COLLECTIVE right that can only be exercised by members of the Utah National Guard.

   ❒ True ❒ False

2. **QUESTION:** A person who does not have a concealed weapon permit may legally carry a gun containing bullets in a holster on a public street ("open carry") as long as it is not concealed and is "unloaded" (even though it contains ammunition).

   ❒ True ❒ False

3. **QUESTION:** A person with a concealed weapon permit may carry his firearm openly ("open carry") or concealed and, in either event, may carry it fully loaded.

   ❒ True ❒ False

4. **QUESTION:** Under Utah law, a gun "containing ammunition" is not necessarily "loaded."

   ❒ True ❒ False

5. **QUESTION:** A double action revolver is considered loaded even if there is not a bullet aligned with the barrel, if the next cylinder to rotate to line up with the barrel contains a cartridge.

   ❒ True ❒ False

6. **QUESTION:** A person, without a concealed weapon permit, can keep a loaded gun in his car as long as it is locked in either the console, trunk or glove compartment.

   ❒ True ❒ False

7. **QUESTION:** Utah's public colleges and universities have no legal authority to prevent students, faculty or other college employees with concealed weapon permits from possessing a firearm for self defense on campus.

   ❒ True ❒ False

8. **QUESTION:** Because the state of Utah has given cities and counties the authority to enact ordinances that will preserve the "health, welfare and safety" of their citizens, cities and counties have the authority to regulate firearms even more restrictively than state statutes.

   ❒ True ❒ False

9. **QUESTION:** A Utah concealed weapon permit allows you to conceal a pocket knife with a three-inch blade.

   ❒ True ❒ False

10. **QUESTION:** When certifying students to carry a concealed weapon, Mitch places HEAVY emphasis on the laws of self and home defense because most of his criminal cases arise from incidents in which police and prosecutors allege the defendant has threatened or used more force than legally justified under the circumstances.

    ❒ True ❒ False

11. **QUESTION:** If you make it a habit of buying and selling used guns at a profit, you could be indicted for a federal felony.

    ❐ True ❐ False

12. **QUESTION:** If I am charged for threatening, shooting at or shooting someone in self defense and my attorney wins a "Not Guilty" verdict, the government prosecuting the case will have to reimburse me for attorney fees.

    ❐ True ❐ False

13. **QUESTION:** If you have justification to use deadly force to defend yourself and your assailant survives the shooting, you should make sure he is dead before the police arrive for at least two reasons (1) dead men tell no lies and (2) damages in a wrongful death lawsuit are often not as high as for a serious injury.

    ❐ True ❐ False

14. **QUESTION:** Likewise, if you shoot someone trying to break into your home and they fall outside, you should drag them into your home before the police arrive!

    ❐ True ❐ False

15. **QUESTION:** A person who has a guardianship or conservatorship placed over him or his financial estate may lose his right to bear arms.

    ❐ True ❐ False

16. **QUESTION:** A person who has taken another person's prescription drug may not legally possess a handgun.

    ❐ True ❐ False

17. **QUESTION:** A person without a concealed weapon permit, who is otherwise hunting legally, may conceal a handgun if its barrel length exceeds 4 inches.

    ❐ True ❐ False

18. **QUESTION:** To be convicted of "carrying" a concealed weapon, a person must have a weapon hidden somewhere on his body or under his clothing.

    ❐ True ❐ False

19. **QUESTION:** If you are going through a divorce and your wife lies about you threatening her with a gun, or she claims she's afraid of you simply because you have a dozen or so guns, your right to bear arms is in serious jeopardy and you had better tell your divorce lawyer to consult immediately with an expert in firearms law.

❒ True ❒ False

20. **QUESTION:** It's legal to shoot from a vehicle as long as the vehicle is at least 200 feet from a highway, you don't shoot across the highway, and you are at least 600 feet from a building.

❒ True ❒ False

21. **QUESTION:** If you accidently shoot someone, your homeowner's insurance company will probably cover your defense as well as any damages up to the policy limit. However, most, if not all insurance policies exclude (won't cover) an intentional shooting.

❒ True ❒ False

22. **QUESTION:** Guns are prohibited in national forests.

❒ True ❒ False

23. **QUESTION:** If one of your friendly postal employees goes "postal" while you are sending a package, you'll just have to die along with that person's expendable co-workers.

❒ True ❒ False

24. **QUESTION:** A Utah citizen 21 years of age or older with a clean criminal record MUST be issued a concealed weapon permit, whether she has a good reason for having one or not.

❒ True ❒ False

25. **QUESTION:** A concealed weapon permit is valid throughout the state without restriction.

❒ True ❒ False

26. **QUESTION:** A person who has been acquitted of murder charges on the grounds of self defense, cannot be sued by the heirs of the person he killed.

    ❐ True ❐ False

27. **QUESTION:** Cities and towns have been given authority by the Legislature to pass ordinances regulating the discharge of firearms, but the counties can only pass ordinances regulating spotlighting and night hunting.

    ❐ True ❐ False

28. **QUESTION:** The concept of repentance is recognized under Utah state law in that a person convicted of a crime can usually have his criminal record cleansed after a specific length of time, depending on the seriousness of the crime.

    ❐ True ❐ False

29. **QUESTION:** You pass through a school zone on the way home from the deer hunt. Your deer rifle is unloaded and zipped in a gun case behind your seat. You do not have a concealed weapon permit. You are guilty of a crime punishable up to 5 years in prison and if convicted, you could lose the right to possess a firearm or ammunition for the rest of your life.

    ❐ True ❐ False

30. **QUESTION:** Federal law prohibits a gun dealer from selling a handgun to an individual under the age of 21. However, a Utah resident who is not a gun dealer can sell a handgun to another Utah resident who is 18 years of age or older but less than 21 years of age if the non-dealer did not have the intent to resell the gun to the resident 18 - 21 year old at the time the non-dealer bought the gun.

    ❐ True ❐ False

31. **QUESTION:** You can hunt on a farmer's hay field as long as it is not posted "No Hunting!"

    ❐ True ❐ False

32. **QUESTION:** Neither an individual nor a small group of persons can have much effect on the government in which they live.

❐ True ❐ False

Pancho's Wisdom

Armed Patriot and Proud of it!

CHAPTER IV

ANSWERS TO GUN OWNERS' GAUNTLET

Pancho's Wisdom

Pancho defines "Depression" as "being out of ammo."

1. ANSWER: FALSE. Utah's Constitution, Article I, Section 6 guarantees the right to keep and bear arms to each INDIVIDUAL Utahn. Article I, Section 1 tells us that the right to defend ourselves in an "inalienable" (fundamental) right. Chapter VI.

2. ANSWER: TRUE. See discussion of U.C.A. 76-10-505 in Chapter VII. Theoretically, anyone can "open carry" with an UNLOADED gun, but he must be careful no one claims that wearing a gun is intended as a threat.

3. ANSWER: TRUE. People with a concealed weapon permit can carry either openly or concealed with a loaded gun. See "Commentary" following discussion of U.C.A. 76-10-505 in Chapter VII. Unfortunately, not all cops or prosecutors believe this yet. Therefore, although Pancho lets his pistolas show from time to time to make a political statement, he carries a **concealed lawyer** around wherever he goes!

4. **ANSWER: TRUE.** See U.C.A. 76-10-502. When weapon deemed loaded. Chapter VII. In other words, a Glock 17 with a fully-loaded 17 round pre-ban magazine is" unloaded" under Utah law as long as there is no round in the chamber! Fun, huh?

5. ANSWER: TRUE. See U.C.A. 76-10-502. When weapon deemed loaded. Chapter VII.

6. ANSWER: FALSE. Without a concealed weapon permit, a person may not have a loaded gun in his vehicle, period. U.C.A. 76-10-505 in Chapter VII. Although Utah law does not specifically address locked glove boxes or consoles, those places are off limits for non-permit holders. See definition of "securely encased" U.C.A. 76-10-501(18) (Chapter VII).

The key to carrying a gun in a car WITHOUT a concealed weapon permit is to carry it (1) UNLOADED and (2) NOT CONCEALED. Example: Carry it on your passenger seat with a fully-loaded magazine in the gun but without a bullet in the chamber. When exiting the car, the gun could be "securely encased to prevent theft by putting it, still "unloaded," into a completely zipped up "gun rug," whether or not locked, under the car seat. It could not be legally placed in the console or glove box. "Car Carry" is complicated stuff unless you have a concealed weapon permit.

WITH a Concealed Weapon Permit, however, the weapon could be carried loaded AND concealed anywhere in the car, including the glove box or console. U.C.A. 76-10-505 and 523, Chapter VII.

7. ANSWER: TRUE. In September of 2006, the Utah Supreme Court held that the University of Utah's "No Weapon" policy violated U.C.A. 63-98-102. See Commentary after U.C.A. 76-10-500 in Chapter VII.

8. ANSWER: FALSE. Utah's Uniformity Law keeps gun-hating urban liberal mayors and councilmen from legislating gun owner's rights out of existence. See U.C.A. 76-10-500(2), Chapter VII.

9. ANSWER: TRUE. See U.C.A. 76-10-523 excepting concealed weapon holders from the applications of sections 504(1)(a)(b) in Chapter VII. These statutes refer to "weapons," not just "firearms."

10. ANSWER: TRUE. In most of my criminal cases, the prosecutor claims the defendant's conduct with a firearm was "over the top" of what was reasonably justifiable self defense under the circumstances. To spare my students the anguish of being charged criminally, I focus heavily on the law of self defense in my concealed carry classes. See Chapter XI on Self Defense.

11. ANSWER: TRUE. As ridiculous as it sounds, you could be indicted for the felony of dealing guns without a federal gun dealer's license (FFL). See discussion in Chapter XIII of 18 U.S.C. § 922(a)(1).

12. ANSWER: FALSE - It is a question of fact whether or not a person claiming self defense acted reasonably under the circumstances. Judges and juries decide questions of fact based upon evidence presented under oath at the trial in the case. Therefore, if there is enough evidence that a defendant could be convicted (eg. the bad guy says defendant started the fight and there were no other witnesses), it is usually "fair game" to put the defendant through the ugly expense of a preliminary hearing or even a trial unless he is willing to agree to a plea bargain. So it's the phrase "reasonably believes" in the self defense statutes (see Chapter XI) that justifies police and prosecutors in bringing charges even if the defendants are ultimately acquitted. Most self defense schools suggest that if you are going to carry a gun for self defense, you had better begin building a fund to pay defense costs if the unspeakable occurs and you live through it.

13. ANSWER: FALSE! - You may NEVER use more force than is reasonably necessary to stop deadly force against you or a third person. Once the threat of unlawful force against you is over, you must stop your use of force. If your killing of an assailant is "overkill" you could be charged and convicted of manslaughter or murder. Furthermore, witness tampering and obstruction of justice are serious crimes in and of themselves. Read Chapter XI carefully and anticipate with baited breath (not breath that smells like bait) my new book which focuses exclusively on the law of self defense.

14. ANSWER: Again FALSE! - Ever watch CSI? Don't you suppose the forensic people will know your carpet-burned assailant was dragged across the sidewalk and onto your white carpet? Again, tampering with evidence is an attempt to obstruct justice and suggests you have a guilty conscience about what you did. Don't do it! Read Chapter XI as well as my highly anticipated book about Utah's law of Self Defense. And before I forget, you "brass hounds" had better remember the conviction of U.S. Border Patrol Agent Ramos who shot a drug smuggler and then picked up his brass. Tampering with evidence is a serious crime and will hurt your case.

15. ANSWER: TRUE - A person who is protected by a conservatorship or guardianship must be either mentally or physically incapacitated under the Utah Probate Code. If the person is mentally incapacitated this could be construed to be the same thing as mentally defective within the meaning of U.C.A. 76-10-503(1)(b)(vii) and federal law 18 U.S.C. Sec. 922 (g)(4). My computerized legal research did not reveal that the term "mentally defective" was defined anywhere in the United States Code or Code of Federal Regulations. See Chapters VII and XIII. As more mass shootings are committed by persons with some type of mental disorder, the more broadly the courts will interpret the term "mentally defective" against gun owners.

16. ANSWER: TRUE - U.C.A. 76-10-503(1)(b)(3), Chapter VII. (What if a patrol officer has a rough day and takes one of his wife's anti-inflammatories because he has a backache. Did the Legislature intend to disarm him?)

17. ANSWER: TRUE - U.C.A. 76-10-504(4), Chapter VII.

18. ANSWER: FALSE - See *State v. Williams*, 636 P.2d 1092 (Utah 1981) discussed in Chapter VII. The defendant was convicted of "carrying a concealed weapon" for concealing a pistol in a bag on the passenger's seat of his car. The court held that a concealed weapon need not be concealed under a person's clothing, if it is easily ACCESSIBLE to him or her.

19. ANSWER: TRUE - See in Chapter XIII the Commentary relating to 18 USC 922(g)(8) [protective orders after notice and a hearing] and (9) [convictions of "misdemeanor domestic violence."]

20. ANSWER: FALSE - You can't shoot from a vehicle, PERIOD (See U.C.A. 76-10-508 in Chapter VII). The only exception is for those who are disabled within the meaning of Utah law (See R657-12-4 and the Big Game proclamation provided by the Utah Division of Wildlife Resources).

21. ANSWER: TRUE - Most homeowner liability insurance policies cover you for acts of <u>negligence</u> up to your policy limits. You do not have to be home or on your own property for this coverage to apply. If you check with your insurance agent, you might be surprised at how affordable a million dollar "umbrella policy" is on your cars and home. It's called an "umbrella policy" because it "covers" or is added to your basic coverage. If you have $250,000 coverage on your basic policy, for a fairly affordable premium you can add another $1 Million to it giving you $1.25 Million dollars in protection in the event you are sued for negligent use of a firearm (or automobile or whatever). The insurance contract may allow you to choose the lawyer you want to represent you.

MOST insurance contracts will not cover you for injuring someone intentionally. Here's the argument I use to persuade my client's homeowner's insurance company to cover my client after a defensive incident. Although he or she may have intentionally pulled the trigger, his intent was simply to stop the progression of deadly force against himself or others, NOT to injure. If an unjustifiable or unforseen injury occurred, I argue , at worst, it involved the negligent, not intentional, use of excessive force. See discussion in Chapter X.

22. ANSWER: FALSE - However, there are some restrictions on shooting (as opposed to possessing) guns in national forests. See discussion entitled 36 CFR 261.10 & 261.58 [Shooting and Hunting in National Forests] Chapter XIII.

23. ANSWER: TRUE - The federal government has declared postal property to be a "weapon free zone" so that patrons and employees can enjoy a false sense of violence-free-soft-cuddlies while sending and handling Easter Bunny mail. Refer to 18 USC 930, "Possession of firearms and dangerous weapons in Federal facilities" and 39 C.F.R. § 232.1, "Conduct on postal property" in Chapter XIII.

24. ANSWER: TRUE - This is why they call Utah and over 30 other states "Must Issue" States. See discussion in Chapter VIII and U.C.A. 53-5-704.

25. ANSWER: FALSE - Notice the word "except" after the phrase "throughout the state without exception" in section U.C.A. 53-5-704. Therefore, even concealed weapon holders cannot carry weapons into "secured areas" at courthouses, prisons, jails, airports and federal buildings. These issues are discussed in detail primarily in Chapters VII, VIII and XIII.

26. ANSWER: FALSE - A "Not Guilty" verdict does not protect you in a later civil lawsuit for damages. You can be found innocent of murder, but still be held liable in money damages for killing or injuring another. If you don't believe us, ask O.J.

Simpson! On the other hand, it's arguable that a guilty verdict of murder could be used against the guilty person in a later civil case. See discussion in Chapters X and XI.

27. ANSWER: TRUE - See the discussion in U.C.A. 10-8-47 and Chapter IX. I had a client who was arrested for violating Salt Lake County's ordinance prohibiting the discharge of a firearm anywhere in the county except shooting ranges. The Salt Lake County prosecutor dismissed the case when I proved to him that counties have never been given the authority to regulate the discharge of firearms except during night hunting.

28. ANSWER: TRUE - If they have gone without an offense or conviction for a long time, even felons can sometimes have their criminal records wiped clean. The process is known as "EXPUNGEMENT." Through expungement, a convicted criminal can have his civil rights restored. See U.C.A. 77-18-10 *et.seq.*, Chapter XII. However, those convicted of a capital felony, first degree felony, second degree forcible felony or a sexual act against a minor, can forget about expungement. Those not eligible for an expungement may nevertheless be able to get a court to reduce their convictions to a misdemeanor through a process known as a "402 Motion" (check with a local attorney for details). Finally, I am not aware of any process by which a FEDERAL felony may be expunged short of a Presidential Pardon.

29. ANSWER: TRUE - You cannot possess a firearm in a school zone, 18 U.S.C. § 922(q), Chapter XIII, even if it's unloaded, unless it's locked in a gun rack or case. Because the gun, in this example, is in a zipper case (the way many deer hunters carry their guns in Utah) and not in a locked container, you would be guilty of a crime punishable of up to 5 years in prison, 18 U.S.C. 924(4). If convicted of a crime punishable for more than one year in prison, you cannot legally possess a gun or ammunition, 18 U.S.C. § 922(g). If federal agents set up road blocks in school zones during the 10 day Utah deer hunt, they could use this law to send ten thousand Utah deer hunters to prison and strip them of their right to bear arms! Fortunately, concealed weapon permit holders are exempt from this outrageously overly-broad federal statute (see discussion of the Gun Free School Zone Act in Chapter XIII).

30. ANSWER: TRUE - As long as the non-dealer isn't acting as a "middle man" to help gun dealers sell handguns and handgun ammo to individuals under 21 years of age. The non-dealer cannot have the intent to transfer the handgun to an individual who is less than 21 years of age at the time he, the non-dealer, purchases the gun from the dealer (see Chapter XIII). This assumes also, that the seller is not aware of any facts that would make the 18-20 year old buyer a "prohibited person" under state (U.C.A. 76-10-503) or federal (18 USC 922(g)) law.

31. ANSWER: FALSE - A cultivated field is PRESUMED to be posted "No Trespassing." (See U.C.A. 23-20-14, Chapter IX.)

32. ANSWER: FALSE - See discussion in the Conclusion of this book (Chapter XV).

CHAPTER V

FELONY TRAPS FOR GUN OWNERS

Pancho's Wisdom

IF judges had S-T-R-E-T-C-H-E-D the Second Amendment as far as they've S-T-R-E-T-C-H-E-D the First Amendment (eg. Adult Porn = Freedom of Speech), it would be a CRIME for gun owners NOT to shoot rapists, robbers, kidnapers and carjackers ON SIGHT!

Felons do not have the right to bear arms under either federal or state law. Unfortunately, there are several ways shooters and hunters can unwittingly commit a felony and lose their right to bear arms. Many state felonies can be expunged (cleansed off your record) after a certain number of years (see Chapter XII for details), but federal felonies can't. This chapter alerts Utah gun owners to some of the ways gun owners could inadvertently commit a felony and consequently lose the right to carry a firearm.

1. Point a gun at someone without legal justification (eg. not in legal self defense - see Chapter XI). If you **point a gun** at someone and you are **not justified**, you can be charged with aggravated assault, a **third degree felony**.

2. Conceal a handgun while riding the UTA OR TRAX without a concealed weapon permit (U.C.A. 76-10-1504, Chapter VII).

3. Knowingly possess a firearm that has had the serial number filed off of it or altered. This is a FIVE YEAR FEDERAL FELONY (**18 U.S.C. 922(k)**, Chapter VII).

4. Make a profit buying and selling guns without a gun dealer's license (See Chapter XIII, 18 USC §922(a)(1)).

5. Let your 17-year-old neighbor handle your UNLOADED, fully automatic M-16 machine gun for ten seconds to admire it (See 76-10-509.4(2) and (4), Chapter VII). (This assumes you have complied with the federal laws that permit you to own and possess a fully automatic weapon.)

6. Intentionally give false information to a gun dealer when purchasing a handgun (U.C.A. 76-10-527, Chapter VII).

7. As a gun dealer, sell a handgun to a person whom you know cannot legally own or possess one (U.C.A. 76-10-527, Chapter VII).

8. Buy a handgun from a dealer with the intent to transfer it to someone you know can't legally own or possess one, for example, a felon or a person under 21 years of age (U.C.A. 76-10-527, Chapter VII). This is now referred to as a "straw purchase."

9. Take someone else's prescription medication or possess illegal drugs and possess a firearm (U.C.A. 76-10-503(3)(a)(iii), Chapter VII).

10. Concealed weapon permit holder or not, attempt to take your gun into a "secured area" of a jail, prison, mental institution or courthouse. Most offenses under these sections are third degree felonies if committed "knowingly or intentionally"(U.C.A. 76-10-523.5, 76-8-311.1, 76-8-311.3, and 78-7-6, Chapter VII). It's a big-time federal felony to attempt to take a firearm into the passenger compartment of a commercial airliner (49 U.S.C. 46505, Chapter VII).

11. As a parent, get convicted twice of allowing your problem child, who has been convicted of a violent crime such as manslaughter, rape, robbery, burglary, or house breaking, to possess a firearm (U.C.A. 76-10-509.6, Chapter VII).

12. Possess a firearm if you are under indictment for a felony (U.C.A. 76-10-503(1)(b)(i), Chapter VII).

13. As a minor, pick up the Road Warrior's UNLOADED sawed-off shotgun, having a barrel length of less than 18 inches (U.C.A. 76-10-509.4, Chapter VII).

14. Take a box of bullets to your little brother, who is incarcerated in a mental health facility for drug abuse, to encourage

him to get well soon, so you can go shooting together [Duh!] (U.C.A. 76-8-311.3, Chapter VII).

15. It's a FELONY to intentionally or RECKLESSLY and UNLAWFULLY injure or kill any of the following species of wildlife:

- bison,
- big horn sheep,
- rocky mountain goats,
- moose,
- bear,
- a member of any endangered species (see discussion in Chapter IX),
- elk, (one fellow I know was charged with a felony for shooting an elk a few hundred yards outside his poorly-defined area),
- threatened species (see discussion in Chapter IX),
- trophy deer with an antler spread of 24 inches,
- a pronghorn antelope buck with horns exceeding 14 inches (U.C.A. 23-13-1, U.C.A. 23-20-4, Chapter IX).

16. Illegally and intentionally or recklessly kill or injure two or more non-trophy deer or antelope. U.C.A. 23-20-4.5 gives animals an arbitrary monetary value. If the value exceeds $500, killing the animal without a valid hunting license is a felony. However, for the animals that have been given an arbitrary value of less than $500, if you kill enough animals in that species to equal or exceed $500, you have also committed a felony. Non-trophy deer and antelope have been given an arbitrary value of $400. Poaching two of either of these species, is a felony. The same is true for intentionally or recklessly killing or injuring the following combinations of animals without a license or permit:

a. a non-trophy antelope and a non-trophy deer,
b. a bobcat and two turkeys,
c. five turkeys and a loon (no, we're not talking about O.J.'s legal "dream team!"), and
d. one swan a diving, two sandhill cranes a craning, three Utah milk snakes a milking, one Utah mountain king

snake a reigning (without even killing a partridge in a pear tree). See U.C.A. 23-20-4(4)(f), Chapter IX.

17. You shoot and kill what, at a distance, looks like a "monster" of a moose with gigantic antlers. When you get closer you realize it was just an average moose with embarrassingly small antlers. Because a bull moose hunt is a once-in-a-lifetime hunt, you abandon the moose without tagging it in hopes of finding the bull with enormous antlers you saw while scouting. It's a felony to intentionally abandon the flesh of protected wildlife with assigned values greater than $500 (U.C.A. 23-20-4(1)(c)(ii)).

18. You are deer hunting in Hackberry Canyon in Kane County, with your trusty 7mm strapped over your shoulder. All of a sudden, crawling on the damp rocks on a cliff above the trail, you see the elusive Kanab Ambersnail (Oxyloma Haydeni Kanabensis). You think to yourself how amusing it would be to splatter this slimy mollusk all over the hieroglyphs of this forty-foot-high red rock wall. Now what are you going to do, kiddies?

You carefully place the cross hairs of your Zeiss 16 power scope on the snail's oviduct to avoid the risk of wounding your prey! The adrenaline is rushing and your heart is pounding. In fact, you have "snail fever," so you eject two cartridges without firing. Finally, you get a hold of yourself and squeeze the trigger like your Boy Scout merit badge instructor taught you. You hear the gun's report and feel the dull jolt against your shoulder. The snail disappears from the scope's image. You see a light spray of what appears to be soy sauce descending in the midst of the sun's rays penetrating the narrow gorge. Without warning, three Special Forces Officers from the Division of Wildlife Resources, suddenly rappel from the top of the cliff. They are clad in a full array of bullet-proof vests, black hoods and combat boots. They immediately subdue and handcuff you. As they bring you shamefully before the Federal United States District Court, Central Division, you hang your head as the Judge asks you, "Are you guilty of a felony?" ANSWER: Yes. The Kanab Ambersnail is listed as an endangered species that inhabits Kane County. It's a felony to kill a member of an endangered species, U.C.A. 23-20-4. Kane County residents in the mood for escargot, BEWARE! No wonder there are no French restaurants in Kanab!

19. Shoot carp in the shallow waters of Muddy Creek with your .458 Winchester Magnum, knowing that endangered Razorback suckers are swimming nearby. See U.C.A. 23-20-4, and discussion of endangered species, Chapter IX. See also U.C.A. 76-2-103 that defines "intentional," "knowingly, or with knowledge," and "recklessly or maliciously" also in Chapter IX. You don't necessarily have to INTEND to kill, if you "consciously disregard a substantial and unjustifiable risk" that your actions will result in the death of an endangered species. If there are endangered fish mixed in with carp, which are not endangered, and you shoot, although you can't see what you are shooting at, you could be found guilty of a felony.

20. Simply possess a pipe bomb, U.C.A. 76-10-306(1), (although this doesn't involve using a firearm, we threw it in as a bonus, because some gun enthusiasts like to hear things go "Bang!")

21. Obviously stealing a firearm is a felony (second degree, U.C.A. 76-6-412.) Did you realize that "borrowing" one from a friend without his permission without the intent to deprive him of it permanently is a third degree felony (U.C.A.76-6-404.5. Wrongful Appropriation)?

22. I represented two young men who accidently shot a trophy bull elk in a spike-only area. It was their first big-game hunt without their parents and they hadn't surveyed the area boundaries in order to fully understand the ambiguities found in the hunting proclamation. They were both charged with felonies! Fortunately we were able to convince the prosecutor that they had made an innocent mistake and had not intentionally killed the giant bull outside their area boundaries. Most Utah hunters do not realize that they can be charged with a felony for intentionally or recklessly and unlawfully (like shooting before or after daylight) killing certain big game animals even though they have a license to hunt that particular species. See U.C.A. 23-20-4, Chapter IX.

23. Sell a gun to a minor outside the presence of his parent, e.g., two 17-year-olds trade a gun for a car (See U.C.A. 76-10-509.9, Chapter VII).

24. Kiss your boyfriend under the mistletoe hanging in the doorway of the local bus station (one foot in the bus station and

one foot out) while having an unloaded pistol in your purse (yes, you read it right, UNLOADED), U.C.A. 76-10-1507, Chapter VII.

25. Pretend you're John Dillinger and stick your grandpa's old sawed-off shotgun down your pants (even if you have a concealed weapon permit). It's a second degree felony to conceal a sawed-off shotgun or sawed-off rifle (Chapter VII, U.C.A. 76-10-504 (2)).

CHAPTER VI

UTAH'S CONSTITUTION

PANCHO'S JUDICIAL LITERACY EXAM:

(No judge should be appointed if he/she can't answer this question right!)

"Shall not be infringed" means (Hint: there is only ONE correct answer):

- Congress and State Legislatures can take away all of our guns by passing laws.
- The President and Governors can take away all of our guns by executive order.
- The Courts can take away our guns by establishing judicial precedent.
- Keep yer Freedom-Stranglin' government hands OFF OUR GUNS!!!!

Constitution of Utah, Article I. Declaration of Rights. Sections 1 [Inherent and inalienable rights.] and 6 [Right to bear arms.]

"PLAIN TALK"

Unlike in the Federal Constitution, where the Bill of Rights appear at the end of the document, Utah's Constitution begins, as Article I, with a "Declaration of Rights." The first sentence of the first paragraph of the first Article states that Utahns have an "inalienable right"[meaning that no one, not even liberal judges, can take it away] to defend themselves, their liberties and their property. Article I, Section 6, declares that each individual Utahn has the right to possess firearms to implement the inalienable right of self defense. These two declared rights contain such a powerful statement of the right to possess a firearm to defend one's self and family that it's inconceivable that police, prosecutors and even learned judges tend to think of it as privilege rather than a fundamental right.

The United States Supreme Court has said that each state has the sovereign right to "beef up" the individual rights of its citizens so that they are stronger than those same rights guaranteed under the Federal Bill of Rights. A state has a "sovereign right to adopt in its own Constitution individual liberties more expansive than those conferred by the Federal Constitution." *Pruneyard Shopping Center v. Robins*, 447 U.S. 74, 81 (1980). Utah's right to bear arms fits this profile - it was written to avoid the confusion generated by the "militia" clause of the Second Amendment of the Federal Constitution. Rather than a "militia clause" which has mislead several less-than-fully-informed courts into believing the right to bear arms is somehow connected to service in the National Guard, Utah's right to keep and bear arms begins with an "individual rights" clause. Therefore, each individual Utah citizen has the right to keep and bear arms for "security and defense of self, family, others, property" and the state "as well as for other lawful purposes." The Legislature has the right to define the lawful use of arms, but not to infringe on the right. For example, the Legislature can prohibit the use of a firearm for an "assault with a deadly weapon" and define the parameter's of self defense, but may not legislate away the right to keep and bear arms. This would constitute an infringement. (See Commentary below.) The legislative history is quiet clear, however, that the drafters of the most recent version of Utah's right to keep and bear arms did not intend the right to extend to felons. Furthermore, federal law, as the supreme law of the land, generally takes precedence over Utah law including Utah's Constitution. See Chapter XIII for a discussion of the Brady Act and other very restrictive federal statutes.

ACTUAL TEXT

ARTICLE I DECLARATION OF RIGHTS

Section 1. [Inherent and inalienable rights.] All men have the **inherent and inalienable right** to enjoy and **defend their lives and liberties**; to acquire, possess **and protect property**; . . .

Section 6. [Right to bear arms.] The **individual right** of the people **to** keep and **bear arms** for **security and defense of self, family**, others, **property**, or the state, as well as for other lawful purposes shall not be infringed; but nothing herein shall prevent the Legislature from defining the lawful use of arms. (Emphasis added.)

C. of U. Article 1. Section 6.

COMMENTARY

The Second Amendment of the United States Constitution says, "A well regulated militia, being necessary to the security of a free state, the right of the people to keep and bear arms, shall not be infringed." Unfortunately, many judges, not understanding the historical meaning of the term "militia," have interpreted the right to bear arms as a collective right associated with military service. However, at the time the 2nd Amendment was drafted, "militia" meant "the people" rather than a standing army. "...I ask, who are the militia? They consist now of the whole people, except a few public officers." George Mason, Virginia's U.S. Constitution Ratification Convention, 1788. See also S. Halbrook, *That Every Man Be Armed, The Evolution of a Constitutional Right* (1984). Therefore, the right belongs to all the people, not just a few members of state militia groups. The drafters of the Utah Constitution wanted no misunderstanding. Therefore, they added the adjective "individual" to the phrase, " right to keep and bear arms."

Article I, § 6 is no holdover from the cowboy days. It was a constitutional amendment passed by an overwhelming legislative mandate in 1984 with a 69-1 vote in the Utah House of Representatives and 28-1 in the Senate. Despite a well-organized media blitz against it and a scathing condemnation in the voter information packet by a University of Utah law professor (surprise, surprise!), the voters of this state adopted it by a landslide 61% vote.

Pancho's Wisdom

Left-Wingers argue that the Constitution means what judicial activists say it means; conservatives appoint judges who can read!

CHAPTER VII

THE WEAPON LAWS

Pancho's Wisdom

If you don't instinctively hollar "FREEDOM" when you see an INKBLOT that looks like a GUN, your brain is beginning to rot from "Mad Liberal's" disease!

INTRODUCTION AND WARNING!

If you don't have a concealed weapon permit ("CWP" - also short for "concealed weapon permit holder"), possessing a firearm in your home, your car, on a public street or even within the boundaries of a city limit can be a legal nightmare! There are what I think were unintentional omissions by the Legislature that give police and prosecutors "hidden traps" in the law to snare unsuspecting citizens possessing weapons. I attended a committee meeting during a session of the Utah Legislature in 2006 where several lawmakers admitted to unintentionally carrying a firearm illegally in their vehicles because they didn't fully understand the state's weapons laws! If you don't track the interrelationship of the following definitions and statutes carefully, you could easily be fooled. Getting a CWP for yourself and everyone around you will make your life as a gun owner a LOT easier. I've tried hard to simplify this stuff, but by the time you finish the next two chapters you'll have a lot more empathy for military mine sweepers!

U.C.A. 76-10-500. Uniform Law.

"PLAIN TALK"

Section 500 reaffirms the principle written into Article I, Section 6 that the right to keep and bear arms is an individual right rather than a collective right. This law keeps cities, counties, government agencies and even school districts from enacting ordinances or making rules that conflict with state law. Otherwise , gun owners would find it impossible to travel around the state without violating some obscure ordinance or rule. Without the "uniformity law" the right to carry a firearm for constitutionally protected purposes would become so overly burdensome and inconvenient that it would become meaningless.

ACTUAL TEXT

(1) The individual right to keep and bear arms being a constitutionally protected right, the Legislature finds the need to provide uniform laws throughout the state. Except as specifically provided by state law, a citizen of the United States or a lawfully admitted alien shall not be:

- (a) prohibited from owning, possessing, purchasing, selling, transferring, transporting, or keeping any firearm at his place of residence, property, business, or in any vehicle lawfully in his possession or lawfully under his control; or
- (b) required to have a permit or license to purchase, own, possess, transport, or keep a firearm.

(2) This part is uniformly applicable throughout this state and in all its political subdivisions and municipalities. All authority to regulate firearms shall be reserved to the state except where the Legislature specifically delegates responsibility to local authorities or state entities. Unless specifically authorized by the Legislature by statute, a local authority or state entity may not enact or enforce any ordinance, regulation, or rule pertaining to firearms.

U.C.A. 76-10-500

COMMENTARY

Despite the plain meaning of this statute, many of Utah's public school, college and university administrators continued to enforce school policies prohibiting concealed weapon permit holders who were employees or students from bringing their firearms onto school property. Because the Legislature intended for concealed weapon permit holders to be able to have a means of self defense in schools and universities, it clarified this by passing another law, U.C.A. 63-98-102 under the title of "State Affairs" (not included herein because of its similarity to U.C.A. 76-10-500). The language of 63-98-102 is very similar to 76-10-500 except that it added the wording, "'local authority or state entity' includes public school districts, public schools, and state institutions of higher education." Even after the enactment of U.C.A. 63-98-102 the University of Utah refused to obey the law, claiming it had some sort of educational "autonomy." To prove its point, The U of U sued Attorney General Mark Shurtleff.

The Utah Supreme Court, in a 4 - 1 decision, with Chief Justice Christine Durham dissenting, agreed that only the Legislature had the authority to regulate firearms and told the University that its policy of prohibiting concealed weapon permit holders from possessing firearms on campus was illegal.

Federal law (see discussion of the "Gun Free School Zone Act" in Chapter XIII) and state law (see U.C.A. 76-10-505.5 below) combine to make it unlawful for **EVERYONE <u>EXCEPT</u> CONCEALED WEAPON PERMIT HOLDERS** to have a gun in a school zone or college campus or even within a thousand feet of a school or campus.

Pancho's Nomination for the Darwin Award

"... guns don't belong in the classroom ...In an academic environment, we believe you should be free from fear.. .. we think it's a common-sense policy for the protection of students, staff and faculty ... this will help parents, students, faculty and visitors feel safe on our campus." Warm-Fuzzy Statement by Virginia Tech spokesman, Larry Hincker upon hearing that the Virginia Legislature would allow Virginia Tech to maintain a "gun free campus" a year before the Virginia Tech massacre.

U.C.A. 10-8-47. [The authority of Cities and Towns to Regulate] Firearms .

"PLAIN TALK"

This code section gives Utah CITIES AND TOWNS the authority to regulate the use of firearms. No similar law exists that authorizes COUNTIES to control the use of firearms. The only authority the State has given counties to regulate shooting relates to the spotlighting of varmints at night, like coyotes and skunks. (See U.C. A. 23-13-17 which is discussed in Chapter IX).

ACTUAL TEXT

They **[cities and towns]** . . . **they may regulate and prevent the discharge of firearms,** rockets, powder, fireworks or any other dangerous or combustible material; . . . **(emphasis added).**

U.C.A. 76-10-501. Definitions.

"PLAIN TALK"

The definitions in section 501 create the foundation for restrictions relating to persons with criminal backgrounds and the concealment of weapons. The definition of "dangerous weapon" includes anything that is capable of causing death or serious bodily injury. This could mean a crocheting needle, a sharp stick **["spot-lighting" for vampires?]**, a nail, brass knuckles, a piece of glass, a small pocket knife, a pointed can opener, a screw driver, a hat pin, or a pair of scissors. If you are carrying such items and do not hurt anyone, because most of these objects have lawful uses, you probably would not be arrested or convicted of carrying a concealed dangerous weapon. How many women don't carry one or more of such items around in their purses? Ever wonder why thugs use screw drivers rather than knives to mug people on buses and subways? That's right, so it will be hard to prosecute them for simply carrying the object. If however, someone is robbed or stabbed with such an object, the police and the courts can look at how the object was used and what kind of wound resulted. If your grandma inflicts a "long, deep and ugly" gash with her crochet needle, she could be convicted of assault with a deadly weapon.

"Fully automatic weapon" means a machine gun (eg. M-14 or M-16) or sub-(pistol caliber) machine gun (eg. Uzzi).

The definition of "securely encased" can be confusing. It includes having a gun in a "closed case or container, whether or not locked . . . but not in a glove box or console." What if the case is closed, but not all the way? What if the glove box or console is locked? The code gives no answers to these questions, so you should make sure, if your gun is in a box or container, it is completely closed and avoid putting a gun in the glove box or console, even if locked. "Securely encased" gives people without a concealed weapon permit the option of hiding their gun to prevent theft when they are not in the car. However, to make certain a securely encased gun is not considered a "concealed dangerous weapon" notice that in (2)(b) it must also be unloaded (see section 502 below for the definition of "unloaded.")

The definition of concealed dangerous weapon is troublesome. Notice that in addition to the words "hide" and "secret" the definition uses the word "covered." Does this mean fully covered or partially? It is unclear and the use of the word covered may suggest to a court that the defendant does not have to intend to conceal to be guilty. This could mean that if you were driving down the street with your gun unloaded on the floor boards of the back seat and you slam on your brakes causing your groceries to fall on the gun, you might be found guilty of carrying a concealed weapon. The Legislature should remove the word "covered" from the definition to make it clear that a prosecutor has to prove "specific intent to conceal" to get a conviction under this code section. If the Legislature doesn't fix this problem, the courts should hold this statute void for vagueness When a statute is confusing or vague, **people cannot be expected to understand what it means.** The courts can invalidate laws like this under a doctrine known as "void for vagueness." The concern is that the vague terms will permit law enforcement personnel and the courts to enforce ordinances without giving citizens fair notice of what is illegal. *Coates v. City of Cincinnati,* 402 U.S. 611, 614 (1971).

"House of worship" means a building set apart "primarily for the purpose of worship." This definition is important to concealed weapon permit holders because churches are permitted by law to exclude CWPs from houses of worship. This definition would not seem to apply to buildings such as free standing gymnasiums even though on church property, genealogical libraries, or office buildings where church services are not held. Chapels, temples and synagogues are rather obvious examples of houses of worship.

ACTUAL TEXT

As used in this part:

(1)(a) "Antique firearm" means any firearm:

(i)(A) with a matchlock, flintlock, percussion cap, or similar type of ignition system; and

(B) that was manufactured in or before 1898; or

(ii) that is a replica of any firearm described in this Subsection

(1)(a), if the replica:

(A) is not designed or redesigned for using rimfire or conventional centerfire fixed ammunition; or

(B) uses rimfire or centerfire fixed ammunition which is:

(I) no longer manufactured in the United States; and

(II) is not readily available in ordinary channels of commercial trade; or

(iii) (A) that is a muzzle loading rifle, shotgun, or pistol; and (B) is designed to use black powder, or a black powder substitute, and cannot use fixed ammunition.

(b) "Antique firearm" does not include:

(i) any weapon that incorporates a firearm frame or receiver;

(ii) any firearm that is converted into a muzzle loading weapon; or

(iii) any muzzle loading weapon that can be readily converted to fire fixed ammunition by replacing the:

(A) barrel;

(B) bolt;

(C) breechblock; or

(D) any combination of Subsection (1)(b)(iii)(A), (B), or (C).

(2)(a) "Concealed dangerous weapon" means a dangerous weapon that is covered, hidden, or secreted in a manner that the public would not be aware of its presence and is readily accessible for immediate use.

(b) A dangerous weapon shall not be considered a concealed dangerous weapon if it is a firearm which is unloaded and is securely encased.

(3) "Criminal history background check" means a criminal background check conducted by a licensed firearms dealer on every purchaser of a handgun through the division or the local law enforcement agency where the firearms dealer conducts business.

(4) "Curio or relic firearm" means any firearm that:

(a) is of special interest to a collector because of a quality that is not associated with firearms intended for:

(i) sporting use;

(ii) use as an offensive weapon; or
(iii) use as a defensive weapon;
(b)(i) was manufactured at least 50 years prior to the current date;

and

(ii) is not a replica of a firearm described in Subsection (4)(b)(i);
(c) is certified by the curator of a municipal, state, or federal museum that exhibits firearms to be a curio or relic of museum interest;

(d) derives a substantial part of its monetary value:

(i) from the fact that the firearm is:

(A) novel;

(B) rare; or

(C) bizarre; or

(ii) because of the firearm's association with an historical:

(A) figure;

(B) period; or

(C) event; and

(e) has been designated as a curio or relic firearm by the director of the United States Treasury Department Bureau of Alcohol, Tobacco, and Firearms under 27 C.F.R. § 178.11.

(5)(a) "Dangerous weapon" means any item that in the manner of its use or intended use is capable of causing death or serious bodily injury. The following factors shall be used in determining whether a knife, or any other item, object, or thing not commonly known as a dangerous weapon is a dangerous weapon:

(i) the character of the instrument, object, or thing;
(ii) the character of the wound produced, if any;
(iii) the manner in which the instrument, object, or thing was used;

and

(iv) the other lawful purposes for which the instrument, object, or thing may be used.

(b) "Dangerous weapon" does not include any explosive, chemical, or incendiary device as defined by Section 76-10-306.

(6) "Dealer" means every person who is licensed under crimes and criminal procedure, 18 U.S.C. § 923 and engaged in the business of selling, leasing, or otherwise transferring a handgun, whether the person is a retail or wholesale dealer, pawnbroker, or otherwise.

(7) "Division" means the Criminal Investigations and Technical Services Division of the Department of Public Safety, created in Section 53-10-103.

(8) "Enter" means intrusion of the entire body.

(9)(a) "Firearm" means a pistol, revolver, shotgun, sawed-off shotgun, rifle or sawed-off rifle, or any device that could be used as a dangerous weapon from which is expelled a projectile by action of an explosive.

(b) As used in Sections 76-10-526 and 76-10-527, "firearm" does not include an antique firearm.

(10) "Firearms transaction record form" means a form created by the division to be completed by a person purchasing, selling, or transferring a handgun from a dealer in the state.

(11) "Fully automatic weapon" means any firearm which fires, is designed to fire, or can be readily restored to fire, automatically more than one shot without manual reloading by a single function of the trigger.

(12) (a) "Handgun" means a pistol, revolver, or other firearm of any description, loaded or unloaded, from which any shot, bullet, or other missile can be discharged, the length of which, not including any revolving, detachable, or magazine breech, does not exceed 12 inches.

(b) As used in Sections 76-10-520, 76-10-521, and 76-10-522, "handgun" and "pistol or revolver" do not include an antique firearm.

(13) "House of worship" means a church, temple, synagogue, mosque, or other building set apart primarily for the purpose of worship in which religious services are held and the

main body of which is kept for that use and not put to any other use inconsistent with its primary purpose.

(14) "Prohibited area" means any place where it is unlawful to discharge a firearm.

(15) "Readily accessible for immediate use" means that a firearm or other dangerous weapon is carried on the person or within such close proximity and in such a manner that it can be retrieved and used as readily as if carried on the person.

(16) "Residence" means an improvement to real property used or occupied as a primary or secondary residence.

(17) "Sawed-off shotgun" or "sawed-off rifle" means a shotgun having a barrel or barrels of fewer than 18 inches in length, or in the case of a rifle, having a barrel or barrels of fewer than 16 inches in length, or any dangerous weapon made from a rifle or shotgun by alteration, modification, or otherwise, if the weapon as modified has an overall length of fewer than 26 inches.

(18) "Securely encased" means not readily accessible for immediate use, such as held in a gun rack, or in a closed case or container, whether or not locked, or in a trunk or other storage area of a motor vehicle, not including a glove box or console box.

(19) "State entity" means each department, commission, board, council, agency, institution, officer, corporation, fund, division, office, committee, authority, laboratory, library, unit, bureau, panel, or other administrative unit of the state.

(20) "Violent felony" means the same as defined in Section 76-3-203.5. [U.C.A.76-3-203.5(c)](i)defines **"Violent Felony"** as follows: "Violent felony" means any of the following offenses, or any attempt, solicitation, or conspiracy to commit any of these offenses punishable as a felony:

(A) aggravated arson, arson, knowingly causing a catastrophe, and criminal mischief under Title 76, Chapter 6, Part 1, Property Destruction;

(B) aggravated assault under Title 76, Chapter 5, Part 1, Assault and Related Offenses;

(C) criminal homicide offenses under Title 76, Chapter 5, Part 2, Criminal Homicide;

(D) aggravated kidnaping and kidnaping under Title 76, Chapter 5, Part 3, Kidnaping;

(E) rape, Section 76-5-402;

(F) rape of a child, Section 76-5-402.1;

(G) object rape, Section 76-5-402.2;

(H) object rape of a child, Section 76-5-402.3;

(I) forcible sodomy, Section 76-5-403;

(J) sodomy on a child, Section 76-5-403.1;

(K) forcible sexual abuse, Section 76-5-404;

(L) aggravated sexual abuse of a child and sexual abuse of a child, Section 76-5-404.1;

(M) aggravated sexual assault, Section 76-5-405;

(N) sexual exploitation of a minor, Section 76-5a-3;

(O) aggravated burglary and burglary of a dwelling under Title 76, Chapter 6, Part 2, Burglary and Criminal Trespass;

(P) aggravated robbery and robbery under Title 76, Chapter 6, Part 3, Robbery;

(Q) theft by extortion under Subsection 76-6-406(2)(a) or (b);

(R) tampering with a witness under Subsection 76-8-508(2)(c);

(S) tampering with a juror under Subsection 76-8-508.5(2)(c);

(T) extortion to dismiss a criminal proceeding under Section 76-8-509 if by any threat or by use of force theft by extortion has been committed pursuant to Subsections 76-6-406(2)(a), (b), and (i);

(U) damage or destruction of school or institution of higher education property by explosives or flammable materials under Section 76-8-715;

(V) possession, use, or removal of explosive, chemical, or incendiary devices under Subsections 76-10-306(3) through (6);

(W) unlawful delivery of explosive, chemical, or incendiary devices under Section 76-10-307;

(X) purchase or possession of a dangerous weapon or handgun by a restricted person under Section 76-10-503;

(Y) unlawful discharge of a firearm under Section 76-10-508;

(Z) aggravated exploitation of prostitution under Subsection 76-10-1306(1)(a);

(AA) bus hijacking under Section 76-10-1504; and

(BB) discharging firearms and hurling missiles under Section 76-10-1505; or

(ii) any felony offense against a criminal statute of any other state, the United States, or any district, possession, or territory of the United States which would constitute a violent felony as defined in this Subsection (1) if committed in this state.]

Pancho's Wisdom

There ain't NOBODY as worthless as SOMEBODY with an unloaded gun! Well, Pancho, actually there are people more worthless. . . college students and professors without a gun during a mass shooting on campus, airline pilots without a gun during an attempted hijacking, and employees without guns when a co-employee "goes postal."

U.C.A. 76-10-502. When weapon deemed loaded .

"PLAIN TALK"

A firearm with a bullet in the chamber is loaded. Pistols and revolvers are loaded if the operation of any mechanism once would cause the gun to fire. A double-action revolver with no bullet aligned with the barrel is still considered "loaded" under this definition, if pulling the trigger would cause the cylinder to rotate and fire the gun. A semi-automatic pistol, however, is NOT loaded even if it has a magazine or clip in it, if there is no bullet in the barrel.

ACTUAL TEXT

(1) For the purpose of this chapter, any pistol, revolver, shotgun, rifle, or other weapon described in this part shall be deemed to be loaded when there is an unexpended cartridge, shell, or projectile in the firing position.

(2) Pistols and revolvers shall also be deemed to be loaded when an unexpended cartridge, shell, or projectile is in a position whereby the manual operation of any mechanism once would cause the unexpended cartridge, shell, or projectile to be fired.

(3) A muzzle loading firearm shall be deemed to be loaded when it is capped or primed and has a powder charge and ball or shot in the barrel or cylinders.

U.C.A. 76-10-503. Restrictions on possession, purchase, transfer, and ownership of dangerous weapons by certain persons.

"PLAIN TALK"

This section creates two categories of restricted persons, Category I (really bad dudes - violent felons either as adults or juveniles) and Category II (bad dudes - "normal felons" either as adults or juveniles, druggies, mentally deficient persons, illegal aliens etc.). None of these people can possess a firearm, but Category I restricted persons are subject to a higher classification of felony than Category II restricted persons. Those who plead not guilty by reason of insanity and who are mentally incompetent to stand trial cannot possess a firearm. Most of these people are already restricted under the Gun Control Act of 1968; why not let the feds prosecute them for possessing a firearm (refer to explanation of federally restricted persons in Chapter XIII)? After all, the Feds boast, "Federal Gun crime convictions have zero possibility of parole. Zero."

ACTUAL TEXT

(1) For purposes of this section:

(a) A Category I restricted person is a person who:

(i) has been convicted of any violent felony as defined in Section 76-3-203.5;

(ii) is on probation or parole for any felony;

(iii) is on parole from a secure facility as defined in Section 62A-7-101; or

(iv) within the last ten years has been adjudicated delinquent for an offense which if committed by an adult would have been a violent felony as defined in Section 76-3-203.5.

(b) A Category II restricted person is a person who:

(i) has been convicted of or is under indictment for any felony;

(ii) within the last seven years has been adjudicated delinquent for an offense which if committed by an adult would have been a felony;

(iii) is an unlawful user of a controlled substance as defined in Section 58-37-2;

(iv) is in possession of a dangerous weapon and is knowingly and intentionally in unlawful possession of a Schedule I or II controlled substance as defined in Section 58-37-2;

(v) has been found not guilty by reason of insanity for a felony offense;

(vi) has been found mentally incompetent to stand trial for a felony offense;

(vii) has been adjudicated as mentally defective as provided in the Brady Handgun Violence Prevention Act, Pub.L. No. 103-159, 107 Stat. 1536 (1993), or has been committed to a mental institution;

(viii) is an alien who is illegally or unlawfully in the United States;

(ix) has been dishonorably discharged from the armed forces; or

(x) has renounced his citizenship after having been a citizen of the United States.

(2) A Category I restricted person who intentionally or knowingly agrees, consents, offers, or arranges to purchase, transfer, possess, use, or have under his custody or control, or who intentionally or knowingly purchases, transfers, possesses, uses, or has under his custody or control:

(a) any firearm is guilty of a second degree felony; or

(b) any dangerous weapon other than a firearm is guilty of a third degree felony.

(3) A Category II restricted person who purchases, transfers, possesses, uses, or has under his custody or control:

(a) any firearm is guilty of a third degree felony; or

(b) any dangerous weapon other than a firearm is guilty of a class A misdemeanor.

(4) A person may be subject to the restrictions of both categories at the same time.

(5) If a higher penalty than is prescribed in this section is provided in another section for one who purchases, transfers, possesses, uses, or has under this custody or control any dangerous weapon, the penalties of that section control.

(6) It is an affirmative defense to a charge based on the definition in Subsection (1)(b)(iv) that the person was:

(a) in possession of a controlled substance pursuant to a lawful order of a practitioner for use of a member of the person's household or for administration to an animal owned by the person or a member of the person's household; or

(b) otherwise authorized by law to possess the substance.

U.C.A. 76-10-504. Carrying concealed dangerous weapon — Penalties.

"PLAIN TALK"

Unless you have a concealed weapon permit (CWP), it's illegal to carry a concealed weapon. If you don't have a CWP, if you are going to carry a firearm on your person, you must carry it **OPENLY** (i.e. it must be visible). Notice the draconian definition of a "concealed dangerous weapon" in section 500 (2) above and my concerns about it in the "Plain Talk" box preceding the actual text of that section. Keep in mind that a hidden weapon "readily accessible for immediate use" is considered a concealed weapon even though you are not totin'it.

Those without CWPs occupying a vehicle or being present on a public street or in a "posted" city limit which prohibits the discharge of firearms, must keep their firearm UNLOADED (see discussion and commentary for section 505 below).

It is a class B misdemeanor if you conceal a knife or other dangerous weapon that is not a firearm unless you're at home, on your property or at your place of business.

For persons who have no CWP, concealing a firearm that does not contain ammunition is a class B misdemeanor, but it is a Class A misdemeanor if it contains ammunition. Remember, a gun can be "unloaded" but still contain ammunition (U.C.A. 76-10-502).

Interestingly, section (1)(b) which refers to firearms does not have the same exception for non-CWPs that subsection (a) has for those possessing other weapons i.e. allowing citizens to keep the weapon concealed at their residence, property or business under their control. This appears to be an oversight by the Legislature. Certainly people without CWPs should not be prosecuted for having a concealed firearm in their homes whether they keep a firearm unloaded in their dresser drawers or closets or loaded under their pillows for protection against home invaders or burglars. Concealed weapon holders are exempt from paragraph (1)(a) and (b) of Section 504, but are not exempt from the remaining provisions of the Section. Even a concealed weapon permit holder cannot legally conceal a sawed-off shotgun or sawed-off rifle. He can legally pretend he is Wyatt Earp, who carried a loaded Buntline Special on his hip, but not John Dillinger, who reportedly concealed a sawed-off shotgun in his baggy trousers.

Persons hunting protected or unprotected wildlife may legally conceal a handgun having a barrel length of over 4 inches without a CWP so long as they do not stray into a city limit or onto a public highway while "taking wildlife." The purpose of allowing hunters to carry a concealed weapon without a permit is for personal protection NOT for the purpose of taking wildlife UNLESS the concealed weapon meets the specific requirements of that particular hunt. For example, if you are hunting big game and the game regulations require the use of a firearm with 500 ft. pounds of energy at the muzzle and a barrel length of 6 inches (see R657-5-10 in Chapter IX), if your concealed pistol fits this description you may legally use it to hunt big game. If, however, you are on a muzzle loader or bow hunt you may NOT use your concealed weapon to take wildlife.

ACTUAL TEXT

(1) Except as provided in Section 76-10-503 and in Subsections (2) and (3):

(a) a person who carries a concealed dangerous weapon, as defined in Section 76-10-501, which is not a firearm on his person or one that is readily accessible for immediate use which is not securely encased, as defined in this part, in a place other than his residence, property, or business under his control is guilty of a class B misdemeanor; and

(b) a person without a valid concealed firearm permit who carries a concealed dangerous weapon which is a firearm and that contains no ammunition is guilty of a class B misdemeanor, but if the firearm contains ammunition the person is guilty of a class A misdemeanor.

(2) A person who carries concealed a sawed-off shotgun or a sawed-off rifle is guilty of a second degree felony.

(3) If the concealed firearm is used in the commission of a violent felony as defined in Section 76-3-203.5, and the person is a party to the offense, the person is guilty of a second degree felony.

(4) Nothing in Subsection (1) shall prohibit a person engaged in the lawful taking of protected or unprotected wildlife as defined in Title 23, Wildlife Resources Code, from carrying a concealed weapon or a concealed firearm with a barrel length of four inches or greater as long as the taking of wildlife does not occur:

(a) within the limits of a municipality in violation of that municipality's ordinances; or

(b) upon the highways of the state as defined in Section 41-6a-102.

U.C.A. 76-10-505. Carrying loaded firearm in vehicle, on street, or in prohibited area.

"PLAIN TALK"

This code section and the preceding section (504) govern how persons WITHOUT concealed weapon permits (CWP) must carry guns in vehicles, public streets and posted prohibited areas. In the definitions section, 501(19) above, "prohibited areas" are defined as "any place where it is unlawful to discharge a firearm." In the discussion of U.C.A. 10-8-47 at the beginning of this chapter, you read that cities and towns have the authority to prohibit the discharge of firearms. Most cities, in their city ordinances, prohibit the discharge of firearms. However, not all of them post this prohibition for public view.

In any event, if you are not a CWP, if you are going to carry a firearm, you must carry it OPENLY and UNLOADED when carrying it in a vehicle, on a public street or within the city limits of a city that has posted signs warning of their ordinance against discharging a firearm. A gun that is securely encased (see definition in section 500(18) above) is not concealed. Securely encased does NOT mean within the console or glove box of a vehicle.

ACTUAL TEXT

(1) Unless otherwise authorized by law, a person may not carry a loaded firearm:

 (a) in or on a vehicle;

 (b) on any public street; or

 (c) in a posted prohibited area.

(2) A violation of this section is a class B misdemeanor.

U.C.A. 76-10-505

COMMENTARY - "OPEN CARRY"

This section and the preceding one provide a segway to a discussion of the topic of "OPEN CARRY." In my CWP classes and other public presentations I generally am asked two separate but related questions about open carry. First, can a person who does not have a CWP strap on his leather holster and walk around town with his smoke wagon on his hip, like in the Old West? Second, is a CWP guilty of a crime if he inadvertently allows his concealed firearm to show? Another form of the second question is, "can a CWP open carry?"

The simple answer is: Both CWPs AND nonCWPs can OPEN CARRY, but only CWPs can carry a loaded firearm in a vehicle, on a public street and in a posted city limit. Both, however, should be careful not to give anyone the impression that their act of carrying a firearm openly is intended as a threat. For example, see U.C.A. 76-10-506 below entitled **"Threatening with or using a dangerous weapon in a fight or quarrel."**

By carrying openly in a mall in some urban liberal Hellhole you could subject yourself to a "disturbing the peace" ordinance. Personally I believe gun-hating-city-dwellers should see as many peaceful, law-abiding citizens as possible carrying guns. It will either help them get over their hoplophobia (a clinical abnormality manifested by the unnatural fear of weapons), or they'll move to some other metropolitan cesspool in a "blue state" or to Eastern Canada like they promised after President Bush was reelected. I open carry in my community just so my fellow suburbanites experience healthy balanced viewing times between Spandex and

Polymer. But then again, my Utah State Bar card rests reassuringly up against my concealed weapon permit.

Legal Analysis: You've probably noticed that neither sections 504 nor 505 come right out and say you can "OPEN CARRY." But 504 makes it clear that people without a CWP MUST open carry to avoid the penalties of carrying a concealed weapon. 505 obviously refers to people without CWPs because section 523 below EXEMPTS CWPs from 505 ("Section 76-10-505 [does] not apply to any person to whom a permit to carry a concealed firearm has been issued. . . ."). 505 when read together with 523 says that people without CWPs who MUST carry openly, can carry a firearm in a vehicle, on a public street (like in the Old West) or in a posted city limit as long as the gun is UNLOADED (meaning it may contain ammunition if compliant with section 502). Because CWPs are exempt from the evils of carrying a loaded or concealed firearm, they may, by inference carry OPENLY AND LOADED! Furthermore, nowhere in the Utah Code does it say that a CWP may NOT carry OPENLY!

Pancho's Personal Advice - If you have a CWP, don't carry openly unless you are willing to accept the risk of being arrested because (1) some police and prosecutors don't understand the law and (2) criminals lie. If there were no witnesses, there is a good possibility your assailant will lie to keep himself out of trouble and get you into trouble. If he has seen your gun, he can vividly describe it to the police and tell them you pointed it at him when all you did is stand there with your big iron on your hip. Under those circumstances (unless the police check the liar's criminal record before they slap the cuffs on you) you will be arrested for Third Degree Felony Aggravated Assault (pointing a gun at another without justification). Even if you say you did it in self defense, the police and prosecutors will probably justify the arrest and subsequent charges by telling themselves, "we'll just let the jury decide." The problem with that is that you could've bought a new SUV with what you will have to pay your lawyer to defend you against felony charges.

The tragic shooting deaths of at least two law enforcement officers WITH THEIR OWN GUNS within the last couple of years highlight the TACTICAL reason you should not carry openly. It's too easy for someone to grab your gun away from you.

U.C.A. 76-10-505.5. Possession of a dangerous weapon, firearm, or sawed-off shotgun on or about school premises — Penalties

"PLAIN TALK"

It is illegal under both state and federal law (see Chapter XIII) to take a gun or other type of dangerous weapon into a school zone. State law defines "school zone" as property within a 1000 feet of a public or private elementary, secondary, vocational school, postsecondary institution, in those portions of any building, park, stadium, or other structure or grounds which are, at the time of the act, being used for an activity sponsored by or through a school or institution, or a preschool or child-care facility (see U.C.A. 76-3-203.2 below). Dangerous weapon includes a "facsimile" of a weapon. Utah case law says you can be convicted of using a dangerous weapon if you make others believe you have one, even if you don't.

The exceptions are concealed weapon permit holders, U.C.A. 53-5-704, temporary concealed weapon permit holders, U.C.A. 53-5-705, people keeping a loaded weapon at their temporary residences, residences or camps, U.C.A. 76-10-511, federal and state police officers, mail carriers making deliveries, concealed weapon permit holders from other states, non-residents with unloaded weapons that are securely encased, and judges, U.C.A. 76-10-523. Nearby businesses and private automobiles are also exempted. Federal law, however, requires firearms in the vehicles of those who do not have a concealed weapon permit to be unloaded and locked in a case to be lawful in a school zone. We discuss this topic again in Chapter XIII to show how it relates to the federal statute known as the Gun Free School Zone Act. When successful applicants for a Utah concealed weapon permit receive their permit in the mail, they get a letter from the Bureau of Criminal Investigation (BCI) specifically telling them they can take their concealed weapons onto school property.

ACTUAL TEXT

(1) A person may not possess any dangerous weapon, firearm, or sawed-off shotgun, as those terms are defined in Section 76-10-501, at a place that the person knows, or has reasonable cause to believe, is on or about school premises as defined in Subsection 76-3-203.2(1).

(2) (a) Possession of a dangerous weapon on or about school premises is a class B misdemeanor.

(b) Possession of a firearm or sawed-off shotgun on or about school premises is a class A misdemeanor.

(3) This section does not apply if:

(a) the person is authorized to possess a firearm as provided under Section 53-5-704, 53-5-705, 76-10-511, or 76-10-523, or as otherwise authorized by law;

(b) the possession is approved by the responsible school administrator;

(c) the item is present or to be used in connection with a lawful, approved activity and is in the possession or under the control of the person responsible for its possession or use; or

(d) the possession is:

(i) at the person's place of residence or on the person's property;

(ii) in any vehicle lawfully under the person's control, other than a vehicle owned by the school or used by the school to transport students; or

(iii) at the person's place of business which is not located in the areas described in Subsection 76-3-203.2(1)(a)(i), (ii), or (iv).

(4) This section does not prohibit prosecution of a more serious weapons offense that may occur on or about school premises.

U.C.A. 76-3-203.2. Definitions — Use of dangerous weapon in offenses committed on or about school premises — Enhanced penalties.

(1)(a) As used in this section and Section 76-10-505.5, "on or about school premises" means any of the following:

(i) in a public or private elementary, secondary, or on the grounds of any of those schools;

(ii) in a public or private vocational school or postsecondary institution or on the grounds of any of those schools or institutions;

(iii) in those portions of any building, park, stadium, or other structure or grounds which are, at the time of the act, being used for an activity sponsored by or through a school or institution under Subsections (1)(a)(i) and (ii);

(iv) in or on the grounds of a preschool or child-care facility; and

(v) within 1,000 feet of any structure, facility, or grounds included in Subsections (1)(a)(i), (ii), (iii), and (iv).

(b) As used in this section:

(i) "Dangerous weapon" has the same definition as in Section 76-1-601.

(ii) "Educator" means any person who is employed by a public school district and who is required to hold a certificate issued by the State Board of Education in order to perform duties of employment.

(iii) "Within the course of employment" means that an educator is providing services or engaging in conduct required by the educator's employer to perform the duties of employment.

(2) Any person who, on or about school premises, commits any offense and uses or threatens to use a dangerous weapon, as defined in Section 76-1-601, in the commission of the offense is subject to an enhanced degree of offense as provided in Subsection (4).

(3)(a) Any person who commits an offense against an educator when the educator is acting within the course of employment is subject to an enhanced degree of offense as provided in Subsection (4).

(b) As used in Subsection (3)(a), "offense" means:

(i) an offense under Title 76, Chapter 5, Offenses Against The Person; and

(ii) an offense under Title 76, Chapter 6, Part 3, Robbery.

(4) If the trier of fact finds beyond a reasonable doubt that the defendant, while on or about school premises, commits any offense and in the commission of the offense uses or threatens to use a dangerous weapon, or that the defendant committed an offense against an educator when the educator was acting within the course of his employment, the enhanced penalty for a:

(a) class B misdemeanor is a class A misdemeanor;

(b) class A misdemeanor is a third degree felony;

(c) third degree felony is a second degree felony; or

(d) second degree felony is a first degree felony.

(5) The enhanced penalty for a first degree felony offense of a convicted person:

(a) is imprisonment for a term of not less than five years and which may be for life, and imposition or execution of the sentence may not be suspended unless the court finds that the interests of justice would be best served and states the specific circumstances justifying the disposition on the record; and

(b) is subject also to the dangerous weapon enhancement provided in Section 76-3-203.8 except for an offense committed under Subsection (3) that does not involve a firearm.

(6) The prosecuting attorney, or grand jury if an indictment is returned, shall provide notice upon the information or indictment that the defendant is subject to the enhanced degree of offense or penalty under Subsection (4) or (5).

(7) In cases where an offense is enhanced pursuant to Subsection (4)(a), (b), (c), or (d), or under Subsection (5)(a) for an offense committed under Subsection (2) that does not involve a firearm, the convicted person is not subject to the

dangerous weapon enhancement in Section 76-3-203.8.

U.C.A. 76-1-601. Definitions.

(5) "Dangerous weapon" means:

(a) any item capable of causing death or serious bodily injury; or

(b) a facsimile or representation of the item; if:

(i) the actor's use or apparent intended use of the item leads the victim to reasonably believe the item is likely to cause death or serious bodily injury; or

(ii) the actor represents to the victim verbally or in any other manner that he is in control of such an item.

Pancho's Wisdom

The same people who wouldn't declaw a cat, would disarm a college coed.

U.C.A. 53B-3-103. Power of board to adopt rules and enact regulations.

"PLAIN TALK"

This code section, although numerically out of order, was placed here because it provides the current rule for public colleges and universities. This code section reiterates that state owned colleges and universities have no independent autonomy to regulate firearms except as allowed by the Utah Legislature. In this code section , the Legislature has said that colleges and universities may only prohibit firearms in one disciplinary hearing room set up as a secured area. Otherwise they may not prohibit firearms. They may create a rule, however, that allows students living in college dormitories to choose whether or not they want to have a roommate who has a concealed weapon permit.

> Caution: This does not apply to private colleges and universities like BYU, Westminster College and LDS Business College. Also, because of the prohibitions in 76-10-505.5 above, no one may possess a firearm within 1000 feet of a college or university campus except concealed weapon permit holders and property owners who have homes or businesses within a 1000 feet of a school.

ACTUAL TEXT

(1) The board may enact regulations governing the conduct of university and college students, faculty, and employees.

(2)(a) The board may:

(i) enact and authorize higher education institutions to enact traffic, parking, and related regulations governing all individuals on campuses and other facilities owned or controlled by the institutions or the board; and

(ii) acknowledging that the Legislature has the authority to regulate, by law, firearms at higher education institutions:

(A) authorize higher education institutions to establish no more than one secure area at each institution as a hearing room as prescribed in Section 76-8-311.1 , but not otherwise restrict the lawful possession or carrying of firearms; and

(B) authorize a higher education institution to make a rule that allows a resident of a dormitory located at the institution to request only roommates who are not licensed to carry a concealed firearm under Section 53-5-704 or 53-5-705 .

(b) In addition to the requirements and penalty prescribed in Subsections 76-8-311.1(3), (4), (5), and (6), the board shall make rules to ensure that:

(i) reasonable means such as mechanical, electronic, x-ray, or similar devices are used to detect firearms, ammunition, or dangerous weapons contained in the personal property of or on the person of any individual attempting to enter a secure area hearing room;

(ii) an individual required or requested to attend a hearing in a secure area hearing room is notified in writing of the requirements related to entering a secured area hearing room under this Subsection (2)(b) and Section 76-8-311.1;

(iii) the restriction of firearms, ammunition, or dangerous weapons in the secure area hearing room is in effect only during the time the secure area hearing room is in use for hearings and for a reasonable time before and after its use; and

(iv) reasonable space limitations are applied to the secure area hearing room as warranted by the number of individuals involved in a typical hearing.

(3) The board and institutions may enforce these rules and regulations in any reasonable manner, including the assessment of fees, fines, and forfeitures, the collection of which may be by withholding from moneys owed the violator, the imposition of probation, suspension, or expulsion from the institution, the revocation of privileges, the refusal to issue certificates, degrees, and diplomas, through judicial process or any reasonable combination of these alternatives.

U.C.A. 76-10-506. Threatening with or using dangerous weapon in fight or quarrel.

"PLAIN TALK"

You can't legally threaten someone with a dangerous weapon, such as a firearm, unless your threat is necessary to defend yourself from bodily harm from that person. If you threaten without justification, it's a class A misdemeanor. The wording, "in the presence of two or more persons" is unclear. It appears there must be two or more witnesses to convict someone of this offense. This language could lead one to believe that this statute was enacted to keep gangs from threatening each other with weapons. Unfortunately, this statute is being used to prosecute law-abiding citizens simply trying to defend themselves from someone who is threatening them, their property or another person.

Although it's not obvious from the language of this section (506) and the Aggravated Assault statute, U.C.A.76-5-103, my experience in defending gun owners against these charges seems to indicate that the difference between misdemeanor "threatening (brandishing)" and felony aggravated assault is that the misdemeanor generally arises from merely showing the gun and the felony comes from pointing the gun at a person. I see these charges brought most often when the defender has a gun and feels threatened by two or more individuals who don't appear to have weapons. Police and prosecutors don't seem to be as convinced of the necessity of threatening with a gun against two or more threatening individuals as some of my fellow CWP instructors who teach that a "disparity of numbers" justifies the threat or use of deadly force. (See detailed discussion of the law of self defense in Chapter XI. Also, look for my new book written exclusively about Utah's law of self defense.)

After successfully defending computer icon Dell Schanze ("SUPERDELL") against the charge of threatening with a weapon (aka "brandishing"), I decided that there is more to explain to Utah gun owners about the topic of self defense than I can realistically put in one chapter in this book. So I am writing a separate book on the subject. You will finally get the whole story of the SUPERDELL- Brandishing Case rather than just the bits and pieces the media wanted you to hear. I'm including the ENTIRE transcript of the trial in the book's appendix. You'll see how we successfully defended against the State's allegations that Dell wasn't justified in drawing his gun on three "innocent," "concerned neighbors" who objected to Dell driving through their neighborhood at "high speeds" and who only "threatened to break the tail light out on his Jaguar" but "never threatened him [or anyone else]." Furthermore, the book will have a chapter entitled "Thumbs Down Factors" based upon my trial experience and my reading of most of Utah's appellate cases where the gun-toting defendants claimed self defense. This book will teach Utahns what circumstances to avoid, if possible, which cause the police to arrest, prosecutors to prosecute and juries to convict. Every gun owner who possesses a firearm for self defense should add my *Utah Self Defense Law* book to their "must read" list.

ACTUAL TEXT

Every person, except those persons described in Section 76-10-503 **[felons etc.]**, who, not in necessary self defense in the presence of two or more persons, draws or exhibits any dangerous weapon in an angry and threatening manner or unlawfully uses the same in any fight or quarrel is guilty of a class A misdemeanor.

U.C.A. 76-10-506

COMMENTARY

I have represented several clients charged with violating this code section. Unfortunately, these cases often stem from verbal arguments or road rage incidents. Consequently, I train my concealed carry students to set "macho" aside when they are packing heat. The object of concealed carry is to survive, not win arguments or prove that you "had the right of way." Shun verbal disputes before they escalate into conflicts that force you to use a gun to defend yourself. Avoiding gestures with your middle finger, will save wear and tear on your trigger finger (and on your pocket book by not having to hire a lawyer to defend you for committing a crime with your gun).

U.C.A. 76-10-507. Possession of deadly weapon with intent to assault.

"PLAIN TALK"

Possessing a dangerous weapon with the intent to assault is a class A misdemeanor. This statute makes 90% of the rest of the gun laws unnecessary.

ACTUAL TEXT

Every person having upon his person any dangerous weapon with intent to unlawfully assault another is guilty of a class A misdemeanor.

U.C.A. 76-10-508. Discharge of firearm from a vehicle, near highway, or in direction of any person, building, or vehicle - Penalties.

"PLAIN TALK"

You cannot shoot your gun out of or from a vehicle unless you are disabled (see R657-12-4 in Chapter IX entitled "Obtaining Authorization to Hunt from a Vehicle"). U.C.A. 76-10-508 applies to all dangerous weapons including slingshots, blowguns, BB guns, and crossbows. "Vehicle" includes ATVs, motorcycles, dune buggies and Jeeps. U.C.A. 41-6a-102. (33) defines, "Motor vehicle" as "every vehicle which is self-propelled and every vehicle which is propelled by electric power obtained from overhead trolley wires, but not operated upon rails. 'Motor vehicle' does not include vehicles moved solely by human power [like bicycles] and motorized wheel chairs."

You cannot shoot from or across a highway. The term "highway" has a very broad definition under the Utah code. "Highway" means "the entire width between property lines of every way or place of any nature when any part of it is open to the use of the public as a matter of right for vehicular travel" (U.C.A.41-6a-102. (20)). So even if you're off the road, if you are on the "right of way," you can't shoot. It probably doesn't mean dirt roads on private property unless there is a public right of way. If the public has a right of way for vehicular travel over a private dirt road, the road is considered a highway under this definition.

It is a crime to shoot at road signs, communications equipment, railroad equipment, in Utah State Park buildings (duh!), state park camping and picnic sites, overlooks, golf courses, boat ramps, and developed beaches. Don't shoot your gun (or your blowgun for that matter) within 600 feet of any building or structure where a domestic animal is kept, without the permission of the owner or person in charge of the property. Police officers and people acting in self defense are exceptions to the prohibitions contained in this code section.

ACTUAL TEXT

1(a) A person may not discharge any kind of dangerous weapon or firearm:

(i) from an automobile or other vehicle;

(ii) from, upon, or across any highway;

(iii) at any road signs placed upon any highways of the state;

(iv) at any communications equipment or property of public utilities including facilities, lines, poles, or devices of transmission or distribution;

(v) at railroad equipment or facilities including any sign or signal;

(vi) within Utah State Park buildings, designated camp or picnic sites, overlooks, golf courses, boat ramps, and developed beaches; or

(vii) without written permission to discharge the dangerous weapon from the owner or person in charge of the property within 600 feet of:

(A) a house, dwelling, or any other building; or
(B) any structure in which a domestic animal is kept or fed, including a barn, poultry yard, corral, feeding pen, or stockyard.

(b) It shall be a defense to any charge for violating this section that the person being accused had actual permission of the owner or person in charge of the property at the time in question.

(2) A violation of any provision of this section is a class B misdemeanor unless the actor discharges a firearm under any of the following circumstances not amounting to criminal homicide or attempted criminal homicide, in which case it is a third degree felony and the convicted person shall be

sentenced to an enhanced minimum term of three years in prison:

(a) the actor discharges a firearm in the direction of any person or persons, knowing or having reason to believe that any person may be endangered;

(b) the actor, with intent to intimidate or harass another or with intent to damage a habitable structure as defined in Subsection 76-6-101(2), discharges a firearm in the direction of any building; or

(c) the actor, with intent to intimidate or harass another, discharges a firearm in the direction of any vehicle.

(3) The court shall:

(a) notify the Driver License Division of the conviction for purposes of any revocation, denial, suspension, or disqualification of a driver license under Section 53-3-220(1)(a)(xi); and

(b) specify in court at the time of sentencing the length of the revocation under Subsection 53-3-225(1)(c).

(4) This section does not apply to a person:

(a) who discharges any kind of firearm when that person is in lawful defense of self or others; or

(b) who is performing official duties as provided in Sections 23-20-1.5 and 76-10-523 and as otherwise provided by law.

U.C.A. 76-10-508

COMMENTARY

Sections (1)(a)(i) and (ii) of U.C.A. 76-10-508, which prohibit the discharge of <u>any kind</u> of dangerous weapon or firearm . . .from an <u>automobile or other vehicle</u> or from, upon or across <u>any highway,</u> are too broad. As shown above, the definitions of "vehicle" and "highway" are very expansive. These sections prohibit shooting a slingshot or air rifle on the most remote dirt roads in the most isolated sections of the state. The Legislature should amend these laws to permit shooters and hunters to discharge various weapons from a vehicle, in remote areas, if it can be done with reasonable safety.

Although shooting from a vehicle can be dangerous, many sports, such as rock climbing, horseback riding (e.g., the tragedy surrounding Christopher Reeve's paralysis), kayaking, river running, swimming, and golf, involve some risk. (I once handled a personal injury case where a six-year-old at a city golf clinic drove a chipping wedge through the forehead of another six-year-old!) As most hunters can attest, a Utah general season deer hunt can be spooky. More hunters have probably been killed or injured deer hunting than have ever been shot or killed simply shooting from a vehicle. If safety alone were the issue, why would the state allow disabled persons to hunt big game from a vehicle? (See R657-12-4 Obtaining Authorization to Hunt from a Vehicle, Chapter IX.) No offense to the disabled, but it seems more dangerous to allow a person with a disability to shoot from a vehicle under the excitement of bagging a trophy buck or bull elk, than to allow a healthy individual to shoot jack rabbits out of his truck window thirty five miles northwest of Delta (Dude, we're talking desolate!).

This state statute should be amended to allow hunters to shoot from a vehicle under certain conditions. For example, the activity could be limited to unimproved dirt roads that are not state or county roads. The driver of the vehicle could be prohibited from shooting. Other restrictions could be enacted which could make the sport much safer, including limiting the number of shooters, the types of weapons, and the number of shots per weapon. With a little effort the sport could be made reasonably safe.

Persons protecting their livestock or crops on their own property should be permitted to shoot from a vehicle. By the time a sheep herder climbs out of his truck, marauding coyotes are likely to be loooooonnnnng gone. Subsection (1)(b) seems to give legal authority to shoot from a vehicle or across a private road with permission from the person in charge of the property. I could find no Utah court cases deciding that particular issue.

A reasonable person might consider "highway" to mean a road that is paved and traveled by a substantial number of vehicles. However, the definition in U.C.A. 41-6-1 (15) is broader and may include dirt roads. [**"'Highway' means the entire width between property lines of every way or place of any nature when any part of it is open to the use of the public as a matter of right for vehicular travel", (Utah Code Ann. 41-6-1 (15)).]** The state should define "highway" more narrowly. Most heavily traveled roads contain a federal, state or county road number such as "Interstate 15," "State Road 89," and "County Road 14." The state could enact a law prohibiting the discharge of a firearm from or across any federal, state or county highway or road. Another approach could be to prohibit shooting on interstates, highways, principal roads and improved roads, but allow shooting on unimproved roads, except within 600 feet of another vehicle owned by persons not voluntarily participating in the shooting activity.

Another criticism of sections (i) and (ii) is that they treat all weapons the same. Most cowboys, Indians, medieval knights, and other warriors know that all weapons are not created equal. It's dangerous to zing a .223 caliber 55 grain boat tail at light speed out of your truck window on Interstate 15, three miles south of Cedar City. But it's not unsafe to shoot a .45 Long Colt out of the back of your Jeep, twenty five miles southwest of Trout Creek on a dirt road that hasn't seen another vehicle besides yours, in forty five days. Section 508 does not distinguish between the two situations. The .223 boat tail has a muzzle velocity of over 3200 feet per second, but the .45 Colt, depending on the powder charge, pushes a 250 grain bullet at only 750 to 900 feet per second. The boat tail might skip on a rock and cause injury up to a mile away. My experience has been that a .45 Colt 250 grain lead round nose travels a hundred yards at most after it hits the ground. The statute could be rewritten as follows:

U.C.A. 76-10-508:

(1)(a) A person may not discharge any kind of dangerous weapon or firearm:

(i) from an automobile or other vehicle:

(a) <u>during daylight hours (1/2 hour before sunrise until 1/2-</u>

hour after sunset], while said automobile is on an interstate, paved highway, principle road, or an improved road, or within 600 feet of other persons or vehicles occupied by persons not participating in the same shooting activity as the person discharging the firearm or dangerous weapon; and the shooting activity must be in compliance with all other state laws and city ordinances;

[b] at night time [1/2 hour after sunset until 1/2 hour before sunrise], except as provided in U.C.A. 23-13-17 [the state spotlighting statute] and in accordance with the county ordinances pertaining to spotlighting; or within 600 feet of other persons or vehicles occupied by persons not participating in the same shooting activity as the person discharging the firearm or dangerous weapon; and the shooting activity must be in compliance with all other state laws and city ordinances; and in addition thereto,

- [i] participants in the shooting activity may not use weapons propelling projectiles faster than 1000 ft./sec.
- [ii] a participant may not discharge any weapon while driving a vehicle or holding a spotlight.
- [iii] ~~from, upon, or across any highway;~~ from, upon, or across any interstate, paved highway, principle road, or an improved road, or within 600 feet of other persons or vehicles occupied by persons not participating in the same shooting activity as the person discharging the firearm or dangerous weapon; and the shooting activity must be in compliance with all other state laws and city ordinances.

I invite members of various archery associations to propose reasonably safe changes under this code section relating to archery, including the use of crossbows. I see no reason why archery equipment could not be used to spotlight various varmints and predators. In fact, archery equipment, including cross bows, could be the weapon of choice for predator control near more populated areas. Several eastern state cities have permitted bow hunting of white tail deer which have become overpopulated and pose a serious safety risk to city residents. The State of Utah's Department of Wildlife Resources could obtain a wealth of information from such cities.

U.C.A. 76-10-509. Possession of dangerous weapon by minor.

"PLAIN TALK"

GUNS, MINORS AND JUVENILES — Utah State gun laws refer to persons under 18 years of age as "minors." Federal gun laws call them "juveniles." This Utah statute creates two categories of minors. Minors 14 to 18 years of age can possess a dangerous weapon if their parents give permission. Minors under 14 years of age must be accompanied by a responsible adult to have a dangerous weapon in their possession. Remember, "dangerous weapon" could mean anything that could kill or cause severe injury, such as a pocket knife, a blow gun, or a slingshot.

Without referring to our "Youngsters, Guns and Ammo" chart, Appendix F, it is almost impossible for anyone, including attorneys, peace officers and even BATF agents, to keep straight all the state and federal laws placing age limitations on firearms use. Don't rely on U.C.A. 76-10-509 without referring to Appendix F.

ACTUAL TEXT

(1) A minor under 18 years of age may not possess a dangerous weapon unless he:

  (a) has the permission of his parent or guardian to have the weapon; or

  (b) is accompanied by a parent or guardian while he has the weapon in his possession.

(2) Any minor under 14 years of age in possession of a dangerous weapon shall be accompanied by a responsible adult.

(3) Any person who violates this section is guilty of:

(a) a class B misdemeanor upon the first offense; and

(b) a class A misdemeanor for each subsequent offense.

U.C.A. 76-10-509

COMMENTARY

Federal law goes a step further than state law when it comes to juveniles possessing handguns for legitimate purposes. Under state law, the parent can give oral permission, accompany the child or ask another person 21 or older to accompany the minor. Federal law requires WRITTEN PERMISSION [a piece of paper] which must be kept on the juvenile at all times, even if the parent or guardian accompanies the juvenile in possession of the handgun (see 18 U.S.C. 922(x)(1) which we cover at length in Chapter XIII). The form in "Appendix A" may be used by parents to give written permission to their children to possess a handgun for the purposes referred to on the form. The juvenile should keep the consent form with him at all times while possessing the pistol or revolver.

U.C.A. 76-10-509.4. Prohibition of possession of certain weapons by minors.

"PLAIN TALK"

Section (1) says minors cannot possess a handgun. But there are several exceptions found in Section 512 below, including target shooting at amusement parks, attending a firearm safety course, practicing at a shooting range or other place where the discharge of a firearm is not prohibited by state or local law (outside all city limits and off of all highways and at least 600 feet from any person or building or enclosure where domestic animals are kept). Section 512 also permits minors to hunt with handguns.

Minors cannot possess sawed-off shotguns or rifles or fully automatic weapons "except as provided under federal law." The only exceptions under federal law seem to be in connection with military service.

ACTUAL TEXT

(1) A minor under 18 years of age may not possess a handgun.

(2) Except as provided by federal law, a minor under 18 years of age may not possess the following:

  (a) a sawed-off rifle or sawed-off shotgun; or

  (b) a fully automatic weapon.

(3) Any person who violates Subsection (1) is guilty of:

  (a) a class B misdemeanor upon the first offense; and

  (b) a class A misdemeanor for each subsequent offense.

(4) Any person who violates Subsection (2) is guilty of a third degree felony.

U.C.A. 76-10-509.5. Penalties for providing certain weapons to a minor.

"PLAIN TALK"

This section penalizes anyone assisting minors to obtain the weapons prohibited above.

ACTUAL TEXT

(1) Any person who provides a handgun to a minor when the possession of the handgun by the minor is a violation of Section 76-10-509.4 is guilty of:

  (a) a class B misdemeanor upon the first offense; and

  (b) a class A misdemeanor for each subsequent offense.

(2) Any person who transfers in violation of applicable state or federal law a sawed-off rifle, sawed-off shotgun, or fully automatic weapon to a minor is guilty of a third degree felony.

U.C.A. 76-10-509.6. Parent or guardian providing firearm to violent minor.

> **"PLAIN TALK"**
>
> It is a Class A Misdemeanor for a parent or guardian to knowingly allow a minor, convicted of a violent felony, as defined in U.C.A. 76-10-501(18) and U.C.A.. 76-3-203.5 above, to possess a firearm. The parent or guardian commits a third degree felony for every additional violation of this code section.

ACTUAL TEXT

(1) A parent or guardian may not intentionally or knowingly provide a firearm to, or permit the possession of a firearm by, any minor who has been convicted of a violent felony as defined in Section 76-3-203.5 or any minor who has been adjudicated in juvenile court for an offense which would constitute a violent felony if the minor were an adult.

(2) Any person who violates this section is guilty of:

 (a) a class A misdemeanor upon the first offense; and

 (b) a third degree felony for each subsequent offense.

U.C.A. 76-10-509.7. Parent or guardian knowing of minor's possession of dangerous weapon.

> **"PLAIN TALK"**
>
> A parent who knows a minor illegally possesses a dangerous weapon or a firearm (meaning without the parent's or guardian's permission or outside his or her presence) and fails to make reasonable efforts to take the weapon or handgun away from the minor, is guilty of a Class B Misdemeanor.

ACTUAL TEXT

Any parent or guardian of a minor who knows that the minor is in possession of a dangerous weapon in violation of Section 76-10-509 or a firearm in violation of Section 76-10-

509.4 and fails to make reasonable efforts to remove the firearm from the minor's possession is guilty of a class B misdemeanor.

U.C.A. 76-10-509.9. Sales of firearms to juveniles.

"PLAIN TALK"

No one can sell a firearm to a minor outside the presence of his parent or guardian. To do so is a third degree felony.

ACTUAL TEXT

(1) A person may not sell any firearm to a minor under 18 years of age unless the minor is accompanied by a parent or guardian.

(2) Any person who violates this section is guilty of a third degree felony.

U.C.A. 76-10-509.9

COMMENTARY

Caution gun dealers! This code section suggests it's legal to sell handguns to minors accompanied by a parent or guardian. However, federal law states, "It shall be unlawful for a person to sell . . .[a handgun] to a person who the transferor knows or has reasonable cause to believe is a juvenile" (see 18 U.S.C.§ 922(x)(1), covered in Chapter XIII of this book). The only exceptions are "temporary" transfers of handguns to minors for farming, ranching, target practicing, hunting and serving in the military. I told you this stuff is complicated. It would be extremely unfortunate for a gun dealer, relying on state law, to lose his dealer's license for violating federal law. This Utah code section should be amended to conform with federal law, 18 U.S.C. § 922(x)(1).

U.C.A. 76-10-511. Possession of loaded weapon at residence authorized.

"PLAIN TALK"

Hallelujah! This is one of the good gun laws. The good guys (and gals, of course) can legally protect themselves and their families with a loaded gun in their homes, hotel rooms, trailers, tents, and sleeping bags while camping.

ACTUAL TEXT

Except for persons described in Section 76-10-503, **[convicted felons, mentally defective persons, drug addicts etc.]** a person may have a loaded firearm at his place of residence, including any temporary residence or camp.

U.C.A. 76-10-511

COMMENTARY

This should include dormitories if a student is 18 years of age or older. But it doesn't unless the student is 21 or older and has a valid concealed weapon permit. In my "mind's eye," I see campus administrators biting their nails at the suggestion that students 18 years of age and older should be able to have the same privileges as adult students living off campus. We draft 18 year olds, slap M-16s in their hands, and expect them to sleep together in crowded, wet foxholes in hostile lands. If they are mature enough to do that, they are mature enough to be able to defend their temporary homes if need be, whether on or off campus. It's all about trusting the good guys, isn't it? If our laws hold people criminally and civilly ACCOUNTABLE for injuries caused by firearms, we shouldn't have to place PRIOR RESTRAINTS on the rights of law-abiding citizens to bear arms.

U.C.A. 76-10-512. Target concessions, shooting ranges, competitions, and hunting excepted from prohibitions.

"PLAIN TALK"

Thanks to this code section, we can teach our kids to shoot and hunt with a handgun. Subsection (3) is pretty broad. It says minors can practice using a handgun in ANY place where discharging a firearm is NOT PROHIBITED by state or local law. This means that if a minor has written permission from his parent or guardian to practice shooting a handgun in a remote area, outside city limits, off of highways, at least 600 feet from buildings or enclosures where domestic animals are kept, the minor may legally possess a handgun. Minors under 14 must be accompanied by an adult to possess any dangerous weapon (see U.C.A. 76-10-509(2) above) even if they have written permission. WORDS OF CAUTION: This law must be read in context with several other state laws and the federal law governing juveniles and firearms. Without seeing all these laws in one location and comparing them, they are IMPOSSIBLE to decipher. To help, we compiled a table summarizing them in Appendix F. DON'T LEAVE HOME WITHOUT APPENDIX F (or the consent form in Appendix A, for that matter) anytime you MIX KIDS and GUNS. Otherwise, you could get an "F" which stands for FELONY!

ACTUAL TEXT

The provisions of Section 76-10-509 and Subsection 76-10-509.4 (1) regarding possession of handguns by minors shall not apply to any of the following:

(1) Patrons firing at lawfully operated target concessions at amusement parks, piers, and similar locations provided that the firearms to be used are firmly chained or affixed to the counters.

(2) Any person in attendance at a hunter's safety course or a firearms safety course.

(3) Any person engaging in practice or any other lawful use of a firearm at an established range or any other area where the discharge of a firearm is not prohibited by state or local law.

(4) Any person engaging in an organized competition involving the use of a firearm, or participating in or practicing for such competition.

(5) Any minor under 18 years of age who is on real property with the permission of the owner, licensee, or lessee of the property and who has the permission of a parent or legal guardian or the owner, licensee, or lessee to possess a firearm not otherwise in violation of law.

(6) Any resident or nonresident hunters with a valid hunting license or other persons who are lawfully engaged in hunting.

(7) Any person traveling to or from any activity described in Subsection (2), (3), (4), (5), or (6) with an unloaded firearm in his possession.

U.C.A. 76-10-520. Number or mark assigned to pistol or revolver by Department of Public Safety.

"PLAIN TALK"

Sometimes "low-lifers" file the serial numbers off of guns they intend to use in a crime. As Section 522 below states, this is a crime. Code Section 520 gives the Department of Public Safety the authority to issue a new number to someone who, through legal means, ends up with a pistol or revolver with no serial number. I'm not certain the Department of Public Safety can issue a new number without approval of the Bureau of Alcohol, Tobacco and Firearms (ATF).

ACTUAL TEXT

The Department of Public Safety upon request may assign a distinguishing number or mark of identification to any pistol or revolver whenever it is without a manufacturer's number, or other mark of identification or whenever the manufacturer's number or other mark of identification or the distinguishing number or mark assigned by the Department of Public Safety has been destroyed or obliterated.

U.C.A. 76-10-521. Unlawful marking of pistol or revolver.

"PLAIN TALK"

If you end up with a handgun without a serial number, you can't just stamp one on without getting permission from the Department of Public Safety (DPS). Warning: Acts that are misdemeanors under this section and the following section are federal felonies (see 18 U.S.C. 922(k) and 924 (a)(1)(B)). Some people prefer to buy guns from individuals rather than gun dealers. If you do, you had better check the gun to make sure its serial number hasn't been obliterated, altered or removed; otherwise the gun is a "hot potato" and could get you into BIG trouble. Furthermore, I'm not certain the Department of Public Safety can issue a new number without approval of the Bureau of Alcohol, Tobacco and Firearms (ATF). My legal advice is that you should NEVER take possession of a firearm that has had identifying information on it altered in any manner.

ACTUAL TEXT

(1) Any person who places or stamps on any pistol or revolver any number except one assigned to it by the Department of Public Safety is guilty of a class A misdemeanor.

U.C.A. 76-10-522. Alteration of number or mark on pistol or revolver.

"PLAIN TALK"

It's against the law to grind serial numbers and other I.D. marks off of pistols and revolvers.

ACTUAL TEXT

Any person who changes, alters, removes, or obliterates the name of the maker, the model, manufacturer's number, or other mark of identification, including any distinguishing number or mark assigned by the Department of Public Safety, on any pistol or revolver, without first having secured written permission from the Department of Public Safety to make the change, alteration, or removal, is guilty of a class A misdemeanor.

18 U.S.C. 922(k) [Possessing a firearm with no serial number]

"PLAIN TALK"

It's a five-year federal felony (18 USC 924 (a)(1)(B)) to knowingly possess a firearm that has had the serial number tampered with. HOT POTATO, BABY!!!! Check serial numbers before you buy a gun from a private individual!!!!!!!!!!!! [Before I buy any used gun, I call my local law enforcement people and ask them to run the serial number to make sure I'm not receiving stolen property. The little bit of advice you have gotten in this tiny paragraph is worth the price of this book!]

ACTUAL TEXT

(k) It shall be unlawful for any person knowingly to transport, ship, or receive, in interstate or foreign commerce, any firearm which has had the importer's or manufacturer's serial number removed, obliterated, or altered or to possess or receive any firearm which has had the importer's or manufacturer's serial number removed, obliterated, or altered and has, at any time, been shipped or transported in interstate or foreign commerce.

U.C.A. 76-10-523. Persons exempt from weapons laws.

"PLAIN TALK"

The following persons are exempt from all of the weapon laws referenced in this "part," (part 5), sections 500 to 531:

Federal marshals, federal officials required to carry guns, police officers, judges, freight companies transporting firearms as merchandise, non-residents traveling through the state (as long as the gun is unloaded and securely encased as defined in Section 501).

Federal marshals, police officers and other federal officials that carry guns as part of their work duties, can carry concealed weapons off duty. Utah recognizes permits from all other states and counties even though the rules for getting a permit in those places are less restrictive than in Utah. Because Utah recognizes permits issued in all other states, many of those states recognize Utah's permits. Consequently, Utah's permits have become a coveted item for out-of-staters because it has become one of the most widely recognized permits of all other states. To see which states' permits currently recognize Utah's permits, see the Bureau of Criminal Identification Web page at www.bci.state.ut.us. Please keep in mind that whether a state recognizes Utah's permit could change overnight. Therefore, before traveling to any state, Utah concealed weapon permit holders are encouraged to call the state or states they are traveling to and ask whether that state still recognizes Utah's permit. Unfortunately, the states do not have one particular agency that tracks this information. In Arizona it is the Department of Public Safety. In other states, it is the Attorney General's Office. The most effective way I have found to find out which states recognize our permit is to search the Internet for the name of the state together with the phrase "concealed weapon permit." Keep in mind some states don't have a uniform law provision like Utah's U.C.A. 76-10-500. Therefore, there may be cities and counties within a state that accepts our permit, that have unusual restrictions on concealed weapon permit holders. For example, some states don't authorize permit holders to carry their weapons into school zones, churches or private businesses that post signs. You will not know this unless you call ahead and ask about carrying a concealed weapon in the cities and counties in which you intend to travel. See also www.packing.org for UN-OFFICIAL info about what states accept other state's permits. Some business travelers can afford to hire an attorney to research the issue for them.

Concealed Weapon Holders - This section also gives concealed weapon holders several privileges not enjoyed by those who do not have a concealed weapon permit. Concealed weapon holders can carry concealed dangerous weapons (such as knives) as well as loaded firearms, (U.C.A. 76-10-504(1)(a)). They can carry loaded guns in their vehicles (U.C.A. 76-10-505(1)(a)) and on public streets (U.C.A. 76-10-505(1)(b)). They cannot, however, conceal sawed-off shotguns or sawed-off rifles. Permit holders cannot legally carry their weapons into secured areas within the courts, airports, correctional facilities (jails, prisons, reform schools), and mental health facilities (see sections 523.5 and 529 below).

ACTUAL TEXT

(1) This part and Title 53, Chapter 5, Part 7, Concealed Weapon Act, do not apply to any of the following:

- (a) a United States marshal;
- (b) a federal official required to carry a firearm;
- (c) a peace officer of this or any other jurisdiction;
- (d) a law enforcement official as defined and qualified under Section 53-5-711;
- (e) a judge as defined and qualified in Section 53-5-711;
- (f) a common carrier while engaged in the regular and ordinary transport of firearms as merchandise; or
- (g) a nonresident traveling in or through the state, provided that any firearm is:
    - (i) unloaded; and
    - (ii) securely encased as defined in Section 76-10-501.

(2) The provisions of Subsections 76-10-504(1)(a), (1)(b), and Section 76-10-505 do not apply to any person to whom a permit to carry a concealed firearm has been issued:

- (a) pursuant to Section 53-5-704; or
- (b) by another state or county.

U.C.A. 76-10-523.5. Compliance with rules for secure facilities.

"PLAIN TALK"

This section makes no sense without knowing what Sections 53B-3-103, 76-8-311.1, 76-8-311.3, and 78-7-6 say, so we combined them all together here. In short, it is a third degree felony for persons, including those who have concealed weapon permits, to take firearms into secured areas in jails, mental health facilities and the courts. It is a second degree felony to give them to inmates. Section 529 below gives airports the authority to establish secured areas where even concealed weapon holders may not take firearms.

ACTUAL TEXT

Any person, including a person licensed to carry a concealed firearm under Title 53, Chapter 5, Part 7, Concealed Weapons, shall comply with any rule established for secure facilities pursuant to Sections 53B-3-103, 76-8-311.1, 76-8-311.3, and 78-7-6 and shall be subject to any penalty provided in those sections.

U.C.A. 53B-3-103. Power of board to adopt rules and enact regulations.

"PLAIN TALK"

This section is explained thoroughly in Chapter VIII below.

ACTUAL TEXT

(1) The board may enact regulations governing the conduct of university and college students, faculty, and employees.

(2)(a) The board may:

(i) enact and authorize higher education institutions to enact traffic, parking, and related regulations governing all individuals on campuses and other facilities owned or controlled by the institutions or the board; and

(ii) acknowledging that the Legislature has the authority to regulate, by law, firearms at higher education institutions:

(A) authorize higher education institutions to establish no more than one secure area at each institution as a hearing room as prescribed in Section 76-8-311.1, but not otherwise restrict the lawful possession or carrying of firearms; and

(B) authorize a higher education institution to make a rule that allows a resident of a dormitory located at the institution to request only roommates who are not licensed to carry a concealed firearm under Section 53-5-704 or 53-5-705.

(b) In addition to the requirements and penalty prescribed in Subsections 76-8-311.1(3), (4), (5), and (6), the board shall make rules to ensure that:

(i) reasonable means such as mechanical, electronic, x-ray, or similar devices are used to detect firearms, ammunition, or dangerous weapons contained in the personal property of or on the person of any individual attempting to enter a secure area hearing room;

(ii) an individual required or requested to attend a hearing in a secure area hearing room is notified in writing of the requirements related to entering a secured area hearing room under this Subsection (2)(b) and Section 76-8-311.1;

(iii) the restriction of firearms, ammunition, or dangerous weapons in the secure area hearing room is in effect only during the time the secure area hearing room is in use for hearings and for a reasonable time before and after its use; and

(iv) reasonable space limitations are applied to the secure area hearing room as warranted by the number of individuals involved in a typical hearing.

(3) The board and institutions may enforce these rules and regulations in any reasonable manner, including the assessment of fees, fines, and forfeitures, the collection of which may be by withholding from moneys owed the violator, the imposition of probation, suspension, or expulsion from the institution,

the revocation of privileges, the refusal to issue certificates, degrees, and diplomas, through judicial process or any reasonable combination of these alternatives.

U.C.A. 76-8-311.1. Secure areas — Items prohibited — Penalty.

"PLAIN TALK"

Obviously, taking explosives, firearms or other weapons into a jail or mental institution could create an extremely dangerous situation. The weapon holder could be overpowered by an inmate resulting in death, serious bodily injury or escape. Therefore, Utah law authorizes such facilities to create "secure areas" where such weapons are banned. The facility creating a secure area must post a sign explaining the prohibitions. Facilities having secure areas MUST PROVIDE A STORAGE AREA for weapons, and its employees are responsible for the weapons while gun owners visit the facility. Remember, even concealed weapon permit holders may not enter a secured area without checking their weapons. See "Plain Talk" explanation for section 76-10-523.5 above.

ACTUAL TEXT

(1) In addition to the definitions in Section 76-10-501, as used in this section:

(a) "Correctional facility" has the same meaning as defined in Section 76-8-311.3.

(b) "Explosive" has the same meaning as defined for "explosive, chemical, or incendiary device" defined in Section 76-10-306.

(c) "Law enforcement facility" means a facility which is owned, leased, or operated by a law enforcement agency.

(d) "Mental health facility" has the same meaning as defined in Section 62A-12-602.

(e)(i) "Secure area" means any area into which certain persons are restricted from transporting any firearm, ammunition, dangerous weapon, or explosive.

(ii) A "secure area" may not include any area normally accessible to the public.

(2)(a) A person in charge of a correctional, law enforcement, or mental health facility may establish secure areas within the facility and may prohibit or control by rule any firearm, ammunition, dangerous weapon, or explosive.

(b) Subsections (2)(a), (3), (4), (5), and (6) apply to higher education secure area hearing rooms referred to in Subsections 53B-3-103(2)(a)(ii) and (b).

(3) At least one notice shall be prominently displayed at each entrance to an area in which a firearm, ammunition, dangerous weapon, or explosive is restricted.

(4)(a) Provisions shall be made to provide a secure weapons storage area so that persons entering the secure area may store their weapons prior to entering the secure area.

(b) The entity operating the facility shall be responsible for weapons while they are stored in the storage area.

(5) It is a defense to any prosecution under this section that the accused, in committing the act made criminal by this section, acted in conformity with the facility's rule or policy established pursuant to this section.

(6)(a) Any person who knowingly or intentionally transports into a secure area of a facility any firearm, ammunition, or dangerous weapon is guilty of a third degree felony.

. . . [(6)(b) deals with explosives and is outside the intended coverage of this book.]

U.C.A. 76-8-311.3. Items prohibited in correctional and mental health facilities — Penalties.

"PLAIN TALK"

See "Plain Talk" explanation for section 76-10-523.5 above.

ACTUAL TEXT

(1) As used in this section:

. . .

(c) "Correctional facility" means:

(i) any facility operated by or contracting with the Department of Corrections to house offenders in either a secure or nonsecure setting;
(ii) any facility operated by a municipality or a county to house or detain criminal offenders;
(iii) any juvenile detention facility; and
(iv) any building or grounds appurtenant to the facility or lands granted to the state, municipality, or county for use as a correctional facility.

. . .

(e) "Mental health facility" has the same meaning as defined in Section 62A-15-602.

(f) "Offender" means a person in custody at a correctional facility.

(g) "Secure area" has the same meaning as provided in Section 76-8-311.1.

(2) Notwithstanding Section 76-10-500, a correctional or mental health facility may provide by rule that no firearm, ammunition, dangerous weapon, implement of escape, explosive, controlled substance, spirituous or fermented liquor, medicine, or poison in any quantity may be:

(a) transported to or upon a correctional or mental health facility;

(b) sold or given away at any correctional or mental health facility;

(c) given to or used by any offender at a correctional or mental health facility; or

(d) knowingly or intentionally possessed at a correctional or mental health facility.

(3) It is a defense to any prosecution under this section if the accused in committing the act made criminal by this section:

(a) with respect to a correctional facility operated by the Department of Corrections, acted in conformity with departmental rule or policy;

(b) with respect to a correctional facility operated by a municipality, acted in conformity with the policy of the municipality;

(c) with respect to a correctional facility operated by a county, acted in conformity with the policy of the county; or

(d) with respect to a mental health facility, acted in conformity with the policy of the mental health facility.

(4)(a) Any person who transports to or upon a correctional facility, or into a secure area of a mental health facility, any firearm, ammunition, dangerous weapon, or implement of escape with intent to provide or sell it to any offender, is guilty of a second degree felony.

(b) Any person who provides or sells to any offender at a correctional facility, or any detainee at a secure area of a mental health facility, any firearm, ammunition, dangerous weapon, or implement of escape is guilty of a second degree felony.

(c) Any offender who possesses at a correctional facility, or any detainee who possesses at a secure area of a mental health facility, any firearm, ammunition, dangerous weapon, or implement of escape is guilty of a second degree felony.

(d) Any person who, without the permission of the authority operating the correctional facility or the secure area of a mental health facility, knowingly possesses at a correctional facility or a secure area of a mental health facility any firearm, ammunition, dangerous weapon, or implement of escape is guilty of a third degree felony.

. . .

U.C.A. 78-7-6. Rules — Right to make — Limitation — Security.

"PLAIN TALK"

See "Plain Talk" explanation for section 76-10-523.5 above.

ACTUAL TEXT. . .

(1) Every court of record may make rules, not inconsistent with law, for its own government and the government of its officers; but such rules must neither impose any tax or charge upon any legal proceeding nor give any allowance to any officer for service.

(2)(a) The judicial council may provide, through the rules of judicial administration, for security in or about a courthouse or courtroom, or establish a secure area as prescribed in Section 76-8-311.1.

(b)(i) If the council establishes a secure area under Subsection (2)(a), it shall provide a secure firearms storage area on site so that persons with lawfully carried firearms may store them while they are in the secure area.

(ii) The entity operating the facility with the secure area shall be responsible for the firearms while they are stored in the storage area referred to in Subsection (2)(b)(i).

(iii) The entity may not charge a fee to individuals for storage of their firearms under Subsection (2)(b)(i).

(3)(a) Unless authorized by the rules of judicial administration, any person who knowingly or intentionally possesses a firearm, ammunition, or dangerous weapon within a secure area established by the judicial council under this section is guilty of a third degree felony.

. . . [subsection (b) deals with explosives.]

U.C.A. 78-7-6

COMMENTARY

Restricting a civil right should never be taken lightly. A person disarming another, making him or her vulnerable to attack, takes on a new responsibility, that of protecting the disarmed citizen from assault. Jails, airports, and courts that deprive citizens of this right, should be required to guarantee the safety of such citizens who are no longer armed to protect themselves. Courts throughout the country have held that grocery stores, apartments, hotels, banks with ATMs may be held liable for failing to prevent criminal attacks upon their patrons. Airlines have been held responsible to their passengers for failing to prevent bombings. Civil law (see discussion in Chapter X below) should impose liability for depriving others of a right to defend themselves. The Legislature has made it very plain that if the courts create secure areas, they must provide lock boxes. Thus far most courts have refused to do so. If a court visitor is killed or injured because the courts have failed to provide lock boxes, it seems they should be held liable to the injured person or the family of someone who is killed who could have otherwise defended himself or herself with a firearm.

U.C.A. 76-10-524. Purchase of firearms pursuant to federal law.

"PLAIN TALK"

This state law, coupled with Section 922(b)(3) of the Federal Gun Control Act of 1968 authorizes gun dealers to sell rifles and shotguns to residents of other states if the sale is legal in Utah and the home state of the buyer. The buyer has to buy the gun in person at the dealer's place of business. The dealer has to be "darn sure" the sale is legal in both Utah and the customer's home state. Federal law presumes the dealer knows the laws of both states.

ACTUAL TEXT

This part will allow purchases of firearms and ammunition pursuant to U.S.C. Title 18 Chapter 44 Sec. 922b(3).

ACTUAL TEXT of 18 U.S.C. § 922(b)(3) [of the Federal Gun Control Act of 1968]

(b) It shall be unlawful for any licensed importer, licensed manufacturer, licensed dealer, or licensed collector to sell or deliver—

. . .

(3) any firearm to any person who the licensee knows or has reasonable cause to believe does not reside in (or if the person is a corporation or other business entity, does not maintain a place of business in) the State in which the licensee's place of business is located, except that this paragraph

(A) shall not apply to the sale or delivery of any rifle or shotgun to a resident of a State other than a State in which the licensee's place of business is located if the transferee meets in person with the transferor to accomplish the transfer, and the sale, delivery, and receipt fully comply with the legal conditions of sale in both such States (and any licensed manufacturer, importer or dealer shall be presumed, for purposes of this subparagraph, in the absence of evidence to the contrary, to have had actual knowledge of the State laws and published ordinances of both States), and

(B) shall not apply to the loan or rental of a firearm to any person for temporary use for lawful sporting purposes;

COMMENTARY

I have seen dealers prosecuted for selling handguns to citizens of other states. If anyone, including a dealer, intends to sell a handgun to the citizen of another state, the handgun must be sent to a dealer in the other state. Out of state dealers are required to send an signed copy of their Federal Firearms License (FFL) to the seller or transferor. When the out-of-state FFL receives the handgun, he will first perform a background check to ensure it is legal to transfer the handgun to the citizen of his state who purchased the handgun.

Pancho's Wisdom

If you don't shudder at the hot breath and dripping fangs of government tyranny, your sex-change operation has clouded your sense of self preservation.

U.C.A. 76-10-525. Disposition of weapons after use for court purposes.

"PLAIN TALK"

If your weapon is used as evidence in a legal case, you will probably get it back after the case is over. But if you committed a crime with it, kiss your Kimber goodbye. Handguns owned AND used by criminals to commit crimes get a "Terminator 2" bubble bath (otherwise known as Sarah Brady Stew). It's not what the Founding Fathers had in mind when they envisioned America as a "melting pot!"

ACTUAL TEXT

All police departments and/or sheriff's departments which have in their possession a weapon after it has been used for court purposes shall determine the true owner of the weapon and return it to him; however, if unable to determine the true owner of the weapon, or if the true owner is the person committing the crime for which the weapon was used as evidence, the department shall confiscate it and it shall revert to that agency for their use and/or disposal as the head of the department determines.

U.C.A 76-10-525

COMMENTARY

This law has a horrible conflict of interest built into it. It allows police agencies to use the weapons they seize. This tempts police to arrest gun owners on "trumped up" charges to "get their guns." This law should be amended so that the arresting agency has no financial interest whatever in confiscating a gun. Furthermore, guns should be forfeited only after conviction of felonies, not misdemeanors.

U.C.A. 76-10-526. Criminal background check prior to purchase of a firearm — Fee — Exemption for concealed firearm permit holders.

"PLAIN TALK"

In other words, it now takes an "Act of Congress" and you go through the "Third Degree" to buy a gun. This code section was passed to comply with federal requirements under the Brady Act (see our discussion of the Brady Act in Chapter XIII). You have to show the dealer a photo I.D. on a card issued by a government. Until further notice, the fee for the "Brady check" is $7.50. Denials may be appealed. Old gun owners never die, their firearm-purchase-transaction numbers just eventually (hopefully) fade from the FBI computer. The Utah Bureau of Criminal Investigation (BCI) has the right to research juvenile court records and to deny firearm purchases to persons who were convicted of offenses that would have been felonies had they been adults at the time the offense was committed (See also U.C.A. 76-10-503 above). Other records, including those containing pleas of insanity, findings of mental incompetence to stand trial, and orders of civil commitment are accessible to BCI (U.C.A. 53-10-208 and 208.1, not included in this book). Utah law does not expressly address how those adjudicated mentally deficient may regain their right to possess a firearm in the event they recover from their mental deficiency.

Because the criminal records of concealed weapon holders are checked daily, they do not have to be subjected to or pay for a Brady check. Dealers can sell them a gun upon proof that their concealed weapon permits are still valid.

Even though the proponents of the Brady Act PUBLICIZED it as a law restricting the sale of HANDGUNS (The Brady HANDGUN Violence Prevention Act), as of November 30, 1998, it regulates the sale of RIFLES and SHOTGUNS too. Call it "creeping infringement" which has nearly worn out Pancho's patience and that of every other true Westerner.

ACTUAL TEXT

(1) For purposes of this section, "valid permit to carry a concealed firearm" does not include a temporary permit issued pursuant to Section 53-5-705.

(2) To establish personal identification and residence in this state for purposes of this part, a dealer shall require an individual receiving a firearm to present one photo identification on a form issued by a governmental agency of the state.

(3) A criminal history background check is required for the sale of a firearm by a licensed firearm dealer in the state.

(4)(a) An individual, except a dealer, purchasing a firearm from a dealer shall consent in writing to a criminal background check, on a form provided by the division.

(b) The form shall contain the following information:

(i) the dealer identification number;
(ii) the name and address of the individual receiving the firearm;
(iii) the date of birth, height, weight, eye color, and hair color of the individual receiving the firearm; and
(iv) the Social Security number or any other identification number of the individual receiving the firearm.

(5)(a) The dealer shall send the form required by Subsection (4) to the division immediately upon its completion.

(b) No dealer shall sell or transfer any firearm to an individual until the dealer has provided the division with the information in Subsection (4) and has received approval from the division under Subsection (7).

(6) The dealer shall make a request for criminal history background information by telephone or other electronic means to the division and shall receive approval or denial of the inquiry by telephone or other electronic means.

(7) When the dealer calls for or requests a criminal history background check, the division shall:

(a) review the criminal history files, including juvenile court records, to determine if the individual is prohibited from purchasing, possessing, or transferring a firearm by state or federal law;

(b) inform the dealer that:

(i) the records indicate the individual is so prohibited; or

(ii) the individual is approved for purchasing, possessing, or transferring a firearm;

(c) provide the dealer with a unique transaction number for that inquiry; and

(d) provide a response to the requesting dealer during the call for a criminal background, or by return call, or other electronic means, without delay, except in case of electronic failure or other circumstances beyond the control of the division, the division shall advise the dealer of the reason for the delay and give the dealer an estimate of the length of the delay.

(8)(a) The division shall not maintain any records of the criminal history background check longer than 20 days from the date of the dealer's request if the division determines that the individual receiving the gun is not prohibited from purchasing, possessing, or transferring the firearm under state or federal law.

(b) However, the division shall maintain a log of requests containing the dealer's federal firearms number, the transaction number, and the transaction date for a period of 12 months.

(9) If the criminal history background check discloses information indicating that the individual attempting to purchase the firearm is prohibited from purchasing, possessing, or transferring a firearm, the division shall inform the law enforcement agency in the jurisdiction where the person resides.

(10) If an individual is denied the right to purchase a firearm under this section, the individual may review his criminal history information and may challenge or amend the information as provided in Section 53-10-108.

(11) The division shall make rules as provided in Title 63, Chapter 46a, Utah Administrative Rulemaking Act, to ensure the iden-

tity, confidentiality, and security of all records provided by the division pursuant to this part are in conformance with the requirements of the Brady Handgun Violence Prevention Act, Pub.L. No. 103-159, 107 Stat. 1536 (1993).

(12)(a)(i) All dealers shall collect a criminal history background check fee which is $7.50.

(ii) This fee remains in effect until changed by the division through theprocess under Section 63-38-3.2.

(b)(i) The dealer shall forward at one time all fees collected for criminal history background checks performed during the month to the division by the last day of the month following the sale of a firearm.

(ii) The division shall deposit the fees in the General Fund as dedicated credits to cover the cost of administering and conducting the criminal history background check program.

(13) An individual with a concealed firearm permit issued pursuant to Title 53, Chapter 5, Part 7, Concealed Weapon Act, shall be exempt from the background check and corresponding fee required in this section for the purchase of a firearm if:

(a) the individual presents his concealed firearm permit to the dealer prior to purchase of the firearm; and

(b) the dealer verifies with the division that the individual's concealed firearm permit is valid.

U.C.A. 76-10-527. Penalties.

"PLAIN TALK"

DEALERS, you're in a heap o' trouble if you sell handguns without doing a criminal background check. GUN BUYERS, if you lie to buy a handgun, you'll be singin' the "Jail House Rock." PURCHASERS, it's a felony to use your "squeaky clean" criminal background to buy handguns for ineligible persons such as convicted felons, those who have been convicted of acts of domestic violence, illegal aliens, mental incompetents, minors, citizens from other states and other "undesirables." (Hmmm . . . you'd think discriminating against citizens of other states like this would violate the Privileges and Immunities Clause of the United States Constitution.) ATF refers to such a transaction as a "Straw Purchase." Young adults, 18 or older, but younger than 21, cannot buy handguns or handgun ammo from a dealer. They can, however, buy a handgun and handgun ammo from a "non-dealer," as long as the non-dealer did not purchase the handgun or ammo from a dealer, having the INTENT AT THE TIME OF PURCHASE, to turn around and sell to the young adult. See Appendix F entitled "Youngsters, Guns and Ammo."

ACTUAL TEXT

(1) A dealer is guilty of a class A misdemeanor who willfully and intentionally:

- (a) requests, obtains, or seeks to obtain criminal history background information under false pretenses; or
- (b) disseminates criminal history background information.

(2) A person who purchases or transfers a handgun is guilty of a felony of the third degree who willfully and intentionally makes a false statement of the information required in Subsection 76-10-526(3).

(3) A dealer is guilty of a felony of the third degree if the dealer willfully and intentionally sells or transfers a handgun in violation of this part.

(4) A person is guilty of a felony of the third degree who purchases a handgun with the intent to:

- (a) resell or otherwise provide a handgun to any person who is ineligible to purchase or receive from a dealer a handgun; or
- (b) transport a handgun out of this state to be resold to an ineligible person.

U.C.A. 76-10-528. Carrying a dangerous weapon while under influence of alcohol or drugs unlawful.

"PLAIN TALK"

SIX-GUNS and SIXERS don't mix! If you are too drunk to drive, you are too drunk to "carry" a dangerous weapon. Some prosecutors and police officers take the position that "carry" means "within one's immediate reach." Having re-read this, I'm not sure if this is true. Unlike the statute making it illegal to carry a concealed dangerous weapon without a permit (76-10-504), this statute does not seem to specify that "carrying" means anything other than possessing the weapon on one's person rather than within that person's immediate reach. It will be interesting to see how narrowly or broadly a court interprets the term "carrying" as it relates to someone who is legally intoxicated. Frankly, I don't recommend you have a firearm within your immediate reach, because you will probably be prosecuted and have to pay attorney fees. Furthermore, drinking impairs one's judgement and I've seen gun owners do some pretty stupid things while under the influence of alcohol.

ACTUAL TEXT

(1) Any person who carries a dangerous weapon while under the influence of alcohol or a controlled substance as defined in Section 58-37-2 is guilty of a class B misdemeanor. Under the influence means the same level of influence of blood or breath alcohol concentration as provided in Subsections 41-6a-502(1)(a)(i) through (iii).

(2) It is not a defense to prosecution under this section that the person:

- (a) is licensed in the pursuit of wildlife of any kind; or
- (b) has a valid permit to carry a concealed firearm.

U.C.A. 76-10-529. Possession of dangerous weapons, firearms, or explosives in airport secure areas prohibited — Penalty.

"PLAIN TALK"

Nobody, including concealed weapon permit holders, can carry a gun, bomb (uh, how come?) or other dangerous weapon past the metal detectors (in other words into the "secure area") at an airport. If you do it intentionally, it's a class A misdemeanor. If you forget you have the weapon (don't laugh, it's easy to do when you carry the weapon all the time and get used to it), the penalty is an infraction. But don't be too anxious to pack your PPK onto the plane just because Utah calls it a misdemeanor. Under the guise of deterring terrorism, the feds just beefed up the penalty from 1 year in the slammer to 10 for taking or attempting to take a dangerous weapon onto any aircraft (49 U.S.C. 46505).

ACTUAL TEXT

(1) As used in this section:

(a) "Airport authority" has the same meaning as defined in Section 72-10-102.

(b) "Dangerous weapon" is the same as defined in Section 76-10-501.

(c) "Explosive" is the same as defined for "explosive, chemical, or incendiary device" in Section 76-10-306.

(d) "Firearm" is the same as defined in Section 76-10-501.

(2)(a) Within a secure area of an airport established pursuant to this section, a person, including a person licensed to carry a concealed firearm under Title 53, Chapter 5, Part 7, Concealed Weapon Act, is guilty of:

(i) a class A misdemeanor if the person knowingly or intentionally possesses any dangerous weapon or firearm;

(ii) an infraction if the person recklessly or with criminal negligence possesses any dangerous weapon or firearm; or

(iii) a violation of Section 76-10-306 if the person

transports,possesses, distributes, or sells any explosive, chemical, or incendiary device.

(b) Subsection (2)(a) does not apply to:

(i) persons exempted under Section 76-10-523; and

(ii) members of the state or federal military forces while engaged in the performance of their official duties.

(3) An airport authority, county, or municipality regulating the airport may:

(a) establish any secure area located beyond the main area where the public generally buys tickets, checks and retrieves luggage; and

(b) use reasonable means, including mechanical, electronic, x-ray, or any other device, to detect dangerous weapons, firearms, or explosives concealed in baggage or upon the person of any individual attempting to enter the secure area.

(4) At least one notice shall be prominently displayed at each entrance to a secure area in which a dangerous weapon, firearm, or explosive is restricted.

(5) Upon the discovery of any dangerous weapon, firearm, or explosive, the airport authority, county, or municipality, the employees, or other personnel administering the secure area may:

(a) require the individual to deliver the item to the air freight office or airline ticket counter;

(b) require the individual to exit the secure area; or

(c) obtain possession or retain custody of the item until it is transferred to law enforcement officers.

THE FEDERAL COUNTERPART CARRYING A MINIMUM 10 YEAR SENTENCE SAYS:

49 U.S.C. 46505. Carrying a weapon or explosive on an aircraft

(a) Definition. In this section, "loaded firearm" means a starter gun or a weapon designed or converted to expel a projectile through an explosive, that has a cartridge, a detonator, or powder in the chamber, magazine, cylinder, or clip.

(b) General criminal penalty. An individual shall be fined under title 18, imprisoned for not more than 10 years, or both, if the individual—

(1) when on, or attempting to get on, an aircraft in, or intended for operation in, air transportation or intrastate air transportation, has on or about the individual or the property of the individual a concealed dangerous weapon that is or would be accessible to the individual in flight; **[as is typical of the feds, this is overkill; it doesn't seem to require proof of intent - forget your pistola in your carpet bag and you'll rot in the federal pen! And check out the following provision which gives you 10 years if you forget to unload your piece and check it in your luggage. Forget the fact it ain't even accessible to you in flight! Doesn't anyone in Washington love gun owners?]**

(2) has placed, attempted to place, or attempted to have placed a loaded firearm on that aircraft in property not accessible to passengers in flight; or

(3) has on or about the individual, or has placed, attempted to place, or attempted to have placed on that aircraft, an explosive or incendiary device.

(c) Criminal penalty involving disregard for human life. An individual who willfully and without regard for the safety of human life, or with reckless disregard for the safety of human life, violates subsection (b) of this section, shall be fined under title 18, imprisoned for not more than 15 years, or both.

(d) Non-application. Subsection (b)(1) of this section does not apply to—

(1) a law enforcement officer of a State or political subdivision of a State, or an officer or employee of the United States Government, authorized to

carry arms in an official capacity;

(2) another individual the Administrator of the Federal Aviation Administration by regulation authorizes to carry a dangerous weapon in air transportation or intrastate air transportation; or

(3) an individual transporting a weapon (except a loaded firearm) in baggage not accessible to a passenger in flight if the air carrier was informed of the presence of the weapon.

. . .

U.C.A. 76-10-530. Trespass with a firearm in a house of worship or private residence — Notice — Penalty.

"PLAIN TALK"

U.C.A. 76-10-530 clarifies the criminal trespass statute (U.C.A. 76-6-206). The criminal trespass statute gives a resident on private property who has not invited the public to enter, the right to prohibit access to anyone for any reason. Some were concerned that the language of the concealed weapons statute giving Utahns the right to carry concealed weapons "throughout the state without restriction" might prevent property owners or residents from ousting a gun totin' guest. U.C.A. 76-10-530 unambiguously gives residents the right to ask anyone to leave the resident's home for any reason including the fact that he or she does not want them on the property with a firearm. The same goes for houses of worship. The prohibition may be communicated orally or by posting a sign. Notice that a violation of this code section is an infraction which will not cause the violator to lose his or her concealed weapon permit. Also, the prosecutor will have a tough burden of proving the accused guilty if the defendant claims he didn't know of the restriction. Section (1) requires proof that the defendant "knowingly and intentionally" violated the law. Thus, if the concealed weapon holder carelessly fails to observe a sign prohibiting concealed weapons on the premises, he has a defense because he did not transport his firearm onto the prohibited premises "knowingly and intentionally."

> Although it is clear under Subsection 3 of this new code section that a landlord may not prohibit a renter or lessee from lawfully possessing a firearm on the rented premises, the issue arises as to whether landlord may post a notice in an apartment complex prohibiting guests of the tenants from transporting their legal concealed weapons into the facility. This could be remedied by adding "or invitee" to the phrase "to restrict the renter or lessee from lawfully . . . ."
>
> The Legislature made a distinction between houses of worship, which are only open to "welcome visitors," as opposed to private businesses which invite the public at large. Businesses open to the public, such as grocery or video stores arguably cannot prohibit concealed weapon holders from entering their premises.

ACTUAL TEXT

(1) A person, including a person licensed to carry a concealed firearm pursuant to Title 53, Chapter 5, Part 7, Concealed Weapon Act, after notice has been given as provided in Subsection (2) that firearms are prohibited, may not knowingly and intentionally:

- (a) transport a firearm into:
  - (i) a house of worship; or
  - (ii) a private residence; or
- (b) while in possession of a firearm, enter or remain in:
  - (i) a house of worship; or
  - (ii) a private residence.

(2) Notice that firearms are prohibited may be given by:

- (a) personal communication to the actor by:
  - (i) the church or organization operating the house of worship;
  - (ii) the owner, lessee, or person with lawful right of possession of the private residence; or
  - (iii) a person with authority to act for the person or entity in Subsections (2)(a)(i) and (ii);
- (b) posting of signs reasonably likely to come to the attention of persons entering the house of worship or private

residence;

(c) announcement, by a person with authority to act for the church or organization operating the house of worship, in a regular congregational meeting in the house of worship;

(d) publication in a bulletin, newsletter, worship program, or similar document generally circulated or available to the members of the congregation regularly meeting in the house of worship; or

(e) publication in a newspaper of general circulation in the county in which the house of worship is located or the church or organization operating the house of worship has its principal office in this state.

(3) A church or organization operating a house of worship and giving notice that firearms are prohibited may:

(a) revoke the notice, with or without supersedure, by giving further notice in any manner provided in Subsection (2); and

(b) provide or allow exceptions to the prohibition as the church or organization considers advisable.

(4) (a) (i) Within 30 days of giving or revoking any notice pursuant to Subsection (2)(c), (d), or (e), a church or organization operating a house of worship shall notify the division on a form and in a manner as the division shall prescribe.

(ii) The division shall post on its website a list of the churches and organizations operating houses of worship who have given notice under Subsection (4)(a)(i).

(b) Any notice given pursuant to Subsection (2)(c), (d), or (e) shall remain in effect until revoked or for a period of one year from the date the notice was originally given, whichever occurs first.

(5) Nothing in this section permits an owner who has granted the lawful right of possession to a renter or lessee to restrict the renter or lessee from lawfully possessing a firearm in the residence.

(6) A violation of this section is an infraction.

UTAH BUS PASSENGER SAFETY ACT U.C.A. 76-10-1501 through 76-10-1511

"PLAIN TALK"

This law is confusing at best. It appears to cover both interstate (between states) AND intra-state (inside Utah) bus travel. However, interstate travel is already covered by federal law (see Chapter XIII, TAKING YOUR GUNS ON INTERSTATE CARRIERS (Planes, Trains and Buses) - 18 U.S.C. § 922(e)). Because federal law preempts (trumps) state law, concealed weapon permit holders get no special privileges when riding INTERSTATE BUSES (bus lines whose buses travel between states such as Greyhound, Trailways or Lewis Brothers' Stages) . They, like everyone else, MUST check their guns at the terminal as described in §922(e) (see in Chapter XIII for the details). Violation of the federal law is a federal felony.

On INTRASTATE "buses" (UTA buses and TRAX - the definition in U.C.A. 76-10-1503 seems to be broad enough to cover TRAX vehicles as well as buses) state law applies. Concealed weapon permit holders CAN take concealed weapons into the passenger compartments of such vehicles. Non-permit holders can't. If a non-permit holder violates this state law it is a felony.

ACTUAL TEXT

U.C.A. 76-10-1503. Definitions.

As used in this act:

(1) "Bus" means any passenger bus or coach or other motor vehicle having a seating capacity of 15 or more passengers operated by a bus company for the purpose of carrying passengers or cargo for hire and **includes a transit vehicle**, as defined in Section 17A-2-1004, of a public transit district under Title 17A, Chapter 2, Part 10, Utah Public Transit District Act.

(2) "Bus company" or "company" means any person, group of persons or corporation providing for-hire transportation to passengers or cargo by bus upon the highways in the state, including passengers and cargo in **interstate or intrastate travel.** These terms also include local public bodies, public

transit districts, municipalities, public corporations, boards and commissions established under the laws of the state providing transportation to passengers or cargo by bus upon the highways in the state, whether or not for hire.

. . .

(5) **"Terminal"** means a bus station or depot or any other facility operated or leased by or operated on behalf of a bus company and includes a transit facility, as defined in Section 17B-2a-802, of a public transit district under Title 17B, Chapter 2a, Part 8, Public Transit District Act. This term includes **a reasonable area immediately adjacent to any designated stop along the route traveled by any bus operated by a bus company and parking lots or areas adjacent to terminals. (Emphasis added.)**

U.C.A. 76-10-1504 Bus hijacking — Assault with intent to commit hijacking — Use of a dangerous weapon or firearm — Penalties.

"PLAIN TALK"

It's a third degree felony to get on a intrastate (within Utah only) bus carrying a concealed dangerous weapon. This law does not apply to federal marshals, federal officials required to carry a firearm, peace officers of any jurisdiction, prosecutors or judges with "certificates of qualification" (super permits that allow them to carry a concealed weapon into a courtroom), concealed weapon permit holders or people who have the consent of the bus company to carry a weapon. Remember that under federal law CWPs riding Interstate buses and trains must still check their firearms at the ticket counter just like they are required to do when boarding an airliner (see Chapter XIII, TAKING YOUR GUNS ON INTERSTATE CARRIERS (Planes, Trains and Buses) - 18 U.S.C. § 922(e))."

ACTUAL TEXT

. . .

(4)(a) A person who boards a bus with a concealed dangerous weapon or firearm upon his person or effects is guilty of a third degree felony.

(b) The prohibition of Subsection (4)(a) does not apply to:

(i) individuals listed in Subsections 76-10-523(1)(a), (b), (c), (d), and (e);

(ii) a person licensed to carry a concealed weapon; or

(iii) persons in possession of weapons or firearms with the consent of the owner of the bus or the owner's agent, or the lessee or bailee of the bus.

U.C.A. 76-10-1504

COMMENTARY

TRANSFORMATION INTO A FELON AS SOON AS YOU STEP INTO THE BUS TERMINAL OR ONTO THE BUS - The preceding and following code sections could pose a real problem for citizens who are not concealed weapon permit holders, but who assume that concealing is only a misdemeanor (and it is under most circumstances, see U.C.A. 76-10-504 above). The requirements for a concealed carry permit are very strict and not all law-abiding citizens qualify. Riding the bus can be a frightening experience depending upon the time of day and the area. These two statutes make felons out of people who feel the need to protect themselves with a concealed weapon on the bus or in a bus depot. If they conceal a firearm in the grocery store, they are only guilty of a misdemeanor; if they do so on a bus or in a bus terminal, they become felons. These statutes do not require bus companies to warn citizens of the step-up penalty for riding the bus or entering a bus terminal. Some bus companies warn that no weapons are allowed, but do not mention the penalty. This statute should be amended:

(4) (a) Any person who boards a bus with a concealed dangerous weapon or firearm upon his person or effects is guilty of a ~~third degree felony~~ <u>class B misdemeanor unless the dangerous</u>

<u>weapon is possessed with the intent to assault or harm another without legal jurisdiction, in which case the person is guilty of a second degree felony.</u>

U.C.A. 76-10-1507. Exclusion of persons without bona fide business from terminal — Firearms and dangerous materials — Surveillance devices and seizure of offending materials — Detention of violators — Private security personnel.

"PLAIN TALK"

It's a felony to set foot in a bus terminal if you're carrying a concealed weapon, whether or not it's loaded. Keep in mind that under federal law CWPs riding Interstate buses and trains must still check their firearms in at the ticket counter just like they are required to do when boarding an airliner **(see Chapter XIII, TAKING YOUR GUNS ON INTERSTATE CARRIERS (Planes, Trains and Buses) - 18 U.S.C. § 922(e)).**

ACTUAL TEXT

(1)(a) In order to provide for the safety, welfare and comfort of passengers, a bus company may refuse admission to terminals to a person not having bona fide business within the terminal.

(b) The refusal may not be inconsistent or contrary to state or federal laws or regulations, or to an ordinance of the political subdivision in which the terminal is located.

(c) An authorized bus company representative may require a person in a terminal to identify himself and state his business.

(d) Failure to comply with a request under Subsection (1)(c) or to state an acceptable business purpose is grounds for the representative to request that the person depart the terminal.

(e) A person who refuses to comply with a request made under Subsection (1)(d) is guilty of a class C misdemeanor.

(2)(a) A person who carries a concealed dangerous weapon, firearm, or any highly inflammable or hazardous materials or devices into a terminal or aboard a bus is guilty of a third degree felony.

(b) The prohibition of Subsection (2)(a) does not apply to individuals listed in Subsection 76-10-1504(4).

(c) The bus company may employ reasonable means, including mechanical, electronic or x-ray devices to detect the items concealed in baggage or upon the person of a passenger.

(d) Upon the discovery of an item referred to in Subsection (2)(a), the company may obtain possession and retain custody of the item until it is transferred to a peace officer.

(3)(a) An authorized bus company representative may detain within a terminal or bus any person violating the provisions of this section for a reasonable time until law enforcement authorities arrive.

(b) The detention does not constitute unlawful imprisonment and neither the bus company nor the representative is civilly or criminally liable upon grounds of unlawful imprisonment or assault, provided that only reasonable and necessary force is exercised against the detained person.

(4)(a) A bus company may employ or contract for private security personnel.

(b) The personnel may:

(i) detain within a terminal or bus a person violating this section for a reasonable time until law enforcement authorities arrive; and

(ii) use reasonable and necessary force in subduing or detaining the person.

U.C.A. 76-10-1507

COMMENTARY

Paragraph (5) below should be added to parallel federal law allowing passengers to carry unloaded firearms in baggage not accessible to passengers on board, provided they have informed the bus company of the presence of the weapon, 49 U.S.C. 46505 subsection (d) (We talk about this in Chapter VII under the discussion of U.C.A. 76-10-529).

<u>(5) Subsection (2) of this section does not apply to an individual transporting a weapon (except a loaded firearm) in baggage not accessible to a passenger on the bus, if the bus company was informed of the presence of the weapon.</u>

Pancho's Wisdom

The left keeps claiming the U.S. tortures prisoners. Can we please define torture? Our enemies rammed bamboo shards under our soldiers' fingers and baked them in the sun for months in a dog-sized bamboo cage. That THAT'S torture! U.S. Marine recruits face more emotional and physical challenges during basic training than what has been reported about Abu Ghraib and Guantanamo. If terrorist detainees had to endure the hardships our Navy Seals do to get their berets, the terrorists would have all committed suicide by now. What will it take to keep leftists from shrieking "torture" and hating their own country? How about providing all detainees with an ocean front Miami beach condo? An all-expenses-paid-first-class - six-week furlough to anywhere in the Middle East every six months? Their very own tax-paid-$500/hr. Cochran Firm lawyer? Weekly conjugal visits with their heroine Rosie O'Donnell? A low carb lunch with Michael Moore. Oops! I'm sorry. The average reasonable man would consider conjugal visits with O'Donnell "torture" and lunch with Michael Moore "sicko."

CHAPTER VIII

CONCEALED WEAPON PERMITS

Pancho's Wisdom

It's not brandishing when Pancho reaches for a bag of Doritos Fiery Habanero Chips on the top shelf at the supermarket and his concealed weapon shows; it's a POLITICAL STATEMENT!!!!

U.C.A. 53-5-701. Short title

"PLAIN TALK"

Sections 701 through 711 together with the regulations discussed below, govern the actions of concealed weapon permit holders (hereinafter "CWPs"). Notice the state code does not hyphenate "concealed weapon" when used as an adjective.

ACTUAL TEXT

This part is known as the "Concealed Weapon Act."

U.C.A. 53-5-702. Definitions.

"PLAIN TALK"

These definitions are simple, so we won't bore you by simply restating them. However, please take note that pleas of "nolo contendere" (no contest) and pleas held in abeyance are still considered convictions for purposes of disqualifying a person for concealed weapon permits (CWPs). This also applies to "diversions" (essentially a continuance followed by a dismissal) during the time the diversion is pending, but not after the dismissal is granted.

ACTUAL TEXT

U.C.A. 53-5-702. Definitions.

(1) As used in this part:

(a) "Board" means the Concealed Weapon Review Board created in Section 53-5-703.

(b) "Commissioner" means the commissioner of the Department of Public Safety.

(c) "Conviction" means criminal conduct where the filing of a criminal charge has resulted in:

(i) a finding of guilt based on evidence presented to a judge or jury;
(ii) a guilty plea;
(iii) a plea of nolo contendere;
(iv) a plea of guilty or nolo contendere which is held in abeyance pending the successful completion of probation;
(v) a pending diversion agreement; or
(vi) a conviction which has been reduced pursuant to Section 76-3-402.

(d) "Division" means the Criminal Investigations and Technical Services Division created in Section 53-10-103.

(2) The definitions in Section 76-10-501 apply to this part.

. . .

U.C.A. 53-5-704. Division duties — Permit to carry concealed firearm — Requirements for issuance — Violation — Denial, suspension, or revocation — Appeal procedure.

"PLAIN TALK"

Utah is a "shall issue" state meaning the "good guys and gals" with clean criminal records qualify for a CWP without having to give a reason for having one. Before Utah became a "shall issue" state, applicants had to have a good reason to get a permit like having received a death threat. The permit is valid throughout the state "without restriction" (see discussion under "Commentary" below.)

The things that can disqualify you from getting a CWP are:

- having been convicted of a felony (see Chapter V for examples),
- a crime of violence, **["crime of violence" has been deleted from the definitions in U.C.A. 76-10-501 - the term has been changed to "violent felony" (see U.C.A. 76-10-501(18))]**
- an offense involving alcohol (like driving under the influence of alcohol),
- drug offenses (for example, possession of marijuana or cocaine),
- offenses involving moral turpitude (crimes of dishonesty such as theft, embezzlement, passing bad checks and crimes involving immorality such as prostitution, adultery and lewd behavior),
- domestic violence (physically abusing your spouse or children - careful, this statute is extremely broad and could include breaking a dish or other object in the presence of a spouse or child),
- having been judged mentally incompetent, or
- having a history which shows you could be a threat to yourself or others (threats of suicide or violence against others).

The division can look at juvenile records and expunged records (records which have been sealed by order of the court to wipe your record clean - see discussion below) even though such records are generally confidential. If you were "Psycho Boy" as a teenager, the Division of Public Safety may find out, even though your juvenile records are sealed.

If you are charged with a crime of violence in Utah or any other state, the division must suspend your CWP immediately.

However, if you are acquitted or the charge is dropped, the division has to reinstate your suspended permit. **["crime of violence" has been deleted from the definitions in U.C.A. 76-10-501 - the term has been changed to "violent felony" (see U.C.A. 76-10-501(18))]**

Former police officers with honorable discharges must be issued a concealed weapon permit within 5 years, unless they have a criminal record.

You may be able to get a permit although you have a criminal record. The division can consider "mitigating circumstances," meaning reasons why you should be issued a permit anyway. Several years without an arrest could be a "mitigating circumstance."

Concealed weapon permit applications require:

a. the address of the applicants' permanent residence,

b. one recently dated photograph,

c. one set of fingerprints, and

d. evidence of general familiarity with the types of firearms to be concealed.

Familiarity with a firearm means you know how to safely load, unload, store and carry it. You should also understand the law of self defense including where and when you can use deadly force (see Chapter XI). You must know how to transport and conceal your gun safely and legally. You can satisfy the "general familiarity" requirement by completing a national, state or local firearms training course approved by the division or by being certified by a person who has been approved by the division. This could include a police officer, military firearms instructor, a civilian firearms instructor or a hunter safety instructor. You can also satisfy the requirement by showing that you have equivalent experience by having participated in an organized shooting competition. If you have worked in law enforcement or military service, this could also satisfy the requirement. All permits issued and renewed after May 1, 1998 are valid for 5 years unless suspended or revoked.

The State of Utah is not "vicariously" liable for damages caused by a permit holder. This means that a permit holder may be held civilly liable for causing injury or death (see Chapter X), but the State of Utah is not liable for simply issuing a permit. Likewise, CWP instructors are not vicariously liable for the acts of their students.

If you intentionally give false information to get a permit, you are guilty of a class B misdemeanor and your application may be denied or your permit suspended or revoked when the licensing agency finds out. Your permit may not be denied, suspended or revoked for a single infraction conviction under the weapon laws. If you are denied a concealed weapon permit, you have 60 days from the date of the denial, suspension or revocation to appeal. The denial has to be in writing and must give the general reasons why the permit was denied, suspended or revoked. You have the right to see the information upon which the agency based its decision to revoke, suspend or deny. At the appeal, the agency has the burden of proving by a preponderance of the evidence (meaning more likely than not), that you are not qualified for a concealed weapon permit. The division has to issue an order within 30 days. Once that 30 days is up, the applicant can appeal to a court of law (See Utah Administrative Procedure Act, U.C.A. 63-46b-5 to U.C.A. 63-46b-15).

Instead of making a peace officer submit the paperwork ordinary citizens have to provide to get a concealed weapon permit, subsection (7) allows a peace officer to simply get a letter of "good standing" from his commanding officer.

This code section requires concealed weapon permit instructors to give students a written outline of the course and a certificate of completion. Instructors are now "certified" to teach the CWP course of instruction rather than "approved." Recognizing most people who defend themselves with a firearm never shoot the gun, and if they do, it's from a very short distance, the Legislature astutely refused to require an applicant to demonstrate "proficiency" with a firearm. The applicant must still show "general familiarity" with the type(s) of firearms to be concealed. Legislators who held the line on this issue should be reelected.

ACTUAL TEXT

(1)(a) The division or its designated agent shall issue a permit to carry a concealed firearm for lawful self defense to an applicant who is 21 years of age or older within 60 days after receiving an application, unless during the 60-day period the division finds proof that the applicant is not of good character.

(b) The permit is valid throughout the state for five years, without restriction, except as otherwise provided by Section 53-5-710.

(2)(a) An applicant satisfactorily demonstrates good character if the applicant:

(i) has not been convicted of a felony;
(ii) has not been convicted of a crime of violence;
(iii) has not been convicted of an offense involving the use of alcohol;
(iv) has not been convicted of an offense involving the unlawful use of narcotics or other controlled substances;
(v) has not been convicted of an offense involving moral turpitude;
(vi) has not been convicted of an offense involving domestic violence;
(vii) has not been adjudicated by a state or federal court as mentally incompetent, unless the adjudication has been withdrawn or reversed; and
(viii) is qualified to purchase and possess a firearm pursuant to Section 76-10-503 and federal law.

(b) In assessing good character under Subsection (2)(a), the licensing authority shall consider mitigating circumstances.

(3)(a) The division may deny, suspend, or revoke a concealed firearm permit if it has reasonable cause to believe that the applicant has been or is a danger to self or others as demonstrated by evidence, including:

(i) past pattern of behavior involving unlawful violence or threats of unlawful violence;

(ii) past participation in incidents involving unlawful violence or threats of unlawful violence; or

(iii) conviction of an offense in violation of Title 76, Chapter 10, Part (5) Weapons.

(b) The division may not deny, suspend, or revoke a concealed firearm permit solely for a single conviction for an infraction violation of Title 76, Chapter 10, Part 5, Weapons.

(c) In determining whether the applicant has been or is a danger to self or others, the division may inspect:

(i) expunged records of arrests and convictions of adults as provided in Section 77-18-15; and

(ii) juvenile court records as provided in Section 78-3a-206.

(d)(i) If a person granted a permit under this part has been charged with a crime of violence in any state, the division shall suspend the permit.

(ii) Upon notice of the acquittal of the person charged, or notice of the charges having been dropped, the division shall immediately reinstate the suspended permit.

(4) A former peace officer who departs full-time employment as a peace officer, in an honorable manner, shall be issued a concealed firearm permit within five years of that departure if the officer meets the requirements of this section.

(5) Except as provided in Subsection (6), the licensing authority shall also require the applicant to provide:

(a) the address of the applicant's permanent residence;

(b) one recent dated photograph;

(c) one set of fingerprints; and

(d) evidence of general familiarity with the types of firearms to be concealed as defined in Subsection (7).

(6) An applicant who is a law enforcement officer under Section 53-13-103 may provide a letter of good standing from the officer's commanding officer in place of the evidence required by Subsection (5)(d).

(7)(a) General familiarity with the types of firearms to be concealed includes training in:

- (i) the safe loading, unloading, storage, and carrying of the types of firearms to be concealed; and
- (ii) current laws defining lawful use of a firearm by a private citizen, including lawful self-defense, use of force by a private citizen, including use of deadly force, transportation, and concealment.

(b) Evidence of general familiarity with the types of firearms to be concealed may be satisfied by one of the following:

- (i) completion of a course of instruction conducted by a national, state, or local firearms training organization approved by the division;
- (ii) certification of general familiarity by a person who has been certified by the division, which may include a law enforcement officer, military or civilian firearms instructor, or hunter safety instructor; or
- (iii) equivalent experience with a firearm through participation in an organized shooting competition, law enforcement, or military service.

(c) Instruction taken by a student under Subsection (7)(b) shall be in person and not through electronic means.

(8)(a) An applicant for certification as a Utah concealed firearms instructor shall:

- (i) be at least 21 years of age;
- (ii) be currently eligible to possess a firearm under Section 76-10-503and federal law;
- (iii) have a current National Rifle Association certification or its equivalent as determined by the division; and
- (iv) for certificates issued beginning July 1, 2006, have taken a course of instruction and passed a certification test as described in Subsection (8)(c).

(b) An instructor's certification is valid for three years from the date of issuance, unless revoked by the division.

(c)(i) In order to obtain initial certification or renew a certification, an instructor shall attend an instructional course and pass a test under the direction of the division.

(ii) (A) Beginning May 1, 2006, the division shall provide or contract to provide the course referred to in Subsection (8)(c)(i) twice every year.

(B) The course shall include instruction on current Utah law related to firearms, including concealed carry statutes and rules, and the use of deadly force by private citizens.

(d)(i) Each applicant for certification under this Subsection (8) shall pay a fee of $50.00 at the time of application for initial certification.

(ii) The renewal fee for the certificate is $25.

(iii) The fees paid under Subsections (8)(d)(i) and (ii) may be used by the division as a dedicated credit to cover the cost incurred in maintaining and improving the instruction program required for concealed firearm instructors under this Subsection (8).

(9) A certified concealed firearms instructor shall provide each of the instructor's students with the required course of instruction outline approved by the division.

(10)(a)(i) A concealed firearms instructor is required to provide a signed certificate to a person successfully completing the offered course of instruction.

(ii) The instructor shall sign the certificate with the exact name indicated on the instructor's certification issued by the division under Subsection (8).

(iii)(A) The certificate shall also have affixed to it the instructor's official seal, which is the exclusive property of the instructor and may not be used by any other person.

(B) The instructor shall destroy the seal upon revocation or expiration of the instructor's certification under Subsection (8).

(C) The division shall determine the design and content of the seal to include at least the following:

(I) the instructor's name as it appears on the instructor's certification;

(II) the words "Utah Certified Concealed Firearms Instructor," "state of Utah," and "my certification expires on (the instructor's certification expiration date)"; and

(III) the instructor's business or residence address.

(D) The seal shall be affixed to each student certificate issued by the instructor in a manner that does not obscure or render illegible any information or signatures contained in the document.

(b) The applicant shall provide the certificate to the division in compliance with Subsection (5)(d).

(11) The division may deny, suspend, or revoke the certification of a concealed firearms instructor if it has reason to believe the applicant has:

(a) become ineligible to possess a firearm under Section 76-10-503 or federal law; or

(b) knowingly and willfully provided false information to the division.

(12) A concealed firearms instructor has the same appeal rights as set forth in Subsection (15).

(13) In providing instruction and issuing a permit under this part, the concealed firearms instructor and the licensing authority are not vicariously liable for damages caused by the permit holder.

(14) An individual who knowingly and willfully provides false information on an application filed under this part is guilty of a class B misdemeanor, and the application may be denied, or the permit may be suspended or revoked.

(15)(a) In the event of a denial, suspension, or revocation of a permit, the applicant may file a petition for review with the board within 60 days from the date the denial, suspension, or revocation is received by the applicant by certified mail, return receipt requested.

(b) The denial of a permit shall be in writing and shall include the general reasons for the action.

(c) If an applicant appeals the denial to the review board, the applicant may have access to the evidence upon which the denial is based in accordance with Title 63, Chapter 2, Government Records Access and Management Act.

(d) On appeal to the board, the agency has the burden of proof by a preponderance of the evidence.

(e)(i) Upon a ruling by the board on the appeal of a denial, the division shall issue a final order within 30 days stating the board's decision.

(ii) The final order shall be in the form prescribed by Subsection 63-46b-5(1)(i).

(iii) The final order is final agency action for purposes of judicial review under Section 63-46b-15.

(16) The commissioner may make rules in accordance with Title 63, Chapter 46a, Utah Administrative Rulemaking Act, necessary to administer this chapter.

U.C.A. 53-5-705. Temporary permit to carry concealed firearm — Denial, suspension, or revocation — Appeal.

"PLAIN TALK"

TEMPORARY PERMITS - It could take several weeks before a permanent permit is issued. This could be discomforting to a woman being stalked by an x-con-x-boyfriend who has a fetish for meat cleavers. If her record is clean and the division agrees that "stalking" is an "extenuating circumstance" ("extenuating" is not defined in the code), she will get a temporary permit. If the temporary permit is denied, there is no appeal to the review board - applicants just have to wait to get the "Real McCoy."

ACTUAL TEXT

53-5-705. Temporary permit to carry concealed firearm — Denial, suspension, or revocation — Appeal.

(1) The division or its designated agent may issue a temporary permit to carry a concealed firearm to a person who:

(a) has applied for a permit under Section 53-5-704;

(b) has applied for a temporary permit under this section; and

(c) meets the criteria required in Subsections (2) and (3).

(2) To receive a temporary permit under this section, the applicant shall demonstrate in writing to the satisfaction of the licensing authority extenuating circumstances that would justify issuing a temporary permit.

(3) A temporary permit may not be issued under this section until preliminary record checks regarding the applicant have been made with the National Crime Information Center and the division to determine any criminal history.

(4) A temporary permit is valid only for a maximum of 90 days or any lesser period specified by the division, or until a permit under Section 53-5-704 is issued to the holder of the temporary permit, whichever period is shorter.

(5) The licensing authority may deny, suspend, or revoke a temporary permit prior to expiration if the commissioner determines:

(a) the circumstances justifying the temporary permit no longer exist; or

(b) the holder of the temporary permit does not meet the requirements for a permit under Section 53-5-704. (6) (a) The denial, suspension, or revocation of a temporary permit shall be in writing and shall include the reasons for the action.

(b) The licensing authority's decision to deny, suspend, or revoke a temporary permit may not be appealed to the board.

(c) Denial, suspension, or revocation under this subsection is final action for purposes of judicial review under Section 63-46b-15.

U.C.A. 53-5-707. Permit — Fee — Disposition.

"PLAIN TALK"

Currently it's $65.25 for the permit including the $30.25 charged by the FBI for doing a computer check. Don't be surprised to see these fees increase from time to time.

ACTUAL TEXT

(1) Each applicant for a permit shall pay a fee of $35 at the time of filing an application. The initial fee shall be waived for an applicant who is a law enforcement officer under Section 53-13-103.

(2) The renewal fee for the permit is $10.

(3) The replacement fee for the permit is $10.

(4) The late fee for the renewal permit is $7.50.

. . .

U.C.A. 53-5-708. Permit — Names private.

"PLAIN TALK"

Although the state keeps a record of your personal information when issuing a permit, your name, address, telephone number, date of birth and Social Security Number are confidential, and the state will not disclose this information to anyone else.

ACTUAL TEXT

(1) When any permit is issued, a record shall be maintained in the office of the licensing authority. Notwithstanding the requirements of Subsection 63-2-301(1)(b), the names, addresses, telephone numbers, dates of birth, and Social Security numbers of persons receiving permits are protected records under Subsection 63-2-304 (10).

(2) Copies of each permit issued shall be filed immediately by the licensing authority with the division.

U.C.A. 53-5-710. Cross-references to concealed firearm permit restrictions.

"PLAIN TALK"

CWPs, don't be totin' yo' guns into the secured areas of no airports, jails, prisons, or reform schools, or d' PoPo be haulin' YOUR butt to jail (English don't get no plainer than that)! Churches and private residences are off limits to CWPs when authorized clergy or residents give them sufficient notice by telling them or posting a sign. [For a more scholarly (less plain) explanation of the "secure area" laws, see the "Plain Talk" boxes for code sections U.C.A. 76-10-523.5 and U.C.A. 76-10-529.]

ACTUAL TEXT

53-5-710. Cross-references to concealed firearm permit restrictions. A person with a permit to carry a concealed firearm may not carry a concealed firearm in the following locations:

(1) any secure area prescribed in Section 76-10-523.5 in which firearms are prohibited and notice of the prohibition posted;

(2) in any airport secure area as provided in Section 76-10-529; or

(3) in any house of worship or in any private residence where dangerous weapons are prohibited as provided in Section 76-10-530.

U.C.A. 53-5-711. Law enforcement officials and judges — Training requirements — Qualification — Revocation.

"PLAIN TALK"

Judges, criminal prosecutors and police officers spend most of their professional careers offending hundreds, if not thousands, of dysfunctional people. It's conceivable that some might try to get even. This section invites these state and local officials to get special concealed weapon permits (sometimes referred to as "super permits") if they pass a criminal background check and pay the fee. If they step out of line, their permits will be revoked, just

> like for anyone else. A "super permit" ("certificate of qualification") allows permit holders to pack in secured areas established by state law (as opposed to federal law). Holders of these permits must re-certify yearly.

(1) For purposes of this section and Section 76-10-523:

- (a) "Judge" means a judge or justice of a court of record or court not of record, but does not include a judge pro tem or senior judge.
- (b) "Law enforcement official of this state" means:
  - (i) a member of the Board of Pardons and Paroles;
  - (ii) a district attorney, deputy district attorney, county attorney or deputy county attorney of a county not in a prosecution district;
  - (iii) the attorney general;
  - (iv) an assistant attorney general designated as a criminal prosecutor; or
  - (v) a city attorney or a deputy city attorney designated as a criminal prosecutor.

(2) To qualify for the exemptions enumerated in Section 76-10-523, a law enforcement official or judge shall complete the following training requirements:

- (a) meet the requirements of Sections 53-5-704, 53-5-706, and 53-5-707; and
- (b) successfully complete an additional course of training as established by the commissioner of public safety designed to assist them while carrying out their official law enforcement and judicial duties as agents for the state or its political subdivisions.

(3) Annual requalification requirements for law enforcement officials and judges shall be established by the:

- (a) Board of Pardons and Paroles by rule for its members;
- (b) Judicial Council by rule for judges; and
- (c) the district attorney, county attorney in a county not in a prosecution district, the attorney general, or city

attorney by policy for prosecutors under their jurisdiction.

(4) The division may:

(a) issue a certificate of qualification to a judge or law enforcement official who has completed the requirements of Subsection (1), which certificate of qualification is valid until revoked;

(b) revoke the certificate of qualification of a judge or law enforcement official who fails to meet the annual requalification criteria established pursuant to Subsection (3); and

(c) certify instructors for the training requirements of this section.

Pancho's Wisdom

I'm going through my second childhood and my 200,000th box of bullets!

U.C.A. 53B-3-103. Power of board to adopt rules and enact regulations.

"PLAIN TALK"

This statute involves the infamous SB251 that passed in 2007. In September of 2006 the Utah Supreme Court held that University of Utah's gun ban was illegal. In response the University pressed the Legislature to allow them to ban guns in dormitories and in professors' offices threatening to continue the case in federal court asserting the right to "academic freedom" (undoubtedly found somewhere in the dark corner of unwritten rights in the Bill of Rights near "abortion"). The Legislature called the University's bluff and offered them the right to make a rule allowing dormitory residents to request only roommates who are not licensed to carry concealed weapons. The University accepted the Legislature's offer and dropped its attempt to get guns banned in dorms and professors' offices.

> This statute says that colleges and universities may not ban guns on campus except in one room designated as a disciplinary hearing room set up as a secured area. It also allows campus administrators to make a rule allowing students to request room mates who do not have a CWP. (Like we have "cooties" or something! Does that mean students with CWPs can request roommates who don't have STDs? Who aren't socialists?)

ACTUAL TEXT

(1) The board may enact regulations governing the conduct of university and college students, faculty, and employees.

(2)(a) The board may:

(i) enact and authorize higher education institutions to enact traffic, parking, and related regulations governing all individuals on campuses and other facilities owned or controlled by the institutions or the board; and

(ii) acknowledging that the Legislature has the authority to regulate, by law, firearms at higher education institutions:

(A) authorize higher education institutions to establish no more than one secure area at each institution as a hearing room as prescribed in Section 76-8-311.1, but not otherwise restrict the lawful possession or carrying of firearms; and

(B) authorize a higher education institution to make a rule that allows a resident of a dormitory located at the institution to request only roommates who are not licensed to carry a concealed firearm under Section 53-5-704 or 53-5-705.

(b) In addition to the requirements and penalty prescribed in Subsections 76-8-311.1(3), (4), (5), and (6), the board shall make rules to ensure that:

(i) reasonable means such as mechanical, electronic, x-ray, or similar devices are used to detect firearms, ammunition, or dangerous weapons contained in the personal property of or on the person of any individual attempting to enter a secure area hearing room;

(ii) an individual required or requested to attend a hearing in a secure area hearing room is notified in writing of the requirements related to entering a secured area hearing room under this Subsection (2)(b) and Section 76-8-311.1;

(iii) the restriction of firearms, ammunition, or dangerous weapons in the secure area hearing room is in effect only during the time the secure area hearing room is in use for hearings and for a reasonable time before and after its use; and

(iv) reasonable space limitations are applied to the secure area hearing room as warranted by the number of individuals involved in a typical hearing.

(3) The board and institutions may enforce these rules and regulations in any reasonable manner, including the assessment of fees, fines, and forfeitures, the collection of which may be by withholding from moneys owed the violator, the imposition of probation, suspension, or expulsion from the institution, the revocation of privileges, the refusal to issue certificates, degrees, and diplomas, through judicial process or any reasonable combination of these alternatives.

New Federal Concealed Weapon Statutes for Law Enforcement Officers and Retired Law Enforcement Officers

18 U.S.C. § 926B. Carrying of Concealed Firearms by Qualified Law Enforcement Officers.

"PLAIN TALK"

LEO's can carry concealed nationally. This federal law preempts state laws except (here we go again, giving validation to "gun free zones") laws that permit private persons or entities (presumably businesses) to prohibit CWPs on their property or that prohibit CWPs on government property, including parks. The required ID is issued by the agency that employs the officer. They can't conceal machine guns or silencers. It will be interesting to see how many police officers from outside the state of New York and New Jersey, the two most vicious "gun-hating" states, get arrested and thrown in jail in those two states as they check their firearms in their luggage as required by federal law. If I were a LEO going to either of these two states or to any of the "blue states," I would call ahead to make sure that state's department of public safety has notified their police officers of this provision and that they do not believe any of their state laws supercede this federal law (which they clearly don't, but that doesn't keep you from spending a weekend in jail if they "don't get it.")

ACTUAL TEXT

(a) Notwithstanding any other provision of the law of any State or any political subdivision thereof, an individual who is a qualified law enforcement officer and who is carrying the identification required by subsection (d) may carry a concealed firearm that has been shipped or transported in interstate or foreign commerce, subject to subsection (b).

(b) This section shall not be construed to supersede or limit the laws of any State that—

   (1) permit private persons or entities to prohibit or restrict the possession of concealed firearms on their property; or

   (2) prohibit or restrict the possession of firearms on any State or local government property, installation, building, base, or park.

(c) As used in this section, the term "qualified law enforcement officer" means an employee of a governmental agency who—

   (1) is authorized by law to engage in or supervise the prevention, detection, investigation, or prosecution of, or the incarceration of any person for, any violation of law, and has statutory powers of arrest;

   (2) is authorized by the agency to carry a firearm;

   (3) is not the subject of any disciplinary action by the agency;

(4) meets standards, if any, established by the agency which require the employee to regularly qualify in the use of a firearm;

(5) is not under the influence of alcohol or another intoxicating or hallucinatory drug or substance; and

(6) is not prohibited by Federal law from receiving a firearm.

(d) The identification required by this subsection is the photographic identification issued by the governmental agency for which the individual is employed as a law enforcement officer.

(e) As used in this section, the term "firearm" does not include—

(1) any machinegun (as defined in section 5845 of the National Firearms Act);

(2) any firearm silencer (as defined in section 921 of this title); and

(3) any destructive device (as defined in section 921 of this title).

18 U.S.C. § 926C. Carrying of Concealed Firearms by Qualified Retired Law Enforcement Officers.

"PLAIN TALK"

Retired LEO's can carry concealed nationally. This federal law preempts state laws except laws that permit private persons or entities (presumably businesses) to prohibit CWPs on their property or that prohibit CWPs on government property, including parks. The required ID is issued by the agency that employed the retired officer. In addition to several other requirements listed below, within the last 12 months he must have met the State's standards for training and qualification for active law enforcement officers to carry firearms. I give the same advice to retired officers as I did above for those currently employed - call the department of public safety of any state in which you intend to travel to make sure their peace officers have been told it's legal for you to carry and conceal a firearm in their state.

ACTUAL TEXT

(a) Notwithstanding any other provision of the law of any State or any political subdivision thereof, an individual who is a qualified retired law enforcement officer and who is carrying the identification required by subsection (d) may carry a concealed firearm that has been shipped or transported in interstate or foreign commerce, subject to subsection (b).

(b) This section shall not be construed to supersede or limit the laws of any State that —

(1) permit private persons or entities to prohibit or restrict the possession of concealed firearms on their property; or

(2) prohibit or restrict the possession of firearms on any State or local government property, installation, building, base, or park.

(c) As used in this section, the term "qualified retired law enforcement officer" means an individual who —

(1) retired in good standing from service with a public agency as a law enforcement officer, other than for reasons of mental instability;

(2) before such retirement, was authorized by law to engage in or supervise the prevention, detection, investigation, or prosecution of, or the incarceration of any person for, any violation of law, and had statutory powers of arrest;

(3)(A) before such retirement, was regularly employed as a law enforcement officer for an aggregate of 15 years or more; or

(B) retired from service with such agency, after completing any applicable probationary period of such service, due to a service-connected disability, as determined by such agency;

(4) has a nonforfeitable right to benefits under the retirement plan of the agency;

(5) during the most recent 12-month period, has met, at the expense of the individual, the State's standards for training and qualification for active law enforcement officers to carry firearms;

(6) is not under the influence of alcohol or another intoxicating or hallucinatory drug or substance; and

(7) is not prohibited by Federal law from receiving a firearm.

(d) The identification required by this subsection is—

(1) a photographic identification issued by the agency from which the individual retired from service as a law enforcement officer that indicates that the individual has, not less recently than one year before the date the individual is carrying the concealed firearm, been tested or otherwise found by the agency to meet the standards established by the agency for training and qualification for active law enforcement officers to carry a firearm of the same type as the concealed firearm; or

(2)(A) a photographic identification issued by the agency from which the individual retired from service as a law enforcement officer; and

(B) a certification issued by the State in which the individual resides that indicates that the individual has, not less recently than one year before the date the individual is carrying the concealed firearm, been tested or otherwise found by the State to meet the standards established by the State for training and qualification for active law enforcement officers to carry a firearm of the same type as the concealed firearm.

(e) As used in this section, the term "firearm" does not include—

(1) any machinegun (as defined in section 5845 of the National Firearms Act);

(2) any firearm silencer (as defined in section 921 of this title); and

(3) a destructive device (as defined in section 921 of this title).

State Regulations Regarding Concealed Weapon Permits - Concealed weapon permits are not only governed by state statute, but also by a truckload of "regulations." They are available on the internet at the following address:

http://www.rules.utah.gov/publicat/code/r722/r722-300.htm. Because most of these duplicate the concealed weapon statutes, I have omitted all but a few of those which I consider to be the most important.

R722-300-3. Definitions.

"PLAIN TALK"

These definitions are quite helpful, because they contain definitions of words and phrases used, but not defined, in the Utah Code. Unfortunately, many of the definitions involve multiple references to other code sections. This is reminiscent of the impossible-to-read federal tax code — by the time you get to the fourth reference, you have forgotten what the first and second references said. To keep you from constantly turning pages to check references, we have inserted the text **[using brackets and bold print]** of a few of the most important code sections and regulations referred to in these regulations.

A very disturbing change shows how bureaucrats can "tighten the noose" on the rights of law-abiding citizens without the blessings of our elected officials or by carelessly interpreting the intent of legislators. To qualify for a concealed weapon permit a person must be of "good character." One way to demonstrate good character is never to have been convicted of a crime of moral turpitude (basically immoral). Because the term is not of common daily usage, BCI defines it in this regulation. Before this year it included "firearms violations involving a crime of violence" (**R724-4-3** M. 15.) But the Legislature replaced the term "crime of violence" with the term "violent felony" (see U.C.A. 76-10-503 above). Instead of making the same substitution in this regulation, BCI simply dropped the ending of M.15. as follows, "firearms violations; ~~involving a crime of violence~~." The only thing that keeps a bureaucrat from denying a permit to a person with a petty firearm violation is U.C.A. 53-10-704(3)(b) that prevents denying, suspending or revoking a permit for a single conviction for an infraction under the weapons code. Unfortunately this allows them to revoke a permit for two infractions or for an infraction of the hunting code rather than the weapons code (e.g. shooting 30 minutes and 30 seconds after sundown), or for a petty misdemeanor (e.g. shooting from a pickup at a coyote decimating a flock of sheep). Furthermore, the definition suggests that such violations are immoral and should result in denying or yanking of your permit, which is absurd. M.15. should be changed to read, "firearms violations involving a violent felony." This would conform to legislative intent (and Pancho's peace of mind).

ACTUAL TEXT

Terms used in this rule shall be defined as follows:

(A) "Affidavit" means a written statement made under oath before a notary public.

(B) "Approved firearms instructor" means a person approved by the Division who can certify that an applicant meets the general firearm familiarity requirement of Subsection 53-5-704(8)(a) and is an instructor who is certified pursuant to Section R722-300-13.

(C) "Board" means the Concealed Weapons Review Board referred to in Section 53-5-703.

(D) "Concealed" means that which is covered, hidden, or secreted in a manner that the public would not be aware of its presence and is readily accessible for immediate use.

(E) "Crime of violence" means any crime involving: interference with police officer; fleeing; resisting arrest; failure to obey police officer; obstruction of justice;

(F) "Division" means the Criminal Investigations and Technical Services Division of the Utah Department of Public Safety.

(G) "Domestic violence" means any of the crimes listed in Subsection 77-36-1(2) when committed by one intimate partner against another. **[any criminal offense involving violence or physical harm or threat of violence or physical harm, or any attempt, conspiracy, or solicitation (like "I'll give you 25 bucks to beat up my wife") to commit a criminal offense involving violence or physical harm. This includes assault (an attempt or a threat, accompanied by a show of immediate force or violence, to do bodily injury to another or an act that causes or creates a risk of bodily injury to another), aggravated assault (intentionally causing bodily injury to another or using a dangerous weapon likely to produce death or serious bodily injury), criminal homicide, harassment (a written or recorded threat to commit a violent felony), kidnaping, child kidnaping, or aggravated kidnaping (kidnaping while using or threatening to a dangerous weapon, holding for ransom, taking hostage, afflicting bodily injury, interfering with the performance of a governmental institution, or committing a sexual offense), mayhem (cutting off or disabling a member of the body, putting out an eye, slitting the nose, ear, or lip), sexual offenses (see description below under "unlawful sexual conduct"), stalking (repeatedly maintaining a visual or physical proximity to a person that would make that person fear for himself or a member of his immediate family) unlawfully detaining a person against his or her will, violating a protective order not to contact the person, destroying a person's property by fire or otherwise, possessing a deadly weapon with an intent to assault, discharging a firearm from a vehicle.]**

(H) "Equivalent experience with a firearm through participation in law enforcement" means experience showing that the applicant has within the last five years met the firearms requirement of his/her department as evidenced by verifiable documentation from his/her department.

(I) "Equivalent experience with a firearm through participation in the military" means experience showing that the applicant has within the last five years successfully met the firearms requirements of his/her military organization as evidenced by verifiable documentation from his/her military organization, provided that such training meets the requirements of Subsection 53-5-704(8)(a).

(J) "Equivalent experience with a firearm through participation in an organized shooting competition" means experience showing that the applicant has within the last five years competed in an organized shooting competition as evidenced by verifiable documentation from the organization sanctioning or conducting the organized shooting competition, provided the organized shooting competition meets the requirements of Subsection 53-5-704(8)(a).

(K) "Felony" means any criminal conduct other than those crimes defined as misdemeanors or infractions by the statutes of this state. It also includes any criminal conduct that is punishable by more than one year in prison by a federal statute, or by the statute of some other state.

(L) "Mitigating circumstances" means circumstances which reduce culpability for purposes of assessing good character.

(M) "Moral turpitude" means a conviction for criminal conduct under the statutes of this state or any other jurisdiction involving any of the following offenses:

1. theft;
2. fraud;
3. tax evasion;
4. issuing bad checks;
5. robbery; or aggravated robbery;
6. interference with police officer;
7. fleeing; resisting arrest; failure to obey police officer;
8. obstruction of justice;
9. bribery;
10. perjury;
11. extortion;
12. arson or aggravated arson;

13. criminal mischief;
14. falsifying government records;
15. forgery;
16. receiving stolen property;
17. firearms violations;
18. burglary or aggravated burglary;
19. vandalism;
20. kidnaping, aggravated kidnaping, or child kidnaping;
21. crimes involving unlawful sexual conduct as described in Title 76, Chapter 5, Part 4,**[Unlawful sexual intercourse, rape, rape of a child, object rape (don't ask), object rape of a child (rightfully a first degree felony with a possible life sentence), sodomy, forcible sodomy, sodomy on a child (deserving a life sentence), forcible sexual abuse of adults and children, sexual assault, etc.]** Chapter 5a, Chapter 7, Part 1, **[engaging in activities related to child pornography]** and Chapter 10, Part 13 **[engaging in activities related to prostitution]**; Chapter 9, Part 702-702.5, indecent exposure or public urination may result in revocation, suspension or denial, and
22. violations of the pornographic and harmful materials and performances act, as defined in Title 76, Chapter 10, Part 12.

N. "Offenses involving the use of alcohol" means any of the following offenses:
    1. any violation of Sections 41-6-44 **[Should say 41-6a-502]** through 41-6-44.20 **[Should say 41-6a-526, includes "open container" law]**; including alcohol related reckless driving,
    2. violations of Title 32A, Chapter 12, Part 2 involving the illegal use or consumption of an alcoholic beverage **[including illegally furnishing alcohol to minors]**; and
    3. a violation of Section 76-10-528 **[carrying a deadly weapon while under the influence of alcohol or drugs].**

(O) "Offenses involving the use of narcotics" means any offense involving the use, possession, manufacturing or distribution of any narcotic or drug as defined in Title 58, Chapter 37, 37a, 37b, 37c, 37d, and 37e or a violation of Section 76-10-528.

(P) "Past pattern of behavior" means verifiable incidents, with or without an arrest or conviction, **[do these words worry anyone besides Pancho?]** that would lead a reasonable person to believe that an individual has a violent nature and would be a danger to themselves or others **[like, uh, you spank your kids?]**.

R722-300-12. Requirement to Notify Peace OfficerWhen Stopped.

"PLAIN TALK"

"BY THE WAY, OFFICER, I'M PACKING." - When stopped for questioning by a police officer, a permit holder possessing a concealed firearm must inform the officer of the weapon and the permit. As the following regulation mandates, these should be the first words out of the permit holder's mouth. The permit holder has no duty to do so if he does not have a firearm in his possession.

ACTUAL TEXT

When a concealed firearm permit holder or certificate of qualification holder is stopped for questioning by a peace officer based on reasonable suspicion in accordance with Section 77-7-15 and the holder has a concealed firearm in his/her possession, the holder shall immediately advise the peace officer that he/she is a lawful holder and has a concealed firearm in his/her possession. [**U.C.A. 77-7-15. Authority of peace officer to stop and question suspect - Grounds** . "A peace officer may stop any person in a public place when he has a reasonable suspicion to believe he has committed or is in the act of committing or is attempting to commit a public offense and may demand his name, address and an explanation of his actions."]

R722-300-16. Records Access.

> **"PLAIN TALK"**
>
> The division cannot release information about a permit applicant to other agencies. Even the applicant cannot access the file, unless the division denies the permit. If an application is denied, the applicant may then review the file to find out what records formed the basis of the denial.

ACTUAL TEXT

(A) The purpose of this section is to define access to concealed firearm permit and certificate of qualification records in accordance with Title 63, Chapter 2, and Subsection 53-5-708(1).

(B) Except as provided in Subsection 53-5-708(1), information supplied to the Division by an applicant shall be considered "private" in accordance with Subsection 63-2-302(2)(d).

(C) Information gathered by the Division and placed in the applicant's file shall be considered "protected" in accordance with Subsections 63-2-304(8) and (9). However, if such information is used as the basis for denial of a concealed firearm permit or certificate of qualification, such information shall be considered "private" in accordance with Subsection 63-2-302(2)(d) and the applicant shall have access to it in accordance with Subsection 53-5-704(16)(c).

R722-300-17. Adjudicative Procedures.

> **"PLAIN TALK"**
>
> If your permit to carry a concealed weapon or to instruct, has been denied, suspended or revoked, you can appeal within 60 days of the notice of the suspension, denial or revocation. You can't appeal to a court of law, though, until you "exhaust" (complete) all administrative appeals.

ACTUAL TEXT

(A) Any applicant denied a concealed firearm permit or certificate of qualification may request a hearing before the board by filing an appeal to the Division within 60 days from the date the notice of denial is issued. This appeal process also applies to a concealed firearm permit holder or certificate of qualification holder whose concealed firearm permit or certificate of qualification has been suspended or revoked.

(B) Board hearings will be conducted informally in accordance with Section 63-46b-5.

(C) Board decisions shall be issued within 30 days from the date of the hearing in accordance with Subsection 53-5-704(16)(e) and shall comply with the requirements of Subsection 63-46b-5(1)(i).

(D) In accordance with Section 63-46b-11 the board may enter a default order against any party who fails to participate in a hearing.

(E) Judicial review of all final actions resulting from informal adjudicative proceedings is available pursuant to Section 63-46b-15.

(F) Denial, suspension, or revocation of a temporary permit is not appealable to the board.

(G) A concealed firearm permit instructor or certificate of qualification instructor has the same appeal rights as set forth in this section for concealed firearm permit holders and certificate of qualification holders.

SUMMARY OF CONCEALED WEAPON LAWS

There are so many interrelated state and federal code sections governing concealed weapons that it may be difficult for the reader to understand exactly where he or she can or cannot carry a concealed weapon. The following summary is a SIMPLIFICATION. Grey areas are specifically discussed in Chapters VII, VIII and XIII.

A. A CWP holder can carry a concealed weapon "throughout the state without restriction" EXCEPT the following places:

1. Secured areas of airports, courthouses, jails, and mental institutions,
2. Private residences or churches if the permit holder is told orally or in writing that firearms are not allowed,
3. Federal facilities and buildings including post offices,
4. In the passenger compartments of airlines and other INTERSTATE modes of travel such as trains (e.g. AMTRAK) and buses (e.g. Greyhound). However, permit holders may carry concealed weapons in INTRASTATE mass transit vehicles such as UTA buses and TRAX.
5. In national parks and monuments (must be unloaded and packed, cased or stored in a manner that will prevent their ready use, see Chapter XIII).
6. In states not recognizing Utah's permit.

B. States that recognize Utah's permit.

States that have reciprocal agreements (they recognize the permits of each other's citizens by formal written agreement) and states that recognize Utah permits without a formal reciprocal agreement have been listed at www.bci.state.ut.us. However, we suggest permit holders traveling out of state call each state they plan to travel through in advance to verify. Keep in mind some states don't have a uniform law provision like Utah's U.C.A. 76-10-500. Therefore, there may be cities and counties within a state that accepts our permit, that have unusual restrictions on concealed weapon permit holders. For example, most states don't authorize permit holders to carry their weapons into school zones, in churches or into private business that post signs. You will not know this unless you call ahead and ask about carrying a concealed weapon in the cities and counties in which you intend to travel. Some business travelers simply pay an attorney to research these issues for them.

C. Areas of Controversy (Utah)

Several state and private institutions claim they can prohibit citizens from defending themselves with a concealed weapon despite clear intent of the Legislature to the contrary. Only the Legislature has the authority to regulate the use of firearms. Policies enacted by political subdivisions that are contrary to state law are unenforceable (see Chapter VII, U.C.A. 76-10-500). Therefore, concealed weapon permit holders may carry firearms for self defense in the following places:

1. In public places, including state libraries and office buildings.
2. On the premises of private businesses where the public has free access.
3. In public schools and on public university campuses, despite school board and university policies to the contrary.

D. "No Weapons Policies" at work

In the case *Hansen et. al. v. America On Line* (AOL) the Utah Supreme Court held that employees who are fired for violating their employer's "No Weapons Policies" cannot sue for wrongful termination.

Pancho's Wisdom

Remember the AOL- amo! Make sure that any business that discriminates against gun owners goes broke; politician s who support gun control lose elections and judges who don't understand the phrase "shall not be infringed" get booted during the next "retention election!"

CHAPTER IX

HUNTING LAWS AND REGULATIONS

(As they relate to the use of firearms)

Pancho's Wisdom

If liberals knew what they were missing, they'd give up drugs, sex and rock-n-roll for hunting and shooting. . .but then the rest of us would never draw an elk tag. . . so to Hell with 'em!

INTRODUCTION

There are hundreds of code sections and regulations that govern hunting in the State of Utah. Most of Utah's hunting rules and regulations are found in State hunting proclamations or on the website of the Utah Division of Wildlife Resources (DWR). Because of this, I have not included most of them in this chapter (see discussion under "State Hunting Rules and Regulations" below.

WARNING: In Pancho's humble opinion, the Utah Hunting Proclamations STILL do not adequately warn hunters that acts they might consider harmless can result in FELONY convictions and forfeitures of tens of thousands of dollars. Most hunters think of "poaching" as intentionally killing a valuable game animal out of season; not killing a trophy buck a few minutes after the hunting day formally ends or a couple of leaps over a poorly-defined boundary. Of course there should be rules and consequences, but hunters should be clearly and adequately warned of life and career-ruining "bad" acts.

The previous edition criticized the DWR for prohibiting modern firearms during several different types of hunts eg. bow hunts, muzzle loader, bear and cougar chase etc. It appears the state at least partially took "Pancho's" advice by correcting these regulations to comply with Utah's Concealed Weapon statutes. If you recall, I wrote in the previous edition that state code sections permitting citizens to carry a concealed weapon throughout the state except where prohibited by statute, preempted regulations promulgated by the DWR prohibiting modern weapons. The DWR has corrected this in most of its regulations, recognizing that a person with a concealed weapon permit may carry the gun as long as he doesn't use it to violate the rules of hunting, for example, shoot a deer on a bow hunt with a pistol and then stick an arrow in the hole (and if you do, they'll catch you because they have a CSI - DWR). This still doesn't answer the question of whether you can defend yourself if you are attacked by a wild animal during a hunt or a "chase." There appear to be no hunting codes or regulations that say you can kill an animal in "self defense" (compare the code sections in Chapter XI, discussing the use of deadly force to counter an attack by another human being). Fortunately, even without a code section spelling it out, under the common law (case law as opposed to statutory law), for every criminal act there is always the defense of "justification." A hunter would certainly be justified in killing an attacking bear or cougar without a license to kill that species, if he reasonably believed he was in immediate danger of serious bodily harm or death. That doesn't mean you won't be prosecuted, however, for shooting a bear or cougar for example, during a cougar or bear "chase" (where dogs are used, perhaps trained, to corner a bear or cougar which is then freed rather than killed). If the right to self defense is an "inalienable right" it makes me wonder, why state officials are so quick to prosecute someone who uses a firearm to defend himself or others. Courts should be required to instruct juries that self defense is an inalienable right in addition to instructing them that the state has the burden of proving, beyond a reasonable doubt, that the defendant didn't use a firearm in self defense.

Pancho's Wisdom - Varmint Huntin': As you'll see below, this stuff can be confusing, and we omitted a huge number of hunting codes and regulations because of limited space. You **almost have to be a lawyer to understand this stuff**! So . . . if you've got a varmint problem and don't want to take the chance of violating one of these laws, call "Pancho" at 1.800.530.0222. He'll help you git rid of your pesky varmints FOR FREE. BUT it has to be LEGAL and FUN with a GUN!!!! Pancho V.

U.C.A. 23-13-2. Definitions.

"PLAIN TALK"

Although most of the definitions used in Title 23 are quite understandable, two of the terms, "feral" and "protected wildlife," invite further discussion. Feral animals are those that were once domestic, like cats, dogs, horses, pigs and pigeons, but have run off or flown away and become wild. Feral animals are not wildlife. And speaking of wildlife, notice that everything that has a back bone except coyote, field mouse, gopher, ground squirrel, jack rabbit, muskrat, and raccoon, is considered protected wildlife. Interestingly, rats, were omitted from this exception, hopefully an oversight. This makes RATS, if you can believe it, PROTECTED WILDLIFE!

Elsewhere in Utah law, rats are excluded the definition of "game animal" and are listed as "non controlled." This provides a strong argument that they may be hunted in the daytime without a permit or "certificate of registration" (defined below). However, because they are defined as "protected wildlife," they are probably illegal to hunt at night with a spotlight (see state spotlighting statute, U.C.A. 23-13-17, below). These kinds of ambiguities in the gun laws and hunting regulations leave shooters and hunters nervous and frustrated.

Warning Varmint Hunters: That's not the end of the madness. It appears that feral animals are included in the definition of "animal" under Utah's animal cruelty statute [UCA 76-9-301 - not included in this book because of space limitations. If you frost a feral cat, dog, gerbil, lizard (anything that used to be domesticated, but is now wild), you could be convicted of a serious misdemeanor or even a felony if the bleeding hearts force our

Legislature to pass an "animal torture" statute. Pancho's Advice: Try not to ice an iguana with your Ithaca in a precinct populated predominantly with PETA pea brains.

ACTUAL TEXT

§ 23-13-2. Definitions

As used in this title:

(1) "Activity regulated under this title" means any act, attempted act, or activity prohibited or regulated under any provision of Title 23, Wildlife Resources Code of Utah, or the rules, and proclamations promulgated thereunder pertaining to protected wildlife including:

(a) fishing;

(b) hunting;

(c) trapping;

(d) taking;

(e) permitting any dog, falcon, or other domesticated animal to take;

(f) transporting;

(g) possessing;

(h) selling;

(i) wasting;

(j) importing;

(k) exporting;

(l) rearing;

(m) keeping;

(n) utilizing as a commercial venture; and

(o) releasing to the wild.

(2) "Aquatic animal" has the meaning provided in Section 4-37-103.

(3) "Aquatic wildlife" means species of fish, mollusks, crustaceans, aquatic insects, or amphibians.

(4) "Aquiculture facility" has the meaning provided in Section 4-37-103.

(5) "Bag limit" means the maximum limit, in number or amount, of protected wildlife that one person may legally take during one day.

(6) "Big game" means species of hoofed protected wildlife.

(7) "Carcass" means the dead body of an animal or its parts.

(8) "Certificate of registration" means a document issued under this title, or any rule or proclamation of the Wildlife Board granting authority to engage in activities not covered by a license, permit, or tag.

(9) "Closed season" means the period of time during which the taking of protected wildlife is prohibited.

(10) "Conservation officer" means a full-time, permanent employee of the Division of Wildlife Resources who is POST certified as a peace or a special function officer.

(11) "Dedicated hunter program" means a program that provides:

- (a) expanded hunting opportunities;
- (b) opportunities to participate in projects that are beneficial to wildlife; and
- (c) education in hunter ethics and wildlife management principles.

(12) "Division" means the Division of Wildlife Resources.

(13)(a) "Domicile" means the place:

- (i) where an individual has a fixed permanent home and rincipal establishment;
- (ii) to which the individual if absent, intends to return; and
- (iii) in which the individual and the individual's family voluntarily reside, not for a special or temporary purpose, but with the intention of making a permanent home.

(b) To create a new domicile an individual must:

- (i) abandon the old domicile; and
- (ii) be able to prove that a new domicile has been established.

(14) "Endangered" means wildlife designated as such according to Section 3 of the federal Endangered Species Act of 1973.

(15) "Fee fishing facility" has the meaning provided in Section 4-37-103.

(16) "Feral" means an animal which is normally domesticated but has reverted to the wild.

(17) "Fishing" means to take fish or crayfish by any means.

(18) "Furbearer" means species of the Bassariscidae, Canidae, Felidae, Mustelidae, and Castoridae families, except coyote and cougar.

(19) "Game" means wildlife normally pursued, caught, or taken by sporting means for human use.

(20) (a) "Guide" means a person who receives compensation or advertises services for assisting other person to take protected wildlife.

(b) Assistance under Subsection (20)(a) includes the provision of food, shelter, or transportation, or any combination of these.

(21) "Guide's agent" means a person who is employed by a guide to assist another person to take protected wildlife.

(22) "Hunting" means to take or pursue a reptile, amphibian, bird, or mammal by any means.

(23) "Intimidate or harass" means to physically interfere with or impede, hinder, or diminish the efforts of an officer in the performance of the officer's duty.

(24) "Nonresident" means a person who does not qualify as a resident.

(25) "Open season" means the period of time during which protected wildlife may be legally taken.

(26) "Pecuniary gain" means the acquisition of money or something of monetary value.

(27) "Permit" means a document, including a stamp, which grants authority to engage in specified activities under this title or a rule or proclamation of the Wildlife Board.

(28) "Person" means an individual, association, partnership, government agency, corporation, or an agent of the foregoing.

(29) "Possession" means actual or constructive possession.

(30) "Possession limit" means the number of bag limits one individual may legally possess.

. . .

(32) "Private wildlife farm" means an enclosed place where privately owned birds or furbearers are propagated or kept and which restricts the birds or furbearers from:

(a) commingling with wild birds or furbearers; and

(b) escaping into the wild.

(33) "Proclamation" means the publication used to convey a statute, rule, policy, or pertinent information as it relates to wildlife.

. . .

(35)(a) "Protected wildlife" means wildlife as defined in Subsection (49), except as provided in Subsection (35)(b).

(b) "Protected wildlife" does not include coyote, field mouse, gopher, ground squirrel, jack rabbit, muskrat, and raccoon. **[See, what did I tell ya? Do you see the word "rat" in this sentence anywhere?]**

(36) "Released to the wild" means to turn loose from confinement.

(37)(a) "Resident" means a person who:

(i) has been domiciled in the state for six consecutive months immediately preceding the purchase of a license; and

(ii) does not claim residency for hunting, fishing, or trapping in any other state or country.

(b) A Utah resident retains Utah residency if that person leaves this state:

(i) to serve in the armed forces of the United States or for religious or educational purposes; and

(ii) complies with Subsection (37)(a)(ii).

(c)(i) A member of the armed forces of the United States and dependents are residents for the purposes of this chapter as of the date the member reports for duty under assigned orders in the state if the member:

(A) is not on temporary duty in this state; and

(B) complies with Subsection (37)(a)(ii).

(ii) A copy of the assignment orders must be presented to a wildlife division office to verify the member's qualification as a resident. (d) A nonresident attending an institution of higher learning in this state as a full-time student may qualify as a resident for purposes of this chapter if the student:

(i) has been present in this state for 60 consecutive days immediately preceding the purchase of the license; and

(ii) complies with Subsection (37)(a)(ii).

(e) A Utah resident license is invalid if a resident license for hunting, fishing, or trapping is purchased in any other state or country.

(f) An absentee landowner paying property tax on land in Utah does not qualify as a resident.

(38) "Sell" means to offer or possess for sale, barter, exchange, or trade, or the act of selling, bartering, exchanging, or trading.

(39) "Small game" means species of protected wildlife:

(a) commonly pursued for sporting purposes; and

(b) not classified as big game, aquatic wildlife, or furbearers and excluding turkey, cougar and bear.

(40) "Spoiled" means impairment of the flesh of wildlife which renders it unfit for human consumption.

(41) "Spotlighting" means throwing or casting the rays of any spotlight, headlight, or other artificial light on any highway or in any field, woodland, or forest while having in possession a weapon by which protected wildlife may be killed.

(42) "Tag" means a card, label, or other identification device issued for attachment to the carcass of protected wildlife.

(43) "Take" means to:

- (a) hunt, pursue, harass, catch, capture, possess, angle, seine, trap, or kill any protected wildlife; or
- (b) attempt any action referred to in Subsection (43)(a).

(44) "Threatened" means wildlife designated as such pursuant to Section 3 of the federal Endangered Species Act of 1973.

(45) "Trapping" means taking protected wildlife with a trapping device.

(46) "Trophy animal" means an animal described as follows:

- (a) deer — any buck with an outside antler measurement of 24 inches or greater;
- (b) elk — any bull with six points on at least one side;
- (c) bighorn, desert, or rocky mountain sheep — any ram with a curl exceeding half curl;
- (d) moose — any bull with at least one antler exceeding five inches in length;
- (e) mountain goat — any male or female;
- (f) pronghorn antelope — any buck with horns exceeding 14 inches; or
- (g) bison — any bull.

(47) "Waste" means to abandon protected wildlife or to allow protected wildlife to spoil or to be used in a manner not normally associated with its beneficial use. . . .

(48) "Wildlife" means:

- (a) crustaceans, including brine shrimp and crayfish;
- (b) mollusks; and
- (c) vertebrate animals living in nature, except feral animals.

PANCHO WANTS TO BE THERE WHEN:

- the LAST California condor chokes on lead bullet fragments, aspirates and dies of hypoxia;
- the residents of Kanab, Utah serve the LAST endangered Kanab Amber Snails as escargot HORS D'OEUVRES;
- the raucous town of Mesquite, Nevada hosts a Turtle Soup Festival in honor of St. George developers featuring the LAST of the Desert Tortoises;
- Members of the Sierra Club get caught smokin' the endangered Shivwits milk-vetch aka "loco weed" only found in and around St. Geroge;
- when ENVIRONMENTALISTS become an Endangered Species.

The Endangered Species Act

"PLAIN TALK"

Because the preceding definitions include the terms "endangered" and "threatened" species, and because later code sections make you a felon if you happen to "drill" one of these creatures, we had better discuss the state and federal Endangered Species Acts right here and right now. After I had searched the state and federal codes for hours failing to find a "list" of endangered species, I began to wonder it vanished with the last unicorn. But believing that you can find anything and everything on the Internet, I finally searched there and Wallah!

First, let me say that this book ain't long enough to contain the complete endangered and threatened species list. Second, even if it was, I'd have to publish a new book every day because the list is subject to DAILY CHANGES (just to keep you hunters on yer toes, or is it to bring you to your knees?)! The list contains every endangered and threatened plant and animal in the world and can be found at http://endangered.fws.gov. Fortunately, the list is broken down by country and further by state. The state of Utah keeps its own list at http://dwrcdc.nr.utah.gov/ucdc/

ViewReports/te list.pdf, although it has been changed from time to time (do a "Google" search for "Utah Endangered Species" if you can't find it there).

The federal Endangered Species Act is found in the United States Code at 16 U.S.C. 1531-1543, but it's not included in this book because it doesn't contain the list of endangered species. 16 U.S.C. 1540 contains civil penalties up to $25,000, criminal fines up to $50,000 and prison terms up to 1 year, for ramming a Ruger to its Rareness. And then the state prosecutes Desert Tortoise connoisseurs as felons (see U.C.A. 23-20-4). Pancho's view on this is that unless they are furry, cuddly and have big sad eyes with long eye lashes, we shouldn't use taxpayer's dollars to protect them. If ecogeeks want to protect "slime-ates" (snails, suckers, milkvich, buzzards) they should buy federal land with donations and create a privately-owned, worthless-plants-and-animals preserve.

ACTUAL TEXT

(Subject to daily changes)

Animals — 19

Status Species/Listing Name

E Ambersnail, Kanab (Oxyloma haydeni kanabensis)

T Bear, grizzly lower 48 States, except where listed as an experimental population or delisted (Ursus arctos horribilis)

E Chub, bonytail entire (Gila elegans)

E Chub, humpback entire (Gila cypha)

E Chub, Virgin River (Gila seminuda (=robusta))

E Curlew, Eskimo (Numenius borealis)

T Eagle, bald lower 48 States (Haliaeetus leucocephalus)

E Ferret, black-footed except where XN (Mustela nigripes)

E Flycatcher, southwestern willow (Empidonax traillii extimus)

T Lynx, Canada lower 48 States DPS (Lynx canadensis)

T Owl, Mexican spotted (Strix occidentalis lucida)

E Pikeminnow (=squawfish), Colorado except Salt and Verde R. drainages, AZ (Ptychocheilus lucius)

T Prairie dog, Utah (Cynomys parvidens)

E Sucker, June (Chasmistes liorus)

E Sucker, razorback entire (Xyrauchen texanus)
T Tortoise, desert U.S.A., except in Sonoran Desert (Gopherus agassizii)
T Trout, Lahontan cutthroat (Oncorhynchus clarki henshawi)
E Wolf, gray lower 48 States, except MN and where XN; Mexico (Canis lupus)
E Woundfin except Gila R. drainage, AZ, NM (Plagopterus argentissimus)

COMMENTARY

Me n' Pancho's gotta make a comment about the picture of the caribou lying down near an oil well (found at http://www.anwr.org/features/pdfs/caribou-facts.pdf). As you know environmentalists have their "panties in a wad" over the prospect of Americans drilling for oil near the huge ANWR wildlife refuge (thereby reducing our dependence upon foreign oil). This photo shows a herd of caribou feeling very comfortable near a big oil rig. Now me 'n Pancho have never been to ANWR, but we've been to Wyoming to hunt antelope around the oil rigs. We've seen antelope hangin' out in the shadows o' them rigs because they are curious creatures and besides, hunters can't shoot too close to the rigs. It always struck me odd that the antelope seemed safer and more comfortable close to the oil rigs than they were when they wandered off to places where we could get a safe shot at 'em. We report, you decide!

Pancho's Wisdom

Some people say that Pancho hunts just to drive animal-rights activists crazy; it's not true, they're . . .
ALREADY CRAZY!

U.C.A. 23-13-17. Spotlighting of coyote, red fox, striped skunk, and raccoon — County ordinances — Permits.

"PLAIN TALK"

In counties with spotlighting ordinances, you can hunt coyote, red fox, striped skunk and raccoon at night with a spotlight. If the county fails to enact an ordinance, then the general public, excepting persons protecting their crops and domestic animals, may not spotlight. The good ol' spotlights you used to plug into your car's cigarette lighter aren't legal anymore. Spotlights must be portable, like a flashlight, rather than using a vehicle as a power source. There are several rechargeable models available on the market, but my experience has been that the batteries last no longer than 20 to 30 minutes and it takes hours to recharge them. Unless a hunter owns four or more portable spotlights, his night hunt could be rather short. Hunters cannot occupy or ride in the back of a motor vehicle when spotlighting. The Utah Code definition of "motor vehicle" includes ATV's, Jeeps, motorcycles, snowmobiles and dune buggies. This is a BIG CHANGE from spotlighting in the good old days.

The state statute gives counties broad powers to control night hunting and spotlighting within their boundaries. They can prohibit spotlighting altogether, except for persons protecting their crops or livestock. Counties can control the time of day and seasons spotlighting is allowed, , create "safety zones" by closing areas in the county to spotlighting, control the type of weapons allowed, dictate the penalties for violating the ordinance, restrict the number of hunters spotlighting by limiting the number of permits issued, and require hunters to notify the county sheriff of where and when they will be spotlighting. The counties may charge a fee for the permit to cover the costs of administering the ordinance, but surplus revenues must be turned over to the Division of Wildlife Resources. The ordinance does not apply to animal damage control agents (you know, those government guys who get paid by taxpayers to kill the predators that we're all itchin' to shoot!).

Because every county has the authority to tailor its spotlighting ordinance to its own needs, it takes an entire book to adequately cover the topic of spotlighting. My book *The Utah Spotlighting and Night Hunting Manual*, explains the state spotlighting law and analyzes each county's spotlighting ordinance. It reveals how, when, and where you can legally spotlight in the various counties. It covers additional topics including:

1. spotlighting "unprotected wildlife" (partially addressed in next section),
2. the use of night vision equipment,
3. vague areas in state and county spotlighting laws and ordinances that may be unenforceable against hunters,
4. county ordinances that are unenforceable because they conflict with state law,
5. the full text of each county ordinance,
6. recommendations for change in both state law and county ordinances, and
7. a comparison chart showing the differences in the various county ordinances.

Appendix C contains order forms for *The Utah Spotlighting and Night Hunting Manual*, if you are interested in doing a little spotlighting.

As most of Utah's hunting regulations explain, you CANNOT hunt big game animals, upland game or migratory birds at night with or without a spotlight.

ACTUAL TEXT

(1) Spotlighting may be used to hunt coyote, red fox, striped skunk, or raccoon where allowed by a county ordinance enacted pursuant to this section.

(2) The ordinance shall provide that:

(a) any artificial light used to spotlight coyote, red fox, striped skunk, or raccoon must be carried by the hunter;

(b) a motor vehicle headlight or light attached to or powered by a motor vehicle may not be used to spotlight the animal; and

(c) while hunting with the use of an artificial light, the hunter may not occupy or operate any motor vehicle.

(3) For purposes of the county ordinance, "motor vehicle" shall have the meaning as defined in Section 41-6a-102.

(4) The ordinance may specify:

(a) the time of day and seasons when spotlighting is permitted;

(b) areas closed or open to spotlighting within the unincorporated area of the county;

(c) safety zones within which spotlighting is prohibited;

(d) the weapons permitted; and

(e) penalties for violation of the ordinance.

(5) (a) A county may restrict the number of hunters engaging in spotlighting by requiring a permit to spotlight and issuing a limited number of permits.

(b)(i) A fee may be charged for a spotlighting permit.

(ii) Any permit fee shall be established by the county ordinance.

(iii) Revenues generated by the permit fee shall be remitted to the Division of Wildlife Resources for deposit into the Wildlife Resources Account, except the Wildlife Board may allow any county that enacts an ordinance pursuant to this section to retain a reasonable amount to pay for the costs of administering and enforcing the ordinance, provided this use of the permit revenues does not affect federal funds received by the state under 16 U.S.C. Sec. 669 et seq., Wildlife Restoration Act and 16 U.S.C. Sec. 777 et seq., Sport Fish Restoration Act.

(6) A county may require hunters to notify the county sheriff of the time and place they will be engaged in spotlighting.

(7) The requirement that a county ordinance must be enacted before a person may use spotlighting to hunt coyote, red fox, striped skunk, or raccoon does not apply to:

   (a) a person or his agent who is lawfully acting to protect his crops or domestic animals from predation by those animals; or

   (b) an animal damage control agent acting in his official capacity under a memorandum of agreement with the division.

R657-11-14. Spotlighting

"PLAIN TALK"

You cannot hunt "protected wildlife" at night with a spotlight. Guns, "protected wildlife" and artificial light do not mix. If you get caught with a gun while using artificial light, which could be interpreted to mean a flashlight, this is "prima facie" evidence against you and gives law enforcement officers sufficient authority to make an arrest. This is troubling because, when "nature calls" in bear and cougar country, most hunters I know take a flashlight and gun into the night. Under this code section, a vindictive wildlife officer could arrest someone for spotlighting for merely using the bathroom. Fortunately, subsection (2) requires arresting authorities to prove specific intent to hunt protected wildlife and it recognizes other lawful uses of artificial light near protected wildlife.

Notice that neither U.C.A. 23-13-17 nor the related regulations contain the term "unprotected wildlife." If you recall, coyote, field mouse, gopher, ground squirrel, jack rabbit, muskrat, and raccoon are excepted from the definition of protected wildlife.

Except for coyote and raccoon, both of which are specifically included in the spotlighting statute, the spotlighting of unprotected wildlife is nether controlled nor prohibited. So if you are hunting jack rabbits at night in the unincorporated area of a county, just remember to take your gun, ammo, a legal spotlight and your attorney! This interpretation is discussed at length in my book about spotlighting. Notice that concealed weapon permit holders are exempted from this section as long as they do not use their concealed weapon to hunt animals.

ACTUAL TEXT

(1)(a) Except as provided in Subsection (3), a person may not use or cast the rays of any spotlight, headlight, or other artificial light to locate protected wildlife while having in possession a firearm or other weapon or device that could be used to take or injure protected wildlife; and

(b) the use of a spotlight or other artificial light in a field, woodland, or forest where protected wildlife are generally found is prima facie evidence of attempting to locate protected wildlife. **[Constitutional? - seems to shift burden of proof to a defendant! Notice this presumption is in the regulation, but not in the statute. An attorney could also argue the Legislature did not expressly give the agency the authority to enact this presumption as required by UCA 76-10-500.]**

(2) The provisions of this section do not apply to:

(a) the use of the headlights of a motor vehicle or other artificial light in a usual manner where there is no attempt or intent to locate protected wildlife; or

(b) a person licensed to carry a concealed weapon in accordance with Title 53, Chapter 5, Part 7 of the Utah Code, provided the person is not utilizing the concealed weapon to hunt or take wildlife.

. . .

[The remainder of this regulation says exactly the same thing as the preceding spotlighting statute, U.C. A. 23-13-17.]

U.C.A. 23-19-22. Big game hunting permit.

"PLAIN TALK"

In 2007 this code section was amended to reduce the age to hunt big game from 14 to 12.

ACTUAL TEXT

(1) A person who is at least 12 years old, upon paying the big game hunting permit fee established by the Wildlife Board and possessing a valid hunting or combination license, may apply for or obtain a permit to hunt big game as provided by rules and proclamations of the Wildlife Board.

(2)(a) A person who is 11 years old may apply for or obtain a big game hunting permit consistent with the requirements of Subsection (1) if that person's 12th birthday falls within the calendar year for which the permit is issued.

(b) A person may not use a permit to hunt big game before the person's 12th birthday.

(3)(a) Except as provided by Subsection (3)(b), a person who is younger than 14 years old may not apply for or obtain the following types of big game permits issued by the division through a public drawing:

(i) premium limited entry;
(ii) limited entry;
(iii) once-in-a-lifetime; and
(iv) cooperative wildlife management unit.

(b) A person who is 13 years old may obtain a type of permit listed in Subsection (3)(a) if that person's 14th birthday falls within the calendar year for which the permit is issued.

(4) One dollar of each big game permit fee collected from a resident shall be used for the hunter education program as provided in Section 23-19-17.

U.C.A. 23-20-1. Enforcement authority of conservation officers — Seizure and disposition of property.

"PLAIN TALK"

This is the doozy of a statute you have heard about that permits wildlife officers to take away your car, guns, ammunition, camping gear, camper, boat, airplane or whatever you have used to illegally take protected wildlife. Wait until you see some of the fines for poaching trophy animals in the sections below! If the fines and forfeitures don't discourage poachers, nothing will, short of the death penalty.

This code section gives wildlife officers the authority to "seize" the wildlife you have shot and the "materials and devices" (guns, tree stands, trailers, tents, etc.) used to hunt them. Poaching a species of wildlife given an arbitrary value of $5 can result in the forfeiture of a several-thousand-dollar gun. If the poaching of a particular species results in a felony conviction (see section U.C.A. 23-20-4 below), the division can confiscate all the property, including very expensive vehicles, used to commit the felony. If the poaching offense is a misdemeanor, vehicles must be returned to the owner within 30 days.

ACTUAL TEXT

(1) Conservation officers of the division shall enforce the provisions of this title with the same authority and following the same procedures as other law enforcement officers.

(2)(a) Conservation officers shall seize any protected wildlife illegally taken or held.

(b)(i) Upon determination of a defendant's guilt by the court, the protected wildlife shall be confiscated by the court and sold or otherwise disposed of by the division.

(ii) Proceeds of the sales shall be deposited in the Wildlife Resources Account.

(iii) Migratory wildfowl may not be sold, but must be given to a charitable institution or used for other charitable purposes.

(3) Materials and devices used for the unlawful taking or possessing of protected wildlife shall be seized, and upon a finding by the court that they were used in the unlawful taking or possessing of protected wildlife, the materials and devices shall be subject to criminal or civil forfeiture under the procedures and substantive protections established in Title 24, Chapter 1, Utah Uniform Forfeiture Procedures Act.

(4)(a) Conservation officers may seize and impound a vehicle used for the unlawful taking or possessing of protected wildlife for any of the following purposes:

(i) to provide for the safekeeping of the vehicle, if the owner or operator is arrested;

(ii) to search the vehicle as provided in Subsection (2)(a) or as provided by a search warrant; or

(iii) to inspect the vehicle for evidence that protected wildlife was unlawfully taken or possessed.

(b) The division shall store any seized vehicle in a public or private garage, state impound lot, or other secured storage facility.

(5) A seized vehicle shall be released to the owner no later than 30 days after the date the vehicle is seized, unless the vehicle was used for the unlawful taking or possessing of wildlife by a person who is charged with committing a felony under this title.

(6)(a) Upon a finding by a court that the person who used the vehicle for the unlawful taking or possessing of wildlife is guilty of a felony under this title, the vehicle may be subject to criminal or civil forfeiture under the procedures and substantive protections established in Title 24, Chapter 1, Utah Uniform Forfeiture Procedures Act.

(b) The owner of a seized vehicle is liable for the payment of any impound fee if he used the vehicle for the unlawful taking or possessing of wildlife and is found by a court to be guilty of a violation of this title.

(c) The owner of a seized vehicle is not liable for the payment of any impound fee or, if the fees have been paid, is entitled to reimbursement of the fees paid, if:

(i) no charges are filed or all charges are dropped which involve the use of the vehicle for the unlawful taking or possessing of wildlife;

(ii) the person charged with using the vehicle for the unlawful taking or possessing of wildlife is found by a court to be not guilty; or

(iii) the owner did not consent to a use of the vehicle which violates this chapter.

U.C.A. 23-20-3. Taking, transporting, selling, or purchasing protected wildlife illegal except as authorized — Penalty.

"PLAIN TALK"

The long and short of this code section means that you cannot kill protected wildlife without a valid hunting license. If DWR officers catch you in possession of protected wildlife without a valid license, tag or certificate of registration, they presume you killed it illegally. If you unintentionally kill the wrong animal, you are guilty of a class B misdemeanor. But if the animal you kill has an arbitrary value of over $500 (e.g. moose, elk or trophy deer), you will probably be charged with a felony (see "Plain Talk" of next code section).

ACTUAL TEXT

(1) Except as provided in this title or a rule, proclamation, or order of the Wildlife Board, a person may not:

(a) take or permit his dog to take:

(i) protected wildlife or their parts;

(ii) an occupied nest of protected wildlife; or

(iii) an egg of protected wildlife;

(b) transport, ship, or cause to be shipped protected wildlife or their parts;

(c) sell or purchase protected wildlife or their parts; or

(d) possess protected wildlife or their parts unaccompanied by a valid license, permit, tag, certificate of registration, bill of sale, or invoice.

(2) Possession of protected wildlife without a valid license, permit, tag, certificate of registration, bill of sale, or invoice is prima facie evidence that the protected wildlife was illegally taken and is illegally held in possession.

(3) A person is guilty of a class B misdemeanor if he:

  (a) violates any provision of Subsection (1); and

  (b) does so with criminal negligence as defined in Subsection 76-2-103(4).

U.C.A. 23-20-4. Wanton destruction of protected wildlife — Penalties.

"PLAIN TALK"

Gun owners and hunters, **please read this law with fear and trembling.** This code section assigns an arbitrary (plucked out of the air) value to every species of protected wildlife to determine whether poaching these animals is a misdemeanor or a felony. It is a felony to poach a trophy deer or antelope, an elk, moose or an animal classified as endangered or threatened.

Most people don't equate poaching with shooting a big game animal in the wrong area as long as the hunter has a proper tag. Think Again! DWR has been charging hunters with a felony for shooting animals that have an arbitrary value over $500 (elk, moose, trophy deer etc.) while in the wrong area, after hours, or an animal of the wrong sex even if the hunter didn't realize he was in the wrong. I got a call from one elderly gentleman who was charged with a felony for taking a shot at a spike elk and hitting a mature bull by mistake. State law says a hunter doesn't have to know he or she was breaking the law, if his or her actions were reckless. Lawmakers should either change this to require a proof of intent beyond a reasonable doubt or DWR should do a better job of defining areas and warning hunters of potential felony charges in the hunting proclamations. Otherwise, it's just a matter of time before a hunter who hunts elk and trophy animals regularly will unintentionally violate the law and be charged with a felony. A felony conviction could, of course, result in a permanent loss of the right to bear arms. Pancho believes that there are groups who want to make it so risky for gun owners to shoot and hunt that we'll all just hang up our Peacemakers. . . but Pancho's got news fer 'em . . . He ain't NEVER hangin' up his!!!! Ya hear that Sarah . . . and the rest of you weasels at Handgun [Confiscation] Inc. NEVER!!!!!!!!!!!!!!!!!!!!!!!!!!!!!!!!!!!

ACTUAL TEXT

(1) A person is guilty of wanton destruction of protected wildlife if that person:

(a) commits an act in violation of Section 23-13-4,[1] 23-13-5,[2] 23-13-13,[3] 23-15-6[4] through 23-15-9,[5] 23-16-5,[6] or Subsection 23-20-3(1);[7]

(b) captures, injures, or destroys protected wildlife; and

(c)(i) does so with intentional, knowing, or reckless conduct as defined in Section 76-2-103 **[inserted below following the Commentary to this code section]**,

(ii) intentionally abandons protected wildlife or a carcass;

(iii) commits the offense at night with the use of a weapon;

---

1. Capturing and keeping protected wildlife is illegal, except under certain circumstances (such as owning a private wildlife farm, U.C.A. 23-13-8).
2. Importing or exporting wildlife in and out of Utah or releasing exotic wildlife into the wilds of Utah without written permission from the Division of Wildlife Resources is prohibited. Like the person who released the cayman into Utah Lake!
3. You can't make money buying or selling wildlife, like owning a private wildlife farm, except as otherwise provided by law.
4. It's illegal to pollute waters containing protected aquatic wildlife (game fish) and certain bugs (I'll have a bug light!) that fish eat.
5. Unless you own a fish farm, you can't transport live game fish.
6. Sportsmen cannot hunt and kill more than one species of big game during any year, regardless of how many licenses or permits you purchase, except as otherwise provided in the code for proclamations of the Board of Big Game Control (there are many exceptions to this, particularly regarding antlerless hunts).
7. This is the code section that covers shooting and killing protected wildlife without a valid license, permit, tag, or certificate of registration (for non-game, protected wildlife such as prairie dogs).

(iv) is under a court or division revocation of a license, tag, permit, or certificate of registration; or

(v) acts for pecuniary gain.

(2) Subsection (1) does not apply to actions taken which are in accordance with the following:

(a) Title 4, Chapter 14, Utah Pesticide Control Act;[8]

(b) Title 4, Chapter 23, Agriculture and Wildlife Damage Prevention Act;[9] or

(c) Section 23-16-3.1.[10]

(3) Wanton destruction of wildlife is punishable:

(a) as a third degree felony if:

(i) the aggregate value of the protected wildlife determined by the values in Subsection (4) is more than $500; or

(ii) a trophy animal was captured, injured, or destroyed;

(b) as a class A misdemeanor if the aggregate value of the protected wildlife, other than any trophy animal, determined by the values established in Subsection (4) is more than $250, but does not exceed $500; and

(c) as a class B misdemeanor if the aggregate value of the protected wildlife determined by the values established in Subsection (4) is $250 or less.

(4) Regardless of the restitution amounts imposed under Subsection 23-20-4.5(2), the following values shall be assigned to protected wildlife for the purpose of determining the offense for wanton destruction of wildlife:

(a) $1,000 per animal for:

(i) bison;

(ii) bighorn sheep;

8. You can kill certain "pests" with poison, U.C.A. 4-14-2 (20), (21), which includes rats and snails even though they are "protected wildlife" (see definition on protected wildlife in U.C.A. 23-13-1(35)(a)(b) above). [Sorry for all of the confusing cross references, but I didn't write the code or regs, THEY did!]

9. The Department of Wildlife Resources, as well as property owners under certain conditions, can kill predators and even protected wildlife to protect domestic livestock and crops.

10. Authority for farmers to kill big game animals destroying their crops under certain conditions.

(iii) rocky mountain goat;
(iv) moose;
(v) bear;
(vi) peregrine falcon; or
(vii) endangered species;

(b) $750 per animal for:

(i) elk; or
(ii) threatened species;

(c) $500 per animal for:

(i) cougar;
(ii) golden eagle;
(iii) river otter; or
(iv) Gila monster;

(d) $400 per animal for:

(i) pronghorn antelope; or
(ii) deer;

(e) $350 per animal for bobcat;

(f) $100 per animal for:

(i) swan;
(ii) sandhill crane;
(iii) turkey;
(iv) pelican;
(v) loon;
(vi) egrets;
(vii) herons;
(viii) raptors, except those that are threatened or endangered;
(ix) Utah milk snake; or
(x) Utah mountain king snake;

(g) $35 per animal for furbearers, except:

(i) bobcat;
(ii) river otter; and
(iii) threatened or endangered species;

(h) $25 per animal for trout, char, salmon, grayling, tiger muskellunge, walleye, largemouth bass, smallmouth bass, and wiper;

(i) $15 per animal for game birds, except:

(i) turkey;
(ii) swan; and
(iii) sandhill crane;

(j) $10 per animal for game fish not listed in Subsection (4)(h);

(k) $8 per pound dry weight of processed brine shrimp including eggs; and

(l) $5 per animal for protected wildlife not listed. **["Poach" a rat or crawfish and lose your new Marlin MR-7 30-.06, if BOTH the wildlife officer AND the judge (unlikely, but possible) don't like your looks.]**

(5) For purposes of sentencing for a wildlife violation, a person who has been convicted of a third degree felony under Subsection (3)(a) is not subject to the mandatory sentencing requirements prescribed in Subsection 76-3-203.8(4).

(6) As part of any sentence imposed, the court shall impose a sentence of incarceration of not less than 20 consecutive days for any person convicted of a third degree felony under Subsection (3)(a)(ii) who captured, injured, or destroyed a trophy animal for pecuniary gain.

(7) If a person has already been convicted of a third degree felony under Subsection (3)(a)(ii) once, each separate further offense under Subsection (3)(a)(ii) is punishable by, as part of any sentence imposed, a sentence of incarceration of not less than 20 consecutive days.

(8) The court may not sentence a person subject to Subsection (6) or (7) to less than 20 consecutive days of incarceration or suspend the imposition of the sentence unless the court finds mitigating circumstances justifying lesser punishment and makes that finding a part of the court record.

U.C.A. 23-20-4

COMMENTARY

Let's just go through a couple of examples to show you how easy it could be to commit a felony under this law. While deer hunting, you see what appears to be the most magnificent buck deer you have ever seen partially hidden in the trees. After you shoot it, you discover it was an awesome 6 X 7 BULL ELK instead of a buck deer! A game warden arrests you for poaching. At your trial, a jury of your peers will decide whether or not the kill was intentional (you meant to kill an elk rather than a deer, a felony), reckless (really stupid, also a felony), or simply negligent (stupid, but truly a mistaken identity, not a felony). If you are lucky enough to have a few hunters on the jury who understand "buck fever," they will hopefully find you were negligent (stupid), but not guilty of intending to kill or recklessly killing an elk, a felony.

But what if you shoot a bull moose? Moose are almost black and their antlers look nothing like a deer's. If you do something extremely stupid like that, even the most sympathetic jury might find you guilty of a felony for intentionally poaching a trophy animal [unless you are a California Democrat who voted for Nancy Pelosi which most Utahns understand impliedly fits the Utah Code definition of "mentally defective"].

And don't forget, intentionally or recklessly shooting an animal classified as endangered or threatened is a felony.

U.C.A. 76-2-103. Definitions. [intent, willfulness, recklessness, criminal negligence]

"PLAIN TALK"

This statute defines the state of mind required to convict a person of a crime. Many criminal statutes like the one above require as an element of the crime proof that the gun owner committed the "bad act" "intentionally, knowingly, or recklessly. Following are the definitions of the various states of mind ranging from intentional conduct to criminally negligent conduct.

ACTUAL TEXT

A person engages in conduct:

(1) Intentionally, or with intent or willfully with respect to the nature of his conduct or to a result of his conduct, when it is his conscious objective or desire to engage in the conduct or cause the result.

(2) Knowingly, or with knowledge, with respect to his conduct or to circumstances surrounding his conduct when he is aware of the nature of his conduct or the existing circumstances. A person acts knowingly, or with knowledge, with respect to a result of his conduct when he is aware that his conduct is reasonably certain to cause the result.

(3) Recklessly with respect to circumstances surrounding his conduct or the result of his conduct when he is aware of but consciously disregards a substantial and unjustifiable risk that the circumstances exist or the result will occur. The risk must be of such a nature and degree that its disregard constitutes a gross deviation from the standard of care that an ordinary person would exercise under all the circumstances as viewed from the actor's standpoint.

(4) With criminal negligence or is criminally negligent with respect to circumstances surrounding his conduct or the result of his conduct when he ought to be aware of a substantial and unjustifiable risk that the circumstances exist or the result will occur. The risk must be of a nature and degree that the failure to perceive it constitutes a gross deviation from the standard of care that an ordinary person would exercise in all the circumstances as viewed from the actor's standpoint.

U.C.A. 23-20-4.5. Illegal taking, possession, or wanton destruction of protected wildlife — Restitution — Reimbursable damages — Assessment by magistrates —Disposition of monies.

"PLAIN TALK"

This code section gives guidelines to the courts to impose restitution for poaching different species of wildlife. The code section begins by suggesting restitution of $1,000 per animal for bison, big horn sheep, etc. This section does not allow judges to reduce the restitution amounts for hunters convicted of felonies for killing trophy animals. Section 23-13-1 (see discussion above) defines trophy animal. Generally, a trophy big horn is a ram with a greater than curl, a trophy deer is a buck having antlers with at least a 24-inch spread, and a trophy elk has six points on one of its antlers. The fine for killing a desert or rocky mountain big horn sheep is a whopping $30,000 (You could buy a DODGE RAM for that kind of money)!

The fines go to the Division of Wildlife Resources to help set up programs to help stop poaching. When a hunter is found guilty of poaching and these fines are imposed, the judgment becomes a lien on any real estate the hunter owns in the county where he is convicted.

ACTUAL TEXT

(1) When a person is adjudged guilty of illegal taking, illegal possession, or wanton destruction of protected wildlife, other than any trophy animal, the court may order the defendant to pay restitution as set forth in Subsection (2), or a greater or lesser amount, for the value of each animal taken, possessed, or destroyed, unless the court finds that restitution is inappropriate.

(2) Suggested minimum restitution values for protected wildlife are as follows:

- (a) $1,000 per animal for:
  - (i) bison;
  - (ii) bighorn sheep;
  - (iii) rocky mountain goat;
  - (iv) moose;
  - (v) bear;
  - (vi) peregrine falcon; or
  - (vii) endangered species;
- (b) $750 per animal for:
  - (i) elk; or
  - (ii) threatened species;

(c) $500 per animal for:
   (i) golden eagle;
   (ii) river otter; or
   (iii) gila monster;
(d) $400 per animal for:
   (i) pronghorn antelope; or
   (ii) deer;
(e) $350 per animal for:
   (i) cougar; or
   (ii) bobcat;
(f) $100 per animal for:
   (i) swan;
   (ii) sandhill crane;
   (iii) turkey;
   (iv) pelican;
   (v) loon;
   (vi) egrets;
   (vii) herons;
   (viii) raptors, except those that are threatened or endangered;
   (ix) Utah milk snake; or
   (x) Utah mountain king snake;
(g) $35 per animal for furbearers, except:
   (i) bobcat;
   (ii) river otter; and
   (iii) threatened or endangered species;
(h) $25 per animal for trout, char, salmon, grayling, tiger muskellunge, walleye, largemouth bass, smallmouth bass, and wiper;
(i) $15 per animal for game birds, except:
   (i) turkey;
   (ii) swan; and
   (iii) sandhill crane;
(j) $10 per animal for game fish not listed in Subsection (2)(h);

(k) $8 per pound dry weight of processed brine shrimp including eggs; and

(l) $5 per animal for protected wildlife not listed.

(3) If the court finds that restitution is inappropriate or if the value imposed is less than the suggested minimum value as provided in Subsection (2), the court shall make the reasons for the decision part of the record.

(4) The court shall order any person convicted of a third degree felony under Subsection 23-20-4(3)(a)(ii) to pay restitution. Minimum restitution values for trophy animals are as follows:

(a) $30,000 per animal for bighorn, desert, or rocky mountain sheep;

(b) $8,000 per animal for deer;

(c) $8,000 per animal for elk;

(d) $6,000 per animal for moose or mountain goat;

(e) $6,000 per animal for bison; and

(f) $2,000 per animal for pronghorn antelope.

(5) Any restitution shall be remitted to the division and deposited in the Wildlife Resources Account.

(6) Restitution monies shall be used by the division for activities and programs to help stop poaching, including:

(a) educational programs on wildlife crime prevention;

(b) acquisition and development of wildlife crime detection equipment;

(c) operation and maintenance of anti-poaching projects; and

(d) wildlife law enforcement training.

(7) If restitution is required it shall be in addition to:

(a) any other fine or penalty imposed for a violation of any provision of this title; and

(b) any remedial action taken to revoke or suspend a person's license, permit, tag, or certificate of registration.

(8) A judgment imposed under this section constitutes a lien when recorded in the judgment docket and shall have the same effect and is subject to the same rules as a judgment for money in a civil action.

U.C.A. 23-20-12. Airplanes or terrestrial or aquatic vehicles — Use in taking wildlife unlawful — Exceptions.

"PLAIN TALK"

You can't hunt with an airplane or any other motorized vehicle including hang gliders, ultra light aircraft, 4-wheelers and snowmobiles. However, people who are paralyzed or permanently required to use a wheelchair or crutches may be authorized to hunt from a vehicle.

ACTUAL TEXT

It is unlawful for any person to take any wildlife from an airplane or any other airborne vehicle or device or any motorized terrestrial or aquatic vehicle, including snowmobiles and other recreational vehicles, except as provided by this code or in the rules and regulations of the Wildlife Board. Provided, however, that an individual validly licensed to hunt who is a paraplegic, or otherwise permanently disabled so as to be permanently confined to a wheelchair or the use of crutches, may be authorized to hunt from a vehicle under terms and conditions specified by the Wildlife Board.

U.C.A. 23-20-13. Signs or equipment — Damage or destruction unlawful.

"PLAIN TALK"

Don't "Westernize" (blast holes through) signs erected by the Division of Wildlife Resources, even if you don't like what the signs say.

ACTUAL TEXT

A person may not:

(1) shoot at, shoot, deface, damage, remove, or destroy any division signs or placards located in any part of this state; or

(2) damage, destroy, remove, or cause to be damaged, destroyed, or removed any equipment or devices owned, controlled, or operated by the Division of Wildlife Resources.

U.C.A. 23-20-14. Definitions — Posted property — Hunting by permission — Entry on private land while hunting or fishing — Violations — Penalty — Prohibitions inapplicable to officers — Promotion of respect for private property.

"PLAIN TALK"

Before the 2000 Legislature, property owners had to make it clear to hunters that they could not trespass. They did this by painting their fence posts with bright yellow or fluorescent paint at all corners, where fishing streams cross property lines, at roads, gates and other rights of way entering the land. The 2000 Legislature changed this by making all cultivated land the same as land posted "no trespassing." Hunting on posted land is a class B misdemeanor (U.C.A. 23-20-3.5[not included in book]), but a subsequent conviction within 5 years could cause trespassing hunters to lose their right to hunt for up to 5 years.

ACTUAL TEXT

(1) As used in this section:

- (a) "Division" means the Division of Wildlife Resources.
- (b) "Cultivated land" means land which is readily identifiable as:
  - (i) land whose soil is loosened or broken up for the raising of crops;
  - (ii) land used for the raising of crops; or
  - (iii) pasturage which is artificially irrigated.
- (c) "Permission" means written authorization from the owner or person in charge to enter upon private land

that is either cultivated or properly posted, and must include:

(i) the signature of the owner or person in charge;
(ii) the name of the person being given permission;
(iii) the appropriate dates; and
(iv) a general description of the property.

(d) "Properly posted" means that "No Trespassing" signs or a minimum of 100 square inches of bright yellow, bright orange, or fluorescent paint are displayed at all corners, fishing streams crossing property lines, roads, gates, and rights-of-way entering the land. If metal fence posts are used, the entire exterior side must be painted.

(2)(a) While taking wildlife or engaging in wildlife related activities, a person may not:

(i) without the permission of the owner or person in charge, enter upon privately owned land that is cultivated or properly posted;
(ii) refuse to immediately leave the private land if requested to do so by the owner or person in charge; or
(iii) obstruct any entrance or exit to private property.

(b) "Hunting by permission cards" will be provided to landowners by the division upon request.

(c) A person may not post:

(i) private property he does not own or legally control; or
(ii) land that is open to the public as provided by Section 23-21-4.

(3)(a) A person convicted of violating any provision of Subsection (2) may have his license, tag, certificate of registration, or permit, relating to the activity engaged in at the time of the violation, revoked by a hearing officer.

(b) A hearing officer may construe any subsequent conviction which occurs within a five-year period as a flagrant violation and may prohibit the person from obtaining a new license, tag, certificate of registration, or permit for a period of up to five years.

(4) Subsection (2)(a) does not apply to peace or conservation officers in the performance of their duties.

(5)(a) The division shall provide information regarding owners' rights and sportsmen's duties:

(i) to anyone holding licenses, certificates of registration, tags, or permits to take wildlife; and

(ii) by using the public media and other sources.

(b) The restrictions in this section relating to trespassing shall be stated in all hunting and fishing proclamations issued by the Wildlife Board.

(6) Any person who violates any provision of Subsection (2) is guilty of a class B misdemeanor.

U.C.A. 23-20-15. Destruction of signs or inclosure on private land unlawful.

"PLAIN TALK"

Stop giving "NO TRESPASSING" signs the "Sonny" Corleone treatment.

ACTUAL TEXT

It is unlawful for any person, without the consent of the owner or person in charge of any privately owned land, to tear down, mutilate, or destroy any sign, signboard or other notice which regulates trespassing for purposes of hunting, trapping, or fishing on this land; or to, without such consent, tear down, deface, or destroy any fence or other inclosure on this privately owned land, or any gate or bars belonging to any such fence or inclosure.

U.C.A. 23-20-20. Children accompanied by adults while hunting with weapon.

"PLAIN TALK"

This code section explains when adults must accompany kids who are hunting. But it does not give you the "full picture." For a complete analysis of all of the state and federal laws placing restrictions on minors using firearms, carefully study Appendix F, at the end of this book. It is entitled "Youngsters, Guns and Ammo" and it compares, in table format, all of the laws and regulations relating to juveniles, firearms, hunting and possession of ammunition. Don't take your kids hunting without it.

"Accompany" means being close enough to see and talk to the minor (the rule doesn't tell us whether communicating by walkie talkie satisfies the "verbal communication" requirement). When hunting big game, kids 12 and older, but less than 16, must be accompanied by a parent or guardian, or by an adult, 21 or older who is approved by the parent. When these same kids are hunting small game, the accompanying adult must be 21 or older, but doesn't need to be a parent or guardian, or approved by a parent or guardian. Kids under 14 must always be accompanied by a parent or guardian, or by an adult, 21 or older who is approved of by the parent, while hunting. Minimum age restrictions on hunting turkey and small game were eliminated in 2006 as long as the youth hunter has passed a hunter safety course. (Thank you, Representative Curt Oda, R-Clearfield.)

ACTUAL TEXT

(1) As used in this section:

(a) "Accompanied" means at a distance within which visual and verbal communication is maintained for the purposes of advising and assisting.

(b)(i) "Electronic device" means a mechanism powered by electricity that allows communication between two or more people.

(ii) "Electronic device" includes a mobile telephone or two-way radio.

(c) "Verbal communication" means the conveyance of information through speech that does not involve an electronic device.

(2) A person younger than 14 years old who is hunting with any weapon must be accompanied by:

(a) the person's parent or legal guardian; or

(b) a responsible person who is at least 21 years old and who is approved by the person's parent or guardian.

(3) A person younger than 16 years old who is hunting big game with any weapon must be accompanied by:

(a) the person's parent or legal guardian; or

(b) a responsible person who is at least 21 years old and who is approved by the person's parent or guardian.

(4) A person who is at least 14 years old but younger than 16 years old must be accompanied by a person who is at least 21 years old while hunting wildlife, other than big game, with any weapon.

U.C.A. 23-20-29. Interference with hunting prohibited — Action to recover damages — Exceptions.

"PLAIN TALK"

Militant Vegans, violent animal-rights activists, and other psychologically-unbalanced people who interfere with a hunt, are guilty of a class B misdemeanor. Fortunately, this code section also permits hunters to sue these crazy people for civil damages. I wonder what a Panguitch jury would award an elk hunter who missed bagging a 6 X 7 trophy bull, a once-in-a-lifetime opportunity, because one of these demented souls intentionally interfered with his or her hunt? Hopefully they would render a damage award large enough to bankrupt the radical organizations they belong to that advocate this kind of nonsense.

ACTUAL TEXT

(1) A person is guilty of a class B misdemeanor who intentionally interferes with the right of a person licensed and legally hunting under Title 23, Chapter 19, to take wildlife by driving, harassing, or intentionally disturbing any species of wildlife for the purpose of disrupting a legal hunt, trapping, or predator control.

(2) Any directly affected person or the state may bring an action to recover civil damages resulting from a violation of Subsection (1) or a restraining order to prevent a potential violation of Subsection (1).

(3) This section does not apply to incidental interference with a hunt caused by lawful activities including, but not limited to, ranching, mining, and recreation.

Pancho's Wisdom

ANIMAL-RIGHTS-REEFER SMOKIN' VEGAN (In high winy voice reticent of a vegetarian diet): Does killing Bambi make you feel macho?

PANCHO: No, but when I am pulling out the trachea with blood up to my elbows, it makes me salivate!

STATE HUNTING RULES AND REGULATIONS

"PLAIN TALK"

In the last edition I included a "truckload" of the state's hunting regulations. As I explained at the beginning of this chapter, I chose not to this time around. There are just too many of them and they can be changed at the whim of an administrative agency. Besides, you can always get the current version directly off the web. To access hunting regulations on the internet go to www.wildlife.utah.gov and "click" "rules" and then click "Administrative Rules." These regulations are listed by topic under the letter "R" and then a number. For example, the rules for "Taking Big Game" are found in R657-5. Currently there are 72 rules relating to Big Game, R657-5-1 through R657-5-72. These rules cover everything from seasons and hunting hours to the types of weapons that may be used to hunt big game. Keep in mind these rules and regulations are not like state statutes. Statutes must be amended by the Legislature. Rules and regulations can be changed at any time by the DWR. Therefore, it is better to access them on the web rather than rely on a book which cannot be easily updated after purchase. I included the following few regulations because of their interesting and unusual content. **After you have discovered the general topic of any particular regulation in this book, I suggest you immediately look up the regulation on the Internet to see if and how it may have been amended after I published this edition of the book.**

R657-3-7. Nuisance Birds — Nuisance Porcupine, Striped Skunk, and Squirrel.

"PLAIN TALK"

To hunt some species of "non-game" animals (like certain types of prairie dogs - see discussion under R657-19 below), hunters must have a "certificate of registration" from the state and/or a "federal permit" from the federal government. Neither the state nor the federal government requires such permits to hunt magpies, crows, porcupine, striped skunk or squirrel when their numbers create a nuisance or health hazard, or when they threaten certain plants and animals. The key words are, "when concentrated in such numbers and manner as to constitute a health hazard or other nuisance." These terms are not defined or explained in either Utah or corresponding federal regulations (Sections 50 C.F.R. 21.42 and 21.43). The precautions in the regulation for disposing of feathers and carcasses provide a strong argument that these animals ALWAYS create a health hazard and may, therefore, be hunted at any time. Although the regulation contains language suggesting that only property owners protecting crops or domestic animals may kill these varmints ("allow any federal warden or conservation officer unrestricted access over the premises" . . . "kill crows or magpies . . .only on or over the threatened area"), the regulation plainly refers to "a person" rather than "a property owner or livestock owner" ("A person is not required to obtain a certificate of registration" . . ."A person may kill crows or magpies" . . ."A person may capture"). Therefore, there is a strong argument that anyone who follows these rules can hunt these animals. If Utahns are ever prosecuted for something as "rinky dinky" as shooting crows or magpies, as much of a nuisance they can be to farmers and ranchers, it would be a rallying cry to petition our Congressional delegation for the immediate removal of the attorney or federal agent pushing the case.

ACTUAL TEXT

(1)(a) A person is not required to obtain a certificate of registration or a federal permit to kill American Crows or Black-billed Magpies when found committing, or about to commit, depredations upon ornamental or shade trees, agricultural crops, livestock, or wildlife, or when concentrated in such numbers and manner as to constitute a health hazard or other nuisance, provided:

(i) none of the birds killed pursuant to this section, nor their plumage, are sold or offered for sale; and

(ii) any person killing American Crows or Black-billed Magpies shall:

(A) allow any federal warden or conservation officer unrestricted access over the premises where American Crows or Black-billed Magpies are killed; and

(B) furnish any information concerning the control operations to the division or federal official upon request.

(b) A person may kill American Crows or Black-billed Magpies by any means, excluding bait, explosives or poison, and only on or over the threatened area.

(c) American Crows and Black-billed Magpies killed pursuant to this section shall be collected immediately and must be disposed of at a landfill that accepts wildlife carcasses or must be buried or incinerated.

(d) This subsection incorporates Section 50 CFR 21.42 and 21.43, 2002, ed., by reference.

(2)(a) A person may capture, transport, and kill or release a nuisance porcupine, striped skunk, or squirrel without obtaining a certificate of registration.

(b) A nuisance porcupine, striped skunk, or squirrel may be released only as follows:

(i) within 48 hours of capture;
(ii) within the county in which it was captured; and
(iii) in a location where it does not pose a risk to human health or safety, or create other conflict with humans, agriculture, or other animals.

R657-3-7

COMMENTARY

What?! Can you believe this? The state and federal government both allow us to magpies and crows? You won't find this in the hunting proclamation! But what does "depredating a shade tree" mean? This phrase is not defined either in the state or federal regulations or codes. The law is vague, so it should be amended to eliminate the legal risk of those wanting to help farmers and ranchers rid themselves of these varmints. This regulation was amended to permit varmint hunters to shoot magpies and crows on the ground with varmint rifles. This regulation should be further amended to say:

(1)(a) A person is not required to obtain a certificate of registration or a federal permit to take crows or magpies ~~when found committing, or about to commit, depredations upon ornamental or shade trees, agricultural crops, livestock, or wildlife, or when concentrated in such numbers and manner as to constitute a health hazard or other nuisance,~~ provided:

. . .

Did you know that Virginia has a "crow" season?

I couldn't find a definition for "other nuisance." Ever heard a magpie or crow squawk? "Caw! Caw! Bang! Splat! Thud!"

R657-5-4. Age Requirements and Restrictions.

"PLAIN TALK"

Because U.C.A. 23-19-22 was amended in 2007 to allow kids as young as 12 to hunt big game, this regulation was amended to be consistent and to further define the parameters.

ACTUAL TEXT

(1)(a) Subject to the exceptions in subsection (c), a person 12 years of age or older may apply for or obtain a permit to hunt big game. A person 11 years of age may apply for a permit to hunt big game if that person's 12th birthday falls within the calendar year for which the permit is issued.

(b) A person may not use a permit to hunt big game before their 12th birthday.

(c) A person who is younger than 14 years of age may not apply for or obtain the following types of big game permits issued by the division through a public drawing:

(i) premium limited entry;
(ii) limited entry;
(iii) once-in-a-lifetime; and
(iv) cooperative wildlife management unit.

(d) A person who is 13 years of age may apply for or obtain a type of permit listed in Subsection(1)(c) if that person's 14th birthday falls within the calendar year for which the permit is issued.

(e) antlerless deer, antlerless elk, and doe pronghorn permits are not limited entry, premium limited entry or cooperative wildlife management unit permits for purposes of determining a 12 or 13 year olds eligibility to apply for or obtain through a public drawing administered by the division.

(2)(a) A person at least 12 years of age and under 16 years of age must be accompanied by his parent or legal guardian, or other responsible person 21 years of age or older and approved by his parent or guardian, while hunting big game with any weapon.

(b) As used in this section, "accompanied" means at a distance within which visual and verbal communication are maintained for the purposes of advising and assisting.

R657-5-7. Temporary Game Preserves [weapons restrictions].

"PLAIN TALK"

Unless you have a big game permit to hunt in special areas where trophy animals are found, wildlife officers do not want you to tempt yourself by possessing a gun or bow. Exceptions are upland game hunters carrying a shotgun loaded with birdshot, peace officers carrying service weapons, livestock owners protecting their herds and concealed weapon permit holders as long as they don't use the concealed weapon to hunt big game.

ACTUAL TEXT

(1)(a) A person who does not have a valid permit to hunt on a temporary game preserve may not carry a firearm or archery equipment on any temporary game preserve while the respective hunts are in progress.

(b) "Carry" means having a firearm on your person while hunting in the field.

(2) As used in this section, "temporary game preserve" means all bull elk, buck pronghorn, moose, bison, bighorn sheep, Rocky Mountain goat, limited entry buck deer areas and cooperative wildlife management units, excluding incorporated areas, cities, towns and municipalities.

(3) Weapon restrictions on temporary game preserves do not apply to:

(a) a person licensed to hunt upland game or waterfowl provided the person complies with Rules R657-6 and R657-9 and the Upland Game Proclamation and Waterfowl Proclamation, respectively, and possessing only legal weapons to take upland game and waterfowl;

(b) livestock owners protecting their livestock;

(c) peace officers in the performance of their duties; or

(d) a person licensed to carry a concealed weapon in accordance with Title 53, Chapter 5, Part 7 of the Utah Code, provided the person is not utilizing the concealed firearm to hunt or take protected wildlife.

R657-5-8. Prohibited Weapons [for taking Big Game].

"PLAIN TALK"

Ya cain't use machine guns, night vision or laser sights to hunt big game. Unlike years past, there is no longer a limit on the number of bullets in a rifle magazine.

ACTUAL TEXT

(1) A person may not use any weapon or device to take big game other than those expressly permitted in this rule.

(2) A person may not use:

(a) a firearm capable of being fired fully automatic; or

(b) any light enhancement device or aiming device that casts a beam of light.

R657-5-9. Rifles and Shotguns [Big Game].

"PLAIN TALK"

Hunters can harvest big game with rifles larger than a .22 rimfire firing expanding bullets and shotguns, 20 gauge and larger, shooting slugs or number 4 buckshot.

ACTUAL TEXT

(1) The following rifles and shotguns may be used to take big game:

(a) any rifle firing center-fire cartridges and expanding bullets; and

(b) a shotgun, 20 gauge or larger, firing only number 00 or larger buckshot or slug ammunition.

R657-5-10. Handguns [Big Game].

"PLAIN TALK"

If you use a handgun to hunt big game, it has to be a "MAN'S GUN, not a little sissy gun." Surprisingly, the Division of Wildlife Resources (DWR) considers any handgun caliber less than .24 a "sissy gun," including a Thompson Contender shooting a .223 expanding bullet.

ACTUAL TEXT

(1) A handgun may be used to take deer and pronghorn, provided the handgun is a minimum of .24 caliber, fires a center-fire cartridge with an expanding bullet and develops 500 foot-pounds of energy at the muzzle.

(2) A handgun may be used to take elk, moose, bison, bighorn sheep, and Rocky Mountain goat provided the handgun is a minimum of .24 caliber, fires a center-fire cartridge with an expanding bullet and develops 500 foot-pounds of energy at 100 yards.

R657-5-11. Muzzle Loaders [Big Game].

"PLAIN TALK"

You can hunt big game with a muzzle loader with some restrictions on the size of the lead slug. You can't take your muzzle loader on an archery hunt, and you can't possess modern firearms during a muzzle loader hunt (with the exception of concealed weapon permit holders). However, if you have an upland game permit, you can take a modern shotgun on the muzzle loader hunt (see R657-6-8). Ranchers on a muzzle loader hunt can use modern weapons to protect their livestock from predators.

ACTUAL TEXT

(1) A muzzleloader may be used during any big game hunt, except an archery hunt, provided the muzzleloader:

(a) can be loaded only from the muzzle;

(b) has open sights, peep sights, or a fixed non-magnifying 1x scope;

(c) has a single barrel;

(d) has a minimum barrel length of 18 inches;

(e) is capable of being fired only once without reloading;

(f) powder and bullet, or powder, sabot and bullet are not bonded together as one unit for loading;

(g) is loaded with black powder or black powder substitute, which must not contain nitrocellulose based somkeless powder.

(2)(a) A lead or expanding bullet or projectile of at least 40 caliber must be used to hunt big game.

(b) A 170 grain or heavier bullet, including sabots must be used for taking deer and pronghorn.

(c) A 210 grain or heavier bullet must be used for taking elk, moose, bison, bighorn sheep, and Rocky Mountain goat, except sabot bullets used for taking these species must be a minimum of 240 grains.

(3)(a) A person who has obtained a muzzleloader permit may not possess or be in control of any firearm other than a muzzleloading rifle or have a firearm other than a muzzleloading rifle in his camp or motor vehicle during a muzzleloader hunt.

(b) The provisions of Subsection (a) do not apply to:

(i) a person licensed to hunt upland game or waterfowl provided the person complies with Rules R657-6 and R657-9 and the Upland Game Proclamation and Waterfowl Proclamation, respectively, and possessing only legal weapons to take upland game or waterfowl;

(ii) a person licensed to hunt big game species during hunts that coincide with the muzzleloader hunt;

(iii) livestock owners protecting their livestock; or

(iv) a person licensed to carry a concealed weapon in accordance with Title 53, Chapter 5, Part 7 of the Utah Code, provided the person is not utilizing the concealed firearm to hunt or take protected wildlife.

R657-5-12. Archery Equipment [Big Game - firearms restrictions only]

"PLAIN TALK"

This is a gun law (not bow law) book. . .so we covered only firearms restrictions and omitted a discussion of Lord-of-the-Rings weapons.

ACTUAL TEXT

(1) Archery equipment may be used during any big game hunt, except a muzzleloader hunt, provided:

. . .

(4)(a) A person who has obtained an archery permit may not possess or be in control of a firearm or have a firearm in his camp or motor vehicle during an archery hunt.

(b) The provisions of Subsection (a) do not apply to:

(i) a person licensed to hunt upland game or waterfowl provided the person complies with Rules R657-6 and R657-9 and the Upland Game Proclamation and Waterfowl Proclamation, respectively, and possessing only legal weapons to take upland game or waterfowl;

(ii) a person licensed to hunt big game species during hunts that coincide with the archery hunt;

(iii) livestock owners protecting their livestock; or

(iv) a person licensed to carry a concealed weapon in accordance with Title 53, Chapter 5, Part 7 of the Utah Code, provided the person is not utilizing the concealed firearm to hunt or take protected wildlife.

R657-6-6. Firearms . . .[Upland Game]

"PLAIN TALK"

Upland game means game birds and game rabbits (not including jack rabbits). You can shoot game birds with a shotgun, a handgun (shooting BBs, not bullets) or a bow, but not a crossbow or a rifle. However, you cannot shoot migratory birds with a handgun (see R657-9-9). If you are hunting waterfowl, you must "plug" your shotgun so that it can only hold three shells. Game rabbits (cotton tails and snowshoe hares) may be hunted with any firearm except a machine gun. Spotlighting and laser sights are not allowed.

ACTUAL TEXT

(1) A person may not use any weapon or device to take upland game except as provided in this section.

(2)(a) Upland game may be taken with archery equipment, a shotgun no larger than 10 gauge, or a handgun. Loads for shotguns and handguns must be one-half ounce or more of shot size between no. 2 and no. 8, except:

- (i) migratory game birds may not be taken with a handgun, or a shotgun capable of holding more than three shells, unless it is plugged with a one-piece filler, incapable of removal without disassembling the gun, so its total capacity does not exceed three shells;
- (ii) cottontail rabbit and snowshoe hare may be taken with any firearm not capable of being fired fully automatic;
- (iii) a person hunting upland game on a temporary game preserve as defined in Rule R657-5 may not use or possess any broadheads unless that person possesses a valid big game archery permit for the area being hunted;
- (iv) only shotguns, firing shot sizes no. 4 or smaller, may be used on temporary game preserves as specified in Rule R657-5; and

(v) Sandhill Crane may be taken with any size of non-toxic shot.

(b) Crossbows are not legal archery equipment for taking upland game, except as provided in Rule R657-12.

(3) A person may not use:

(a) a firearm capable of being fired fully automatic; or

(b) any light enhancement device or aiming device that casts a beam of light.

R657-12-4. Obtaining Authorization to Hunt from a Vehicle.

"PLAIN TALK"

Only those permanently confined to a wheelchair or crutches and amputees missing one or both legs may hunt from a vehicle. They have to be accompanied by a licensed hunter who is physically capable of helping them retrieve the animals they have shot. They cannot load their guns until they are ready to fire at game animals and they can't shoot on or across a road.

ACTUAL TEXT

(1) A person who is paraplegic, or otherwise permanently disabled so as to be permanently confined to a wheelchair or the use of crutches, or who has lost either or both lower extremities, and who possesses a valid license or permit to hunt protected wildlife may receive a certificate of registration to take protected wildlife from a vehicle pursuant to Section 23-20-12.

(2)(a) Applicants for the certificate of registration must provide evidence of disability as provided in Subsections R657-12-3(3)(a), (b), or (d).

(b) Certificates of registration may be renewed annually.

(3) Wildlife may be taken from a vehicle under the following conditions:

(a) Only those persons with a valid hunting license or permit and a certificate of registration allowing them to hunt from a vehicle may discharge a firearm or bow from, within, or upon any motorized terrestrial vehicle;

(b) Shooting from a vehicle on or across any established roadway is prohibited;

(c)(i) Firearms must be carried in an unloaded condition, and a round may not be placed in the firearm until the act of firing begins, except as authorized in Title 53, Chapter 5, Part 7 of the Utah Code; and

(ii) Arrows must remain in the quiver until the act of shooting begins; and

(d) Certificate of registration holders must be accompanied by, and hunt with, a person who is physically capable of assisting the certificate of registration holder in recovering wildlife.

(4) Certificate holders must comply with all other laws and rules pertaining to hunting wildlife, including state, federal, and local laws regulating or restricting the use of motorized vehicles.

R657-19 Taking Non-Game Animals (including Prairie Dogs)

"PLAIN TALK"

Hunters have to be extremely careful hunting prairie dogs because the Utah prairie dog is listed as threatened on the Endangered Species List. You give one of them worthless rats (oops! I meant priceless precious rodents) an enema with your .17 HMR, you could end up "stylin'" with Warren Jeffs in Zebrawear at Purgatory. The only reason we're having this discussion is that someone foolishly named these vermin "dogs" instead of "rats." If they had been given the appropriate name originally, the video "Exploding Varmints" would have been the top movie in box offices for the past nine years!

Before shooting prairie dogs be sure you have thoroughly investigated the rules currently found in R657-19. For your convenience, however, I have included R657-19-10 relating to Gunnison and White-tailed prairie dogs below. If you're still confused after you read it, you can always take me hunting with you and make sure I have enough ammo and Mountain Dew to last the entire trip (I know, I drive a HARD bargain).

ACTUAL TEXT

R657-19-10. White-tailed and Gunnison Prairie Dogs.

(1)(a) A license or certificate of registration is not required to take either white-tailed or Gunnison prairie dogs.

(b) There are no bag limits for white-tailed or Gunnison prairie dogs for which there is an open season.

(2)(a) White-tailed prairie dogs, Cynomys leucurus, may be taken in the following counties from January 1 through March 31, and June 16 through December 31:

(i) Carbon County;
(ii) Daggett County;
(iii) Duchesne County;
(iv) Emery County;
(v) Morgan;
(vi) Rich;
(vii) Summit County;
(viii) Uintah County, except in the closed area as provided in Subsection (2)(b)(i);
(ix) Weber; and
(x) all areas west and north of the Colorado River in Grand and San Juan counties.

(b) White-tailed prairie dogs, Cynomys leucurus, may not be taken in the following closed area in order to protect the reintroduced population of black-footed ferrets, Mustela nigripes:

(i) Boundary begins at the Utah/Colorado state line and Uintah County Road 403, also known as Stanton Road, northeast of Bonanza; southwest along this road to SR 45 at Bonanza; north along this highway to Uintah County Road 328, also known as Old Bonanza Highway; north along this road to Raven Ridge, just south of US 40; southeast along Raven Ridge to the Utah/Colorado state line; south along this state line to point of beginning.

(3) The taking of White-tailed prairie dogs, Cynomys leucurus, is prohibited from April 1 through June 15, except as provided in Subsection (5).

(4)(a) The taking of Gunnison prairie dogs, Cynomys gunnisoni, is prohibited in all areas south and east of the Colorado River, and north of the Navajo Nation in Grand and San Juan counties from April 1 through June 15.

(b) Gunnison prairie dogs may be taken in the area provided in Subsection (4)(a) from June 16 through March 31.

(5) Gunnison prairie dogs and White-tailed prairie dogs causing agricultural damage or creating a nuisance on private land may be taken at any time, including during the closed season from April 1 through June 15.

R651-614-5. Hunting with Firearms [near State Park Facilities]

"PLAIN TALK"

You can't hunt with rifles or handguns within 1 mile of a state park "facility." This means buildings, camps, picnic sites, overlook, golf courses, boat ramps and developed beaches. You can't hunt with shotguns and archery equipment within a quarter mile of those types of areas.

ACTUAL TEXT

Hunting with rifles and handguns on park areas designated open is prohibited within one mile of all park area facilities including but not limited to buildings, camp/picnic sites, overlooks, golf courses, boat ramps, and developed beaches. Shotguns and archery equipment are prohibited within one-quarter mile of above stated areas.

R651-614-5

COMMENTARY

This section is too broad. It prohibits HUNTING, whereas, it should only prohibit the DISCHARGE OF A WEAPON. If you are legally hunting in a state park, you may have to walk within a mile or quarter mile of a park facility. If you do not discharge a weapon, the law should not punish you. By passing through the mile perimeter, you are technically still hunting, but you are no danger to anyone unless you discharge your weapon. Therefore, the regulation should be amended to say:

~~Hunting with~~ The discharge of rifles and handguns on park areas designated open is prohibited within one mile of all park area facilities including but not limited to buildings, camp/picnic sites, overlooks, golf courses, boat ramps, and developed beaches. The discharge of shotguns and archery equipment ~~are~~ is prohibited within one-quarter mile of above stated areas.

R651-612-1. Weapons Prohibited [in State Park].

"PLAIN TALK"

You can't possess a loaded gun in a state park unless you are on a legal hunt or are a concealed weapon permit holder. Although this law was changed to conform to the concealed weapon statutes, the regulation still conflicts with the state law that preserves a person's right to protect his camp with a loaded firearm.

ACTUAL TEXT

Possession or use of firearms, including air and gas powered types, traps and all other devices capable of launching a projectile which could immobilize, injure, or kill any person or animal or damage property are prohibited in the park system unless:

(1) The weapon or device is unloaded and cased or otherwise packed away to prevent its use in the park area.

(2) The weapon or device is being used for the legal pursuit of wildlife, see R651-614, or in accordance with U.C.A. 53-5-701 Concealed Weapons Act.

(3) The weapon or device is being used by authorized enforcement officers in the performance of their official duties.

R651-612-1

COMMENTARY

This regulation was recently amended to conform to the Concealed Weapons Act. Nevertheless, it still conflicts with the code section that permits persons who are not concealed weapon permit holders to keep loaded weapons to protect their camps. This regulation should be further amended so that it doesn't violate the uniformity statute, U.C.A. 76-10-500, discussed in Chapter VII above. Only the Legislature has the power to regulate the use of firearms, NOT the Director of State Parks. A paragraph (4)should be added to read:

(4) <u>This section shall also not apply to persons protecting their temporary residences and camps with a loaded firearm as permitted under U.C.A. 76-10-511.</u>

Pancho's Wisdom

1% commit the crimes; but gun control infringes the innocent 99%!

Proposition 5

"PLAIN TALK"

Proposition 5, a constitutional amendment passed by Utah voters on November 3, 1998, makes it more difficult to change Utah's hunting laws through a process known as a "statewide initiative." A statewide initiative allows the "people," as opposed to the "Legislature," to initiate changes in the law. Before a statewide initiative can be placed upon the ballot during a general election, its proponents have to collect enough signatures to total

10% of the number of people who voted for governor in the last general election in at least 20 of Utah's 29 counties (U.C.A. 20A-7-201). Once the signatures are obtained, the proposed changes in the law can be placed on the ballot for vote of the people. This process completely bypasses the Legislature. The technique has been used in the past by various anti-hunting organizations who, through a media blitz and incomplete information, have persuaded voters to make drastic changes in the hunting laws of other states. Proposition 5 does not prevent either the Legislature or the Division of Wildlife Resources from changing Utah hunting laws. It prevents sweeping changes in the hunting laws as a result of a statewide voter initiative, unless the initiative passes by 66 2/3% of the vote rather than by a simple majority. In short, it makes it a lot harder for anti-hunters to stampede voters into passing anti-hunting laws. Because Proposition 5 was a constitutional amendment, two-thirds of each house of the Utah Legislature had to vote for it before it could be placed on the 1998 ballot. This suggests a strong, philosophical foundation in our Legislature favoring wholesome ideals such as hunting, the individual right to bear arms in self defense, and trusting law-abiding citizens with concealed weapons. Our current legislators didn't get elected in a vacuum. Their beliefs reflect those of their constituents. Utahns and their elected representatives know that the answer to violent crime is to make criminals, not law-abiding citizens, accountable. This is why, despite repeated verbal attacks by First-Amendment-loving-Second-Amendment-hating news editors, the Legislature refuses to place further restrictions on concealed weapon permit holders and law-abiding gun owners. This shows great wisdom and commitment to virtuous ideals in the face of unrelenting pressure from a misguided press. Although Proposition 5 was challenged by a liberal group that apparently had a lot of money, it was declared legal by Judge Tina Campbell of the U.S. District Court here in Salt Lake. Judge Campbell was affirmed by the 10th Circuit Court of Appeals, and the Supreme Court refused to hear the case. Therefore, Proposition 5 was validated by the federal courts and remains the law of Utah.

ACTUAL TEXT

ARTICLE VI, SECTION 1

Be it resolved by the Legislature of the state of Utah, two-thirds of all members elected to each of the two houses voting in favor thereof:

Section 1. It is proposed to amend Utah Constitution **Article VI, Section 1,** to read:

Article VI, Section 1. [Power vested in Senate, House and People.]

The Legislative power of the State shall be vested:

1. In a Senate and House of Representatives which shall be designated the Legislature of the State of Utah.
2. In the people of the State of Utah, as hereinafter stated:

   The legal voters or such fractional part thereof, of the State of Utah as may be provided by law, under such conditions and in such manner and within such time as may be provided by law, may initiate any desired legislation and cause the same to be submitted to a vote of the people for approval or rejection, or may require any law passed by the Legislature (except those laws passed by a two-thirds vote of the members elected to each house of the Legislature) to be submitted to the voters of the State before such law shall take effect. *Legislation initiated to allow, limit, or prohibit the taking of wildlife or the season for or method of taking wildlife shall be adopted upon approval of two-thirds of those voting.*

(Note: This amendment took effect on January 1, 1999)

PANCHO'S ENVIRONMENTAL PLEASURES

- Hearing a .40 TMJ smack a jumping jack rabbit.
- Watching a PETA member react to Pancho's description of a .40 TMJ smacking a jumping jack rabbit!
- Turning off balance and one-handedly peppering a fleeting starling with the 870 Express bought at Wal-Mart.
- Wearing a full length Coyote fur coat to an animal rights protest at the furrier's on South Temple and pointing out to the crowd that was about to beat you to death that they just stepped on the last living Kanab Amber Snail as they were rushing you.
- Ordering Humpback whale steak ("medium rare") on a whale watching cruise.
- Reading that the last California Condor died in the loving arms of the Executive Director of PETA causing its anal spincter to relax.

Pancho vs. Pirates of the Caribbean

CHAPTER X

CIVIL LIABILITY ARISING FROM USE OF FIREARMS

Pancho's Wisdom

Life ain't easy for a boy named "Sue."
Johnny Cash

Civil liability makes people ACCOUNTABLE for their actions. ACCOUNTABILITY provides a disincentive to those who carelessly or intentionally misuse firearms to injure or kill others. This in turn, reduces the number of injuries and deaths. In contrast, gun control laws do nothing more than deprive law-abiding citizens of weapons, making them more vulnerable to criminal attack. If criminal and civil laws hold violent felons ACCOUNTABLE for their actions, we DON'T NEED gun control.

Up to this chapter, we have been talking about criminal penalties under Utah's gun laws. If you break a criminal law, you go to jail or pay a fine. Civil liability is different. If you negligently (carelessly) hurt someone, you become liable to that person for money damages. Because neither the law nor the wrongdoer can restore an injured person's health, the law imposes an award of money damages in an attempt to restore an injured person to his or her pre-injury life style. For example, if an injured person earned $30,000 a year before an injury, but can only earn $15,000 because of an accident, the defendant ("tortfeasor") is required to make up the difference. If the injured person is thirty years from retirement at the time of injury, it could be expensive for the defendant. Civil law (also called "tort law") also requires the defendant to reimburse the injured person for all out-of-pocket expenses such as medical bills, rehabilitation expenses, and property damage.

Because of an intense propaganda campaign by the insurance industry, the idea of civil liability offends many people. They think there are too many lawsuits. Although it's true that some people take advantage of the system, civil liability is GOOD because it makes wrongdoers ACCOUNTABLE for their actions. This beats taking gun rights away from innocent, law-abiding citizens in an attempt to reduce "gun violence." Think about it, which is the greater deterrent — getting sued for a $100,000 for negligently injuring someone or getting fined $1,000 for committing a misdemeanor (two pizzas or one pizza)?

The concept of accountability is best illustrated by the criminal and civil trials involving O.J. Simpson. If O.J. actually killed Nicole Simpson and Ron Goldman, one might say that he "got away with murder." But he didn't really, because the victims' families won enormous civil verdicts against Simpson. The civil justice system held Simpson accountable for his actions, even though the criminal justice system failed (assuming Simpson is guilty - duh). Likewise, if a person intentionally or negligently injures someone with a firearm, the victim should not have to bear the burden of the injury; the aggressor should.

A. Negligence in General

Liability for negligence arises from the notion that everyone has a duty to use "reasonable care" to avoid injuring others. Utah Courts use the following jury instruction to explain to juries what negligence means:

> A person has a duty to use reasonable care to avoid injuring other people or property. "Negligence" simply means the failure to use reasonable care. Reasonable care does not require extraordinary caution or exceptional skill. Reasonable care is what an ordinary, prudent person uses in similar situation. **[You don't have to be an "A" student, just a "C" student.]**
>
> The amount of care that is considered "reasonable" depends on the situation. You must decide what a prudent

person with similar knowledge would do in a similar situation. Negligence may arise in acting **[like shooting wildly into the bushes]** or in failing to act **[like failing to lock your guns away when your child's hyperactive-teenage-mutant-ninja- neighbor friend comes to your house for pizza and video games].**

A party whose injuries or damages are caused by another party's negligent conduct may recover compensation from the negligent party for those injuries or damages. **[Comments in bold and brackets are mine.]**

The weapons laws we discussed in Chapter VII create civil, as well as criminal, liability. For example, it is a misdemeanor to carry a loaded firearm in a vehicle (unless you have a concealed weapon permit). If the loaded gun you leave in your car accidentally discharges injuring a passenger, a jury could find you negligent for violating the law prohibiting loaded firearms in a vehicle.

In a civil case, the fact finder, whether a jury or a judge, also decides if the injured person was negligent. In the example above, if the injured passenger knew the guns were loaded and did nothing about it, a jury would have to decide if this was negligent, and if so, how much of the fault to allocate to the injured passenger. The jury instruction generally given states:

If you find that the defendant was negligent, you must decide if the plaintiff **[the injured person]** was also negligent. If the plaintiff was negligent and the plaintiff's negligence was a proximate cause of the plaintiff's own injuries, the plaintiff's negligence must be compared to the negligence of the defendant.

A plaintiff whose negligence is less than 50 percent of the total negligence causing the plaintiff's injuries may still recover compensation, but the amount will be reduced by the percentage of the plaintiff's negligence. If the plaintiff's negligence is equal to or greater than [the negligence of the defendant] [the total negligence of all defendants], then the plaintiff may recover nothing. For example, if you find the plaintiff's negligence was 30 percent of all negligence causing the injuries, then the plaintiff's recovery will be reduced by 30 percent. On the other hand, if you find the plaintiff's negligence is 50 percent or greater, then the plaintiff will recover nothing.

You can see how the civil law reflected in these two jury instructions holds all wrongdoers, including those injured, accountable for their own actions. In Utah, if the fault of the injured person is equal to or greater than the fault of the person who injured him, the injured person loses the case and collects nothing.

B. Negligence Specifically Related to the Use of Firearms

It would be impossible to try to describe or predict every possible scenario in which gun owners could be held liable for negligence. As explained above, any act of carelessness causing injury could subject a person to liability. The question of whether or not a person's actions rise to the level of negligence or carelessness depends upon the circumstances of each case. Just because an injury occurs does not mean someone was negligent.

For example, suppose a deer hunter on a mountain sees a deer below him in a box canyon. Looking through binoculars, he sees no hunters near the deer. Because he will be shooting downhill into the canyon, he believes his bullets will drill into the ground if he misses. He shoots having no reason to believe his bullet will injure another hunter. The bullet misses the deer and unexpectedly hits a large flat rock submerged inch below the dirt. It ricochets out of the ravine and hits a fellow deer hunter in an adjoining canyon. Is the shooter negligent? Probably not. He is only required to act reasonably, not perfectly. The law does not require him to foresee the unforeseeable. Let's change the facts slightly. Suppose this same hunter takes an "over the hill" shot, discouraged by most safety instructors, and hits another person. Is he liable? He probably is, depending upon how foreseeable it is for someone to be in harm's way. If the shooter is hunting 420 miles from nowhere, a jury would be less likely to find him negligent than if a freeway were located just over the hill from where he took the shot.

Another hunting example illustrates the concept of "comparative negligence." Section (6) of the Utah archery regulations, section R657-5-38, requires bow hunters to wear hunter orange if a rifle hunt is in progress during a bow hunt:

(6) Hunter orange fluorescent material must be worn if a centerfire rifle hunt is also in progress in the same area... Archers are cautioned to study rifle hunt tables and identify these areas described in the...[hunting proclamation ...

Suppose a bow hunter, who is not wearing flourescent orange, hides himself in a thicket during a rifle hunt. During the hunt, a rifle hunter, who doesn't see the bow hunter, shoots him. A jury will have to decide (1) whether the rifle hunter was negligent for failing to see the bow hunter, (2) whether the bow hunter was negligent for failing to wear hunter orange as required by the hunting regulations, (3) whether the negligence of either of the parties caused the injury, (4) what percentage of fault each hunter should be assessed and finally, (5) what the injured bow hunter's damages are.

Several factors could influence how a jury might decide these issues. If, for example, the bow hunter had been so well hidden that no one would have seen him, a jury would probably conclude the rifle hunter was not negligent. That would end the case; the injured bow hunter would lose and the rifle hunter would win. Suppose, however, four other hunters saw the bow hunter and they testified they didn't know how the rifle hunter could have failed to see him. Under these circumstances a jury would probably find the rifle hunter negligent for failing to notice the bow hunter.

After such a finding, the jury would then be required to decide whether the bow hunter was negligent. Anyone who has ever been on a general Utah deer hunt knows that wearing hunter orange is vital; a hunter takes his life into his own hands without it. If, during a rifle hunt, a bow hunter wears camouflage rather than fluorescent orange, he does so at his own peril. Under these circumstances, a jury would probably conclude the bow hunter was negligent. If the jurors believed the rifle hunter would have seen the bow hunter had he been wearing fluorescent orange, then they must conclude that the failure to wear orange caused the accident. At this point the jury would have to compare the fault between the hunters. If they decided the rifle hunter's fault was less than or equal to that of the bow hunter, the bow hunter would recover nothing. If, however, the jury decided the rifle hunter was at least 51% at fault, the bow hunter would recover the percentage of his damages assessed against the rifle hunter. For example, if the rifle hunter were found 75% at fault and the damages were $200,000, the verdict would be $150,000, a reduction by 25% because of the bow hunter's own negligence.

The following two cases involved my own clients. The first case occurred in Birmingham, Alabama. My client kept a .38 caliber revolver in his glove compartment because he worked in the bad part of town. One weekend, several friends came over to my client's home and began working on their cars. Coincidentally, one of the friends had a blank gun that looked REMARKABLY like my client's real gun. The young men, all in their late teens, passed the blank gun back and forth, "shooting" each other with blanks. Sometime later, my client, who owned the real gun, pulled it out of the glove compartment and showed it to his friend who owned the blank gun. He said something like, "I'll bet this gun looks real." The friend thought he said, "this gun really looks real." The friend grabbed the real gun out of my client's hands, thinking it was his own blank gun. Before my client could exclaim that the gun was his own real gun, the blank gun's owner shot him in the stomach with it. The round-nose lead bullet pierced the right side of the abdomen, missed most vital organs including the right kidney and exited out of the right lower part of the back, just above the waist. His doctors, worried about internal bleeding, performed exploratory surgery carving a nasty incision from his diaphragm to his navel. His recovery was extremely painful(the incision hurt more than the bullet).

My client filed a claim against his friend's homeowners insurance alleging the friend had been negligent for grabbing the real gun out of his hands and shooting him with it. The friend's insurance adjuster argued, on the other hand, that my client had been contributorily negligent for pulling the real gun out of his glove box without telling the others about it. In Alabama, unlike Utah, if the plaintiff (injured person) is found to be even 1% at fault he loses the case. Because we believed there was a substantial risk that a jury would find the client partially responsible for his own injury, we settled out of court for a sum substantially below the friend's homeowners insurance policy limits. As a result of the negotiations, the civil justice system held both boys accountable for their actions. The defendant, through his insurance company, had to pay part of my client's medical bills, but my client had to accept far less than his injury was worth because of his own carelessness.

In the second case, my client, who was in his early teens, was visiting a friend of the same age. During the visit and while my client was waiting in his friend's bedroom, the friend took a .12 gauge shotgun out of his father's closet. My client did not know his friend was playing with his dad's guns. Assuming it wasn't loaded, the defendant walked into his room where my client was playing with a model airplane, pointed the shotgun at close range and pulled the trigger. Luckily, the gun was pointed at my client's shoulder rather than his face or chest. The blast blew a 1 inch round hole in his left shoulder, destroying 1/3 of his clavicle. Although there was little disability, the scarring was unsightly and the boy will have lead pellets in his shoulder for the rest of his life. I notified the friend's father's homeowners insurance company of the claim. We had two theories of negligence (1) the father had been negligent for leaving a loaded shotgun accessible to children and (2) the son was negligent, indeed reckless, for pointing a gun at my client and pulling the trigger. The insurance adjuster agreed my client was probably not negligent, because he didn't know his friend would be getting into his dad's guns. The only real issue was the value of my client's injuries.

After the adjuster and I researched the range of verdicts and settlements involving similar injuries, we settled the case amicably without taking the case to trial. The settlement was several times greater than medical bills, because my client was not responsible for the injury. Furthermore, the injuries were serious and permanent. Because my client was a minor, the settlement required court approval. After the judge was satisfied that the best interests of the child would be met by the settlement, he approved it and we set up a trust fund for the boy. Again, the civil justice system held the wrongdoers accountable for their actions and helped to compensate an injured person for injuries suffered through no fault of his own.

It is important to note here that the homeowners insurance in both cases would not have been contractually obligated to pay a verdict or settlement if the shootings had been intentional rather than accidental. It is against public policy for people to avoid accountability for their intentional acts of violence through insurance coverage.

Both cases depict how the civil law makes people accountable for their actions whether they cause an injury to others or to themselves. And certainly, both cases show the wisdom of having homeowner's insurance. Homeowners insurance spreads the risk of household injury among thousands of insureds, rather than requiring a negligent person to bear the entire burden of an injury himself.

C. Negligent Storage of Firearms (Accessibility to Children).

The following case shows how a jury allocated fault and awarded damages to a child injured because an adult left a loaded gun in an unlocked drawer. Think about how a gun safe or trigger lock might have prevented this boy's injury. Better yet, if the curiosity of the youngsters involved had been satisfied by a few trips to the range, we may not have been reading about their tragedy. The injured boy's attorney reported this case in the Journal of the Association of Trial Lawyers of America.

12 year-old Gohl (his first name was not given in the report), visited his friend, Raymond Morales, who lived with his grandfather, Raymon Morales. While playing in the house alone, Gohl and Raymond discovered a semiautomatic pistol and a clip of bullets in an unlocked drawer. The pistol had been left in the drawer by the grandfather's brother, Dolphin. When Dolphin finished visiting his brother, he forgot to take his pistol with him.

Gohl and Raymond took the pistol to a nearby ditch to shoot. Gohl put the clip into the pistol. Raymond, who was apparently unfamiliar with the gun, accidentally pointed the gun at Gohl while trying to figure out how to work the safety. The gun fired unexpectedly, hitting Gohl in the right nostril.

The bullet pierced the front of his skull, shoving bone fragments into his brain. Neurosurgeons had to remove almost 25% of the right temporal lobe of his brain. Gohl now suffers from brain damage and a seizure disorder. His medical expenses were approximately $70,000. Gohl sued the grandfather's brother, Dolphin, for negligently storing his gun in an unlocked drawer. He sued the grandfather, Raymon, who, he claimed, should have reminded his brother to take the pistol with him after his visit. He sued Raymond, his friend, for negligently pointing the gun at him while trying to secure the safety. The defendants in turn, alleged that Gohl, the injured boy, should not have placed the clip in the pistol.

Apparently Raymon and Raymond were insured by a homeowner's insurance policy with a $100,000 limit. Their insurance company paid the limit rather than subject Raymon and Raymond to even greater liability in a jury trial. The jury awarded $480,000 in damages, and allocated 55% of the fault to Dolphin for leaving the unloaded gun in an unlocked drawer. The jury held Raymond 18% responsible for pointing the gun at Gohl and Gohl 17% responsible for loading the gun (Gohl's verdict was reduced by 17% making him partially accountable for his own stupidity). Although the case did not report it, there must have been an additional 10% awarded against the grandfather (the percentages of fault must always total 100%), Raymon, who didn't have to pay the verdict because his insurance had already paid. (The homeowner's insurance paid $100,000 on behalf of Raymon and Raymond. Their total fault was 28%, 10% for Raymon and 18% for Raymond. 28% of the verdict is $134,400. Raymon, Raymond and their insurance company saved $34,400 plus court costs by settling out of court. Their insurance adjuster was a hero for advising them to settle.) Thus, Dolphin became responsible for $264,000 (55%) of the $480,000 judgment plus interest, for negligently leaving a firearm in a place where he should have known it would be accessible to children.

Conclusion

Although we have a right to bear arms, we also have a responsibility to conduct ourselves safely. If our carelessness injures another, we are responsible to that person for the damage we cause. It makes more sense to hold careless people accountable for their actions, than to take guns away from law-abiding citizens. Therefore, clear thinking gun owners should welcome the idea of civil liability related to gun use. The following safety rules would have prevented this accident:

a. storing ammunition and firearm in different locations,
b. keeping all firearms in the house in a locked gun safe or locked closet when not in use,
c. teaching children never to touch or handle a firearm without the supervision of an adult (This is exactly what the NRA's "Eddie Eagle" program teaches),
d. never point a gun at anything or anyone you don't intent to shoot,
e. never rely on the gun's safety to prevent the gun from firing,
f. Never put your finger on the trigger until you are ready to shoot intentionally at a target, and
g. MOST IMPORTANTLY, educate your kids AND the kids they "hang out with" about gun safety AND SATISFY THEIR CURIOSITY. Growing up, my kids AND ALL THEIR FRIENDS knew they didn't have to sneak into my guns to handle them or get a chance to shoot them. All they knew just asking was good for a several-hour session at the range where they could shoot 'til they dropped (from fatigue, not loss of blood!)

CHAPTER XI

THE LAW OF SELF-DEFENSE

(Criminal and Civil)

Pancho's Wisdom

"I never killed any one who didn't need killing."
Porter Rockwell

Since publishing the first Utah Gun Law book I have handled numerous criminal cases involving the issue of self defense, the most high profile of which was the successful defense of former computer magnate Dell Schanze ("SUPERDELL"). As a result of my work in the legal arena of self defense, I realized that the subject deserved more thorough treatment than just one chapter. For this reason, I am publishing a companion to this book entitled *"Utah Self Defense Law"* and have included a "Request to be Notified (when it is published and ready for sale), Appendix E. **EVERY Utahn who would use a weapon to defend himself or a third person should own and study *Utah Self Defense Law.*** Because the public only heard what the media wanted them to hear about the *Schanze* case, I'm having the entire trial, the attorneys' opening statements, the testimony of all the witnesses, and the closing arguments transcribed and included in the self defense law book. I may even include a few of the jury instructions so you can get a better feel for how the jury system works when self defense is an issue. You'll be able to read first hand the testimony that lead the jury to conclude that Dell wasn't guilty of threatening with a weapon even though he took his pistol out of his pocket and some folks got weak-kneed when they saw the gun.

Pancho's Wisdom

It's easier to defend yourself with a BLACK GUN than a BLACK BELT.

A. SELF DEFENSE - CRIMINAL LAW

U.C.A. 76-2-402. Force in defense of person — Forcible felony defined.

"PLAIN TALK"

This statute is the essence of Utah's Law of Self Defense. It defines exactly how much force a person can use in defending himself and others from violent criminals. Basically, a person can use whatever force is necessary to stop unlawful aggression, but **cannot use so much force that he, in turn, becomes the aggressor.** A person may only use as much non-deadly force as is necessary to stop the use of non-deadly force against him. Example, a slap for a slap. Deadly force can be repelled with deadly force. Example, bullets for bullets or bullets to repel an imminent knife or crow-bar attack.

Three critical words in the self defense statutes are the words **"justified,"** **"reasonable"** and **"imminent."** "Justified" means authorized. A person is justified in taking action against another, action that would normally be a crime, if his act is reasonably necessary to defend himself or another person. For example, a threat accompanied by an immediate show of force is an assault. If you assault someone, you are guilty of a crime UNLESS you reasonably believe your actions are necessary to defend yourself or another from an imminet threat from the person you assaulted.

The word **"imminent"** means "immediate" or "about to happen." If a bad guy aims his pistol at you, the danger is "imminent." However, if he is ten miles away at home, loading his pistol and you think he is coming after you, this is not imminent and you cannot legally DRIVE BY his home with guns ablaze!

The **reasonableness** of your actions are decided by a judge or jury. The issue becomes "what would a reasonable person [not an unreasonably paranoid person] do under the circumstances." If your actions in defending yourself exceed what the "reasonable person" would do under the circumstances, you are not justified and will be convicted of a crime, depending upon the degree and severity of force you used beyond what was reasonable.

A person cannot claim self defense if he:

a. starts a fight,

b. attempts to commit, is committing, or running away after committing a felony, or

c. agrees to a fight or duel unless he changes his mind and makes it very clear to the other person that he doesn't want to fight or duel.

In some states a person has to retreat before he uses force to defend himself. This is NOT true in Utah, if he is in a place where he has a lawful right to be (like a public street, supermarket, his house or someone else's house as a guest). Trespassers, however, must retreat.

If someone is using deadly force against you or a third person (like a gun or a knife), you can defend yourself or another using deadly force .

You can also use deadly force to prevent a "forcible felony" which includes the following crimes:

a. aggravated assault (intentionally causing serious bodily injury or threatening with a dangerous weapon likely to cause death or serious bodily injury),

b. mayhem (cutting off or disabling a member of the body or slitting someone's nose, ear or lip),

c. aggravated murder (killing another person under a host of aggravating circumstances defined in U.C.A. 76-5-202 including sexual assault of a child, killing for money, killing while kidnaping, poisoning, torturing, etc.),

d. manslaughter (recklessly but not intentionally killing another),

e. kidnaping,

f. aggravated kidnaping (kidnaping while using a deadly weapon, holding someone for ransom, etc., see U.C.A. 76-5-302),

g. a continuing list of unspeakable crimes which are listed in (4) below, including sexual abuse of children, and

h. arson, robbery, burglary (caution: not burglary of a vehicle - you can't shoot someone who is trying to break into your car, unless you or someone else is in the car).

Sections (5)(d), and (e) of this code section allow juries to look at previous violent acts and patterns of abuse committed by the "victim" (the person you "aerated") to determine if the deadly force used against him was justified. If there were no witnesses, looking at the victim's previous record for acts of violence might help a jury decide who likely was the aggressor, you, with a clean criminal record, or the scumbag, trouble-making "victim," who had a criminal history as long and thick as the Code of Federal Regulations!

If your spouse has nearly beaten you or your children to death in the past several months, and you think he is going to wake up in an hour and do it again, you may be justified (but not necessarily) in planting a bullet in his brain stem. Utah juries have to apply the rules stated in this code section every time the accused claims he or she acted in self defense or in defense of another. Included in the "Commentary" below are a series of short case summaries illustrating the principles contained in Utah's Self Defense Law.

The Problem of the Unarmed "Victim:" An extremely difficult dilemma for a gun owner is being threatened by one or more persons whom he believes may have weapons, but is not sure OR who are close enough and have sufficient strength, either alone or together, to overpower him and take his gun away from him. Unfortunately police and prosecutors are not very understanding if a gun owner, under such circumstances, threatens or uses a gun against such persons (hereinafter referred to as "the victims") who ultimately prove to have been unarmed. My experience has been that when the "victim(s)" do not have weapon(s), but the gun owner threatens or uses a weapon against them, the gun owner will almost always be arrested, charged and prosecuted UNLESS (1) the gun owner is in his own home and the "victims" were not invited in OR (2) the gun owner is a woman who is obviously being sexually assaulted by someone other than her husband. Although the gun owners in such cases are not always convicted, most will tell you being charged and prosecuted for what they thought was a justifiable act of self defense is a life-altering event.

ACTUAL TEXT

(1) A person is justified in threatening or using force against another when and to the extent that he or she reasonably believes that force is necessary to defend himself or a third person against such other's imminent use of unlawful force. However, that person is justified in using force intended or likely to cause death or serious bodily injury only if he or she reasonably believes that force is necessary to prevent death or serious bodily injury to himself or a third person as a result of the other's imminent use of unlawful force, or to prevent the commission of a forcible felony.

(2) A person is not justified in using force under the circumstances specified in Subsection (1) if he or she:

(a) initially provokes the use of force against himself with the intent to use force as an excuse to inflict bodily harm upon the assailant;

(b) is attempting to commit, committing, or fleeing after the commission or attempted commission of a felony; or

(c)(i) was the aggressor or was engaged in a combat by agreement, unless he withdraws from the encounter and effectively communicates to the other person his intent to do so and, notwithstanding, the other person continues or threatens to continue the use of unlawful force; and

(ii) for purposes of Subsection (i) the following do not, by themselves, constitute "combat by agreement":

(A) voluntarily entering into or remaining in an ongoing relationship; or

(B) entering or remaining in a place where one has a legal right to be.

(3) A person does not have a duty to retreat from the force or threatened force described in Subsection (1) in a place where that person has lawfully entered or remained, except as provided in Subsection (2)(c).

(4) For purposes of this section, a forcible felony includes aggravated assault, mayhem, aggravated murder, murder, manslaughter, kidnaping, and aggravated kidnaping, rape, forcible sodomy, rape of a child, object rape, object rape of a child, sexual abuse of a child, aggravated sexual abuse of a child, and aggravated sexual assault as defined in Title 76, Chapter 5, and arson, robbery, and burglary as defined in Title 76, Chapter 6. Any other felony offense which involves the use of force or violence against a person so as to create a substantial danger of death or serious bodily injury also constitutes a forcible felony. Burglary of a vehicle, defined in Section 76-6-204, does not constitute a forcible felony except when the vehicle is occupied at the time unlawful entry is made or attempted.

(5) In determining imminence or reasonableness under Subsection (1), the trier of fact may consider, but is not limited to, any of the following factors:

(a) the nature of the danger;

(b) the immediacy of the danger;

(c) the probability that the unlawful force would result in death or serious bodily injury;

(d) the other's prior violent acts or violent propensities; and

(e) any patterns of abuse or violence in the parties' relationship.

U.C.A. 76-2-402

COMMENTARY

The following summaries come from actual Utah appellate court opinions discussing the law of self defense. Most district court libraries have law books containing these cases. For example, you can find the first case entitled *State v. Knoll*, 712 P.2d 211 (Utah 1985) in volume 712 of the Pacific Reporter at page 211. The Pacific Reporter has cases from Utah and thirteen of our neighbor states including Nevada, Colorado, California, Arizona, Alaska, Idaho, and Wyoming.

This first case illustrates the limits of the use of "REASONABLE FORCE" in defending oneself. Although the defendant in this case did not use a firearm, the case illustrates well the principles of self defense and excessive force. The defendant and the victim were two unemployed people sharing a bottle of wine. There were no witnesses to the killing, but the defendant claims the victim starting punching him in the face and the head. They wrestled to the ground and the defendant struck his head. During the fight, the victim grabbed the defendant's knife and stabbed him in the back of the leg. The defendant grabbed the knife leaving the victim on the ground WITHOUT A WEAPON. The defendant alleged the victim pulled his head down so he couldn't see the victim. Claiming that he was afraid the victim would try to kill him, the defendant started slashing and stabbing with the knife. The victim died of multiple stab wounds which penetrated his heart and liver. Rejecting his claim of self defense, the jury found the defendant guilty of manslaughter. The Appeals Court agreed with the verdict. It said the serious stab wounds could lead a reasonable jury to conclude that the defendant used MORE FORCE THAN WAS NECESSARY, especially against a person with no weapon. Although defendant had a right to defend himself, he should not have killed the victim after disarming him. See *State v. Knoll*, 712 P.2d 211 (Utah 1985). **The force you use in self defense must be completely defensive, not offensive. Force and threats must be used solely for the purpose of stopping the progression of unlawful force against you or another, never in revenge or retaliation.**

The following case illustrates how THE DIFFERENCE IN SIZE AND STRENGTH can make a difference in justifying the use of deadly force in self defense. In this case a small, frail woman who had previously undergone several back surgeries was charged with 2nd degree murder for killing her large, powerful husband. They had both been drinking and had been seen arguing at the husband's workplace. The defendant went home first and her husband arrived later, threatening, "I'm going to kill you, you bitch. You don't deserve to live." There were no witnesses. She claimed she tried to leave, but he slammed the door shut. When she ran upstairs, he grabbed her by the leg and dragged her down the stairs on her back. A medical doctor, who had examined her after the incident, testified that she had a herniated disk in her neck and carpet burns on her back consistent with her story. After she kicked him away, he retreated into the kitchen to pour another drink.

Meanwhile, the defendant ran back upstairs, grabbed a loaded .357 Magnum and returned to the top of the stairs. Her husband started up the stairs shouting threats and obscenities. She pled with him to give her a couple of days to pack her belongings and promised to leave. He kept coming up the stairs threatening to kill her. She finally shot him in the face, killing him instantly.

A trial judge, who heard the case without a jury, concluded that the wife was guilty of manslaughter. He said SHE HAD OTHER OPTIONS when her husband retreated into the kitchen after she kicked him. He had no weapon in his hands as he climbed the stairs toward her. The trial judge held that the danger was not "imminent," she could have called the police, escaped through a window or hit him with a piece of furniture, rather than shooting him in the face with a .357 Magnum. Two of the three judges on the Appeals Court overturned the trial judge's manslaughter conviction and cut the defendant loose. Their decision focused on the fact that the husband was LARGE AND STRONG that the defendant was SMALL AND FRAIL, having had four previous back surgeries. This was a close, two-to-one decision in the Appeals Court. The dissenting judge agreed with the trial judge that the defendant was guilty of manslaughter. He focused on her threat, "as soon as she got her hands on a gun, he was a dead S.O.B." **[What you say during an incident WILL come back to haunt you during the resulting court case.]** This case illustrates how different judges can focus on different facts when trying to decide between a guilty verdict and an acquittal on the grounds of self defense. *State v. Stribe*, 790 P.2d 98 (Utah Ct. App. 1990).

This next case shows how important it is NOT TO BE CONSIDERED THE AGGRESSOR if you are going to plead self defense. The defendant was a juvenile who had driven his father to a liquor store. After buying booze, the defendant's father headed for the car where his son was waiting. As he approached the car, two men followed him asking for money. At that point, the defendant's father fell against the car, either because he had been struck or because he was drunk. As the two men started to leave the scene, the defendant jumped out of the car and called them back. One of the men, Warlie, hit him with a nunchuck and the other struck him with his fist. A nunchuck consists of two hardwood sticks dangling from both ends of a piece of leather lace or a chain. Ouch! The defendant pulled a gun and shot Warlie. Warlie laid his hands on the top of defendant's car, and defendant shot him again. He fell to the ground and later died. The other victim ran across the street with the defendant shooting at him. One shot grazed his head and the other lodged in his belt buckle. The defendant's father had gotten into the car before his son fired any of the shots at Warlie.

The Juvenile Court convicted the defendant of manslaughter. Upholding the conviction, the Utah Supreme Court pointed out that defendant's father had gotten into the car before any of the shots were fired. The Court said the defendant did not need to use deadly force to protect his father, who was safe inside the car when Warlie and his friend began walking away. When the defendant got out of the car and called them back, HE BECAME THE AGGRESSOR. Before that, neither he nor his father was in imminent danger, as required by the self-defense statute. *(State v Ex rel. Gonzales*, 545 P.2d 187 (Utah 1975).

U.C.A. 76-2-405. Force in defense of habitation.

"PLAIN TALK"

In Utah, a "man's (woman's) home is his (her) castle," and he can defend it with deadly force against those who break in, sneak in or who enter with the intent to commit a felony. See *State v. Mitcheson*, 560 P.2d 1120 (Utah 1977). It's his castle whether he is buying, renting or staying temporarily at someone else's place. If a stranger breaks into your home at night, has dark-colored clothing, a hood over his head and a knife or a gun in his hand, you can shoot him dead. What if the intruder is a vacuum-cleaner salesman, dressed in a business suit, "armed" with the latest model Hoover? If, in broad daylight, you shoot him full of holes when he sticks his foot in your door as you attempt to slam it in his face, you're in big trouble! These rules apply to both criminal and civil cases.

This statute says you will not be convicted of murder or manslaughter for killing a person who sneaks or breaks into your home, nor will his heirs win a suit for money damages against you. But if you blow away the vacuum salesman, his heirs could end up owning and living in your house while you're doing time in the "Big House."

ACTUAL TEXT

(1) A person is justified in using force against another when and to the extent that he reasonably believes that the force is necessary to prevent or terminate the other's unlawful entry into or attack upon his habitation; however, he is justified in the use of force which is intended or likely to cause death or serious bodily injury only if:

(a) the entry is made or attempted in a violent and tumultuous manner, surreptitiously, or by stealth, and he reasonably believes that the entry is attempted or made for the purpose of assaulting or offering personal violence to any person, dwelling, or being in the habitation and he reasonably believes that the force is necessary to prevent the assault or offer of personal violence; or

(b) he reasonably believes that the entry is made or attempted for the purpose of committing a felony in the habitation and that the force is necessary to prevent the commission of the felony.

(2) The person using force or deadly force in defense of habitation is presumed for the purpose of both civil and criminal cases to have acted reasonably and had a reasonable fear of imminent peril of death or serious bodily injury if the entry or attempted entry is unlawful and is made or attempted by use of force, or in a violent and tumultuous manner, or surreptitiously or by stealth, or for the purpose of committing a felony.

U.C.A. 76-2-407. Deadly force in defense of persons on real property.

"PLAIN TALK"

This statute is patterned after the home defense statute above, but extends the presumption in favor of property owners to the borders of their real property rather than just to the walls of their home. To date, no Utah appellate courts have interpreted this statute.

ACTUAL TEXT

(1) A person is justified in using force intended or likely to cause death or serious bodily injury against another in his defense of persons on real property other than his habitation if:

(a) he is in lawful possession of the real property;

(b) he reasonably believes that the force is necessary to prevent or terminate the other person's trespass onto the real property;

(c) the trespass is made or attempted by use of force or in a violent and tumultuous manner; and

(d)(i) the person reasonably believes that the trespass is attempted or made for the purpose of committing violence against any person on the real property and he reasonably believes that the force is necessary to prevent personal violence; or

(ii) the person reasonably believes that the trespass is made or attempted for the purpose of committing a forcible felony as defined in Section 76-2-402 that poses imminent peril of death or serious bodily injury to a person on the real property and that the force is necessary to prevent the commission of that forcible felony.

(2) The person using deadly force in defense of persons on real property under Subsection (1) is presumed for the purpose of both civil and criminal cases to have acted reasonably and had a reasonable fear of imminent peril of death or serious bodily injury if the trespass or attempted trespass is unlawful and is made or attempted by use of force, or in a violent and tumultuous manner, or for the purpose of committing a forcible felony.

U.C.A. 76-2-406. Force in defense of property.

"PLAIN TALK"

You can use force to defend your real estate or personal property, just NOT deadly force.

ACTUAL TEXT

A person is justified in using force, other than deadly force, against another when and to the extent that he reasonably believes that force is necessary to prevent or terminate criminal interference with real property or personal property:

(1) Lawfully in his possession; or

(2) Lawfully in the possession of a member of his immediate family;

or

(3) Belonging to a person whose property he has a legal duty to protect.

B. SELF DEFENSE - CIVIL LAW

The difference between self defense under criminal law as opposed to self defense under civil law was dramatically illustrated by the criminal and civil cases involving subway passenger Bernard Goetz. Four members of a black street gang approached Goetz on the New York subway. One of them brandished a screw driver and asked for five dollars. Goetz, who was illegally concealing a revolver, drew it and shot at all four, hitting two of them in the back. After the initial shooting Goetz found one of the gangsters, Darryl Cabey, lying wounded on a subway bench and shot him again. The wounds left Cabey permanently brain damaged and paralyzed from the waste down. New York prosecutors charged Goetz with attempted murder. The jury in the criminal case acquitted Goetz of the attempted murder charge, convicting him only on the misdemeanor charge of possessing an illegal weapon (Goetz had no concealed carry permit). The jury was predominantly white.

Cabey later sued Goetz for civil damages and his lawyer filed the case in a jurisdiction consisting of mostly ethnic jurors. During the civil trial, Cabey's personal injury lawyer convinced the jury that Goetz shot him after Cabey was so badly injured that he could no longer hurt Goetz or anyone else on the subay. The jury returned a verdict against Goetz for 43 million dollars, most of which consisted of punitive damages intended to punish Goetz for EXCEEDING THE BOUNDS OF SELF DEFENSE AND ASSUMING THE ROLE OF AGGRESSOR. This shows that a criminal defendant found "not guilty" of a crime on the theory of self defense, can still be held civilly liable for BIG BUCKS!

In Utah, U.C.A. 76-2-402(1) states "a person is JUSTIFIED in threatening or using force against another when and to the extent that he or she reasonably believes that force is necessary to defend himself or a third person against such other's imminent use of unlawful force" (emphasis added). The key word is "JUSTIFIED." You are relieved of legal responsibility, if you do not use excessive force. In addition, under U.C.A. 76-2-402(4) you can shoot a person who is in the process of committing a "forcible felony" against you or another. Forcible felonies include assault with a deadly weapon, kidnaping, attempted rape and sexual abuse of a child. If you shoot and kill a person attempting to commit one of these heinous crimes against you or a family member, and his heirs sue you for money damages, you win!

Your home is your castle under the civil law as well as the criminal law. U.C.A. 76-2-405 entitled "Force in defense of habitation" states:

> (2) The person using force or deadly force in defense of habitation is PRESUMED for the purpose of both CIVIL and criminal cases to have acted reasonably and had a reasonable fear of imminent peril of death or serious bodily injury if the entry or attempted entry is unlawful and is made or attempted by use of force, or in a violent and tumultuous manner, or surreptitiously or by stealth, or for the purpose of committing a felony. (emphasis added)

KEEP IN MIND, HOWEVER, THAT A "PRESUMPTION" CAN BE REBUTTED! Suppose a person breaks into your home and you disarm him. You hold him while your relatives watch. Later you decide to execute him because he broke into your home. If your relatives testify against you and the jury believes them, the presumption that you "had a reasonable fear of imminent peril" is rebutted. You would be convicted of murder and held liable in a civil case.

The following statute protects Utah gun owners who shoot a person committing a felony on their property.

U.C.A. 78-11-27. Defense to civil action for damages resulting from commission of crime.

"PLAIN TALK"

Utah property owners have an additional statute protecting them from civil damages if they shoot someone committing a felony on their property. Beware, however, that the "clearly retreated" provision in this statute strongly suggests all entrance holes be in the front and all exit holes be in the back instead of visa versa. A computer search into my legal data base did not find any cases in Utah where this statute had come into play.

ACTUAL TEXT

(1) Any person who, with criminal intent, enters the property of another or commits a crime against the person or property of another may not recover any damages to his person or property except as required by a court order of restitution in a related criminal action, unless that person can prove by clear and convincing evidence that:

(a) his actions did not constitute a felony; and

(b) his culpability was less than the person from whom recovery is sought.

(2) The provisions of Subsection (1) shall apply to any next-of-kin or heirs of the person if the person is disabled or killed.

(3) Subsections (1) and (2) do not apply if the person committing or attempting to commit the crime has clearly retreated from the criminal activity.

(4) "Clearly retreated" means that the person committing the criminal act has fully, clearly, and immediately ceased all hostile, threatening, violent, or criminal behavior or activity.

The following several cases involving civil lawsuits illustrate the rules of law we have just discussed. They show how important it is to limit actions to DEFENSE rather than REVENGE. This is particularly true in cases where innocent bystanders are unintentionally injured during a shooting or attempted escape.

Our law firm subscribes to a computer service that allows lawyers to search combinations of words in millions of cases in a matter of seconds. To satisfy my curiosity about civil suits involving negligent self defense, I asked the computer to find all cases containing the words "gun or handgun or pistol or rifle or firearm" in the same paragraph as "negligence or negligent" in the same paragraph as "self defense" excluding criminal cases. "Negligent self defense" means using more force than is necessary to protect oneself from an attacker. I was shocked that there were only 27 cases reported. These cases dated back to the late 1940s. Of the 27 cases, some were criminal cases, although I tried to exclude them from my search. Others dealt entirely with insurance issues, and one or two dealt with the liability of business owners who failed to protect their patrons from criminal attacks. These issues are outside the scope of this chapter. The following five case summaries illustrate the breadth and depth of the civil law of self defense.

A. Attractive Teacher Shoots to Frighten Mouthy Teenager, Reaps Lawsuit.

As Estep, an attractive school teacher was driving her car in the country, she came up behind a slow-moving tractor driven by Williams, a teenager. When Estep pulled along side to pass, Williams, stirred by her resplendence, howled like a lovesick coyote. Not impressed, Estep backed up and furiously chastised him. Hurt and offended, the teenager asked Estep if she wanted her neck broken. He then drove away on his tractor. Apparently fed up with mouthy teenagers, she pulled a .410 shotgun out of her trunk and chased the impertinent youngster. Overtaking Williams, she forced him to the ground at gun point. Confronted with the unfriendly end of a scattergun, Williams dropped to his knees pleading forgiveness. Screaming you "no good S.O.B.," she motioned him to crawl away on his knees. Aiming near his legs, she fired and reloaded twice claiming, with 20 years of shooting experience, that she only intended to scare him. After the shooting, Williams' doctors were not able to remove all of the pellets from the boy's legs and they testified he would be permanently affected by his body's reactions to the lead. Estep's defense was that Williams had provoked her. She had earlier been convicted of an unspecified crime related to the incident and had come before the federal district court asking permission to settle the case for $10,000. The court refused to approve the settlement stating a jury would probably find the shooting unjustified and award damages for far more than what she was offering to pay.

COMMENTARY

It's not funny anymore when a teenage boy threatens to break a woman's neck. But such a comment does not justify what happened here. Estep was not in imminent (immediate) danger from Williams. Her actions quickly transformed her from victim to aggressor. She should have simply driven away and reported the incident to the police. The result would have been the same had this incident occurred in Utah.

B. Bubba Shoots Jukebox Ninja, Verdict Exceeds Homeowner's Insurance Limits.

Harris and Pineset ["Bubba"] got into an argument over who had put quarters into a jukebox at a bar. Harris invited Pineset to "step outside" and Pineset accommodated. While confronting each other in the parking lot, Pineset drew a pistol. Harris tried to grab the gun, but it fired, striking him in the stomach. Surgeons had to remove part of his large bowel. The court held Pineset liable and awarded $203,728 in damages including $38,728 in medical expenses. Unfortunately Pineset only had $100,000 of homeowner's insurance coverage. Pineset appealed claiming he was JUSTIFIED in defending himself with a pistol, because Harris threatened to use KARATE on him. The court disagreed that he was justified in using a firearm (deadly force) but it reduced the verdict by 10% because of Harris' contributory negligence in consenting to the fight in the first place. Pineset still ended up having to pay $83,000 out of his personal assets to satisfy the verdict. The court explained its reasoning:

> Resort to the use of a dangerous weapon to repel an attack is not justifiable except in exceptional cases where the actor's fear of the danger is not only genuine, but is founded upon facts which would be likely to produce similar emotions in men of reasonable prudence. . .

Harris v. Pineset , 499 So. 2d 499 at 503 (La. App. 2d Cir. 1986).

COMMENTARY

A reasonable person might believe a person who threatens to use karate is threatening deadly force. If, before the fight, Harris had put on a "pre-fight" karate demonstration like on T.V., had broken two-by-fours with his bare hands and cinder blocks with his bald head, Pineset may have been justified in using deadly force. He couldn't have been too worried Harris' hands were deadly weapons. He voluntarily agreed to fight Harris. If he was sincerely convinced Harris could kill him with his bare hands, Pineset should have gathered his guests, left the bar and refused to fight. Then, had Harris pursued him, Pineset might have been justified in protecting himself with a pistol. Instead, Pineset lost the case because he agreed to fight. The same result would occur under Utah law. U.C.A. 76-2-402(2) states:

> (2) A person is NOT JUSTIFIED IN USING FORCE under the circumstances specified in Subsection (1) if he or she
>
> . . .
>
> (c)(i) was the aggressor or WAS ENGAGED IN A COMBAT BY AGREEMENT, unless he withdraws from the encounter and effectively communicates to the other person his intent to do so and, notwithstanding, the other person continues or threatens to continue the use of unlawful force; (emphasis added)

C. Cause and Effect: Gas Station Attendant Shoots Fleeing Robber, Robber Runs into Innocent Motorist, Gas Station gets Sued.

Bender, a night manager at a Cleveland, Ohio gas station, lugged a .45 revolver in his overalls while on duty. Three men in an Oldsmobile pulled up, wielded a shotgun and demanded cash. Fearing for his life, Bender handed over $400. The robbers told Bender not to move as they slowly drove away. Before the thugs could get off the premises, Bender drew his handgun and blasted through the back window of the car. The slug penetrated the front seat and plunged deep into the driver's back, perforating his spleen, stomach and heart. Mortally wounded, the driver's legs stiffened, propelling the gas pedal to the floor. The Olds screeched into the street accelerating rapidly. A block and a half east of the station, it crashed head on into a Cadillac driven by an innocent motorist, Strother, who suffered serious injuries. As usual, the criminals had no money or insurance so Strother sued Bender and his employer under the theory of negligent self defense.

Strother's attorney argued that Bender didn't need to shoot to protect himself, the criminals were almost out of the driveway when Bender began shooting. His actions, he alleged, created an unnecessary and unreasonable risk of harm to others. Despite his eloquent presentation, the trial court concluded Bender was not liable to Strother. The appeals court agreed with the trial court, pointing out that the getaway car was still in the gas station parking lot when Bender fired. It held Bender could not have foreseen the Olds would have lunged out of the parking lot to strike an oncoming car. As explained in Chapter X, a person is not liable if he cannot foresee that his actions will cause injury.

COMMENTARY

The most difficult cases for courts to decide involve disputes such as this between two innocent people. Let's face it; Bender and Strother were both victims of a criminal act. Unfortunately most criminals don't have much money, so their victims are often forced to look elsewhere for fair compensation.

This was a close case. Strother's attorney made a strong argument that Bender was not privileged to shoot because the danger had already passed. After all, the car was pulling away as shown by the fact that Bender shot through the back window. Unless there was evidence to show Bender was still in danger, his shots may not have been justified.

The Court had to stretch to hold an injury was not foreseeable to Bender. I agree that it was probably not foreseeable to Bender that his bullet would hit the driver in the back, the driver would stiffen up, pressing on the gas causing him to drive down the street at a high rate of speed, presumably already dead. Nevertheless, I think it is foreseeable that when you are shooting at somebody pulling away in a car, he might panic, "stomp on it" to get away, and cause an accident. This is the very reason many police departments forbid their officers to engage in dangerous, high-speed chases. Certainly Bender could have foreseen some injury, although not the manner or extent of the injury. His bullet could have missed and struck an innocent bystander (see the following case). In Utah, as in most states, if a person can foresee some harm, he is responsible for any injury even though he cannot foresee exactly how the injury will occur. If Bender believed the danger had passed, he should not have shot.

Despite these arguments, Bender and his employer would have had another defense in Utah. Utah law permits a person to use deadly force to prevent the commission of a forcible felony. U.C.A. 76-2-402 above defines robbery as a forcible felony and the robbery statute, U.C.A. 76-6-301, makes it clear that flight after a robbery falls within the definition of the "commission" of a robbery:

(1) A person **COMMITS** robbery if:

. . .

(b) the person intentionally or knowingly uses force or fear of immediate force against another **IN THE COURSE OF COMMITTING A THEFT.**

(2) An act shall be considered **"IN THE COURSE OF COMMITTING A THEFT"** if it occurs in an attempt to commit theft, commission of theft, or **IN THE IMMEDIATE FLIGHT AFTER** the attempt or commission. **(emphasis added)**

Because the bad guys were fleeing after committing a forcible felony, Bender would have been justified in using deadly force in Utah. The jury would be instructed to consider the self defense statute, but would not be bound by it. If the jury felt that Bender's force created an unreasonable risk of harm to third persons, he could still be held liable (see the "Restatement" rule discussed in the next case).

If Bender had been sued and found liable by a Utah court, he still would not have to bear the entire burden of the verdict. Utah law states that no defendant is required to pay more than his proportional share of the fault. As discussed above, the fault of all culpable (guilty) parties is compared. Recently, the Utah Supreme Court held that if the identity of a criminal is known, his fault must be compared by the jury. In this case, if a jury found Bender to be 10% at fault and the criminals to be 90% at fault, Strother would collect only 10% of the verdict from Bender, even if the criminals had no assets.

D. Shots into the Night at Peeping Tom Kill Innocent Bystander.

Another tragic case involving an alleged negligent self defense occurred in Nashville, Tennessee. Late one night in 1956, sixty-eight year old Norman Goodrich was walking home from work through a dark, heavily populated residential area. Meanwhile, a woman named Morgan heard a window rattling and thought it could be a prowler. She grabbed her pistol and went outside to sit on her front porch swing. She spotted a man enter her yard, crouch down on the ground and "peep" through a basement window at a woman undressing. Infuriated, Morgan pointed the handgun and cut loose with several shots. As bullets whizzed by, the intruder fled into the street and disappeared into the darkness, undoubtedly having experienced an immense adrenaline rush! Morgan heard someone call out "I've been shot." The bullet struck Mr. Goodrich in the chest ultimately killing him.

Mrs. Goodrich, wife of the deceased, sued Ms. Morgan for negligence but the trial court dismissed the case. The appeals court, however, sent the case back for a new trial, criticizing Morgan for literally "shooting into the dark" without knowing where her bullets would strike. The neighborhood was densely populated, the sidewalk was obscured by thick shrubbery and the area was poorly lit. The rule of law that the court applied to the case was that "a person using a firearm or other weapon in the exercise of his self defense is not liable for any injury unintentionally inflicted upon a bystander unless he is guilty of some negligence or folly in the use of the weapon." The Court held that there was a question of fact whether Morgan had acted negligently and that a jury should decide that issue and not the trial court judge.

COMMENTARY

There is no question that a person can use deadly force to protect others from deadly force. Here, had the "peeping" intruder confronted the woman in the basement with a deadly weapon, Morgan would have been justified in using deadly force to protect her. Under those circumstances, if the bullet had gone astray and hit Goodrich, Morgan would not have been liable. The Restatement of Torts, which most courts including Utah's, rely heavily upon, explains the rule of law with the following example:

A. points a pistol at B, threatening to shoot him.

B. attempts to shoot A,

but his bullet goes astray and strikes C, an innocent bystander. B is NOT liable to C unless, taking into account the exigency [emergency] which A's act placed B, B fired his self-defensive shot in a manner UNNECESSARILY DANGEROUS to C (emphasis added).

Unfortunately for Morgan, there was no evidence to show that the intruder was armed. He ran away after the first shot. The shots into the street were not intended to defend as much as they were intended to frighten, punish or stop the criminal. The "Peeping Tom" was, at most, guilty of criminal trespass, a misdemeanor. Under these circumstances, a person is not privileged to use deadly force and may be liable for injuring innocent bystanders.

E. Bartender Who Fails to Warn Drunken Patron to "Dance" held Liable for Shooting Patron in Foot.

The facts giving rise to this case occurred in 1948 in Wisconsin. Oshogay, a reservation Indian, had started a fight in the defendant's tavern a couple of weeks earlier. When he revisited the bar, Shultz, the bar owner, refused to serve him alcohol. He asked Oshogay to leave, but Oshogay refused. Finally, Shultz pulled a pistol from behind the bar and aimed near Oshogay's feet intending only to frighten him. The bullet struck Oshogay in the foot. A jury awarded damages in the sum of $1,223.70, a sizeable verdict in 1950. The appeals court upheld the verdict, putting particular emphasis on the fact that the bar owner had not tried to get anyone to help remove the belligerent patron, nor had he summoned the police. *Oshogay v. Schultz*, 257 Wis. 323; 43 N.W.2d 485, Supreme Court of Wisconsin, June 30, 1950.

COMMENTARY

Oshogay had not threatened anyone with deadly force. He was not armed with a gun or a knife. The bartender was not justified in using deadly force (a firearm), and was rightfully held liable for his actions.

F. CONCLUSION - CIVIL LIABILITY

Do not panic because our civil law holds people accountable for their actions. If you ever have to defend yourself or your family with a firearm, the following suggestions should help you avoid civil liability.

a. Don't threaten or use deadly force unless you reasonably believe you are being threatened with deadly force.

b. Stop shooting when your attacker no longer poses a threat.

c. Carry homeowners or renters insurance with a large umbrella policy just in case a jury does not agree with the way you approached the situation. You can buy a $1 million dollar "umbrella" liability policy for about $50 a month.

d. Retreat, if you can do so safely, though Utah law does not require it.

e. Make sure you legally possess and conceal the firearm you use for self defense.

f. If you are involved in an incident involving self defense, always consult with a lawyer before agreeing to give any statements. Have someone else call the police or the ambulance if possible, so that your recorded comments to the dispatcher cannot be used against you in a criminal case or civil suit.

g. Carefully study my new book about Utah's laws of self defense.

Pancho vs. Giant Insurance Companies

CHAPTER XII

MISCELLANEOUS GUN LAWS

Pancho's Wisdom

When they start making computers as reliable as Glocks, I'll stop wantin' to shoot 'em (the computers that is).

INTRODUCTION

We found some of Utah's gun laws in the darnedest places. They appear in code sections dealing with motor vehicles, public education, state lands etc. We threw these "maverick" gun laws altogether in this chapter.

U.C.A. 53A-11-904. Grounds for Suspension or Expulsion from a Public School.

"PLAIN TALK"

If your kid takes a real or play gun to school, he gets expelled for at least a year unless the school district superintendent gives him a break. This prohibition does not apply to college kids who are over 21 years of age and have concealed weapon permits (see "Plain Talk" for UCA 53B-3-103 in Chapter VIII above.)

ACTUAL TEXT

(2)(a) A student shall be suspended or expelled from a public school for any of the following reasons:

(i) any serious violation affecting another student or a staff member, or any serious violation occurring in a school building, in or on school property, or in conjunction with any school activity, including:

(A) the possession, control, or actual or threatened use of a real weapon, explosive, or noxious or flammable material;

(B) the actual or threatened use of a look alike weapon with intent to intimidate another person or to disrupt normal school activities;

COMMENTARY

Uh, so how do you take your gun to school to put on a skit (not a good idea with a real gun) or participate in hunter's safety? An administrator may authorize possession of a firearm. See U.C.A. 76-10-505.5 in Chapter VII above. When I was in high school we regularly took guns to school for school plays and left them in our vehicles so we could go dove or duck hunting immediately after school without going home first. There were never any school shootings in those days.

U.C.A. 58-37-8. Prohibited acts — Penalties.

"PLAIN TALK"

Under this code subsection a court can add 1-5 years to a jail sentence of a convicted drug dealer to run "consecutively" [after] rather than "concurrently" [at the same time] with any other penalty if the defendant used a firearm.

ACTUAL TEXT

. . .

(c) Any person who has been convicted of a violation of Subsection (1)(a)(ii) or (iii) **[sell drugs or possess drugs with intent to sell]** may be sentenced to imprisonment for an indeterminate term as provided by law, but if the trier of fact finds a firearm as defined in Section 76-10-501 was used, carried, or possessed on his person or in his immediate possession during the commission or in furtherance of the offense, the court shall additionally sentence the person convicted for a terms of one year to run consecutively and not concurrently; and the court may additionally sentence the person convicted for an indeterminate term not to exceed five years to run consecutively and not concurrently.

U.C.A. 65A-3-2. Prohibited acts on state lands. [Shooting tracer bullets]

"PLAIN TALK"

You can't shoot tracer bullets on state lands. The excuse for passing this law seems to be the potential fire danger. There is a similar federal law that prohibits firing tracers on National Forest property (36 C.F.R .261.5, the relevant section follows U.C.A. 65A-3-2 below). Notice that these laws don't claim to regulate firearms, but rather fire hazards; therefore, individual counties may have similar ordinances. If you are not on private land, you better check with the governments who claim jurisdiction before you amuse yourself with tracer bullets. The Utah Bureau of Criminal identification takes the position that this prohibits shooting tracers anywhere in the state except military installations, but the title of this code section seems to confine the prohibition to "state lands." You MIGHT be able to get away with shooting tracers on private land. This statute is confusing at best.

ACTUAL TEXT

(1) A person is guilty of a class B misdemeanor who:

. . .

(d) fires any tracer or incendiary ammunition anywhere except within the confines of established military reservations.

36 C.F.R. 261.5 Fire. [Shooting Tracer Bullets in National Forests]

The following are prohibited:

. . .

(b) Firing any tracer bullet or incendiary ammunition.

U.C.A. 76-5-102.8. Disarming a peace officer.

"PLAIN TALK"

Have you ever been tempted to see if you could "quick draw" a peace officer's pistol before he can? Forget it! It is a first degree felony.

ACTUAL TEXT

A person is guilty of a first degree felony who intentionally takes or removes, or attempts to take or remove, a firearm from the person or immediate presence of a person he knows is a peace officer:

(1) without the consent of the peace officer; and

(2) while the peace officer is acting within the scope of his authority as a peace officer.

U.C.A. 76-5-104. Consensual altercation no defense to homicide or assault if dangerous weapon used or participants are engaged in an ultimate fighting match.

"PLAIN TALK"

"It was a fair fight officer; he agreed to meet me in front of Blimpie's at high noon, both of us totin' single action 'hog legs.'" Sorry Stud, consent to a duel or gun fight is no defense to the charge of murder or assault, not even if the victim drew first. [This sure puts the dampers on making a living as a gunslinger!]

ACTUAL TEXT

In any prosecution for criminal homicide under Part 2 of this chapter or assault, it is no defense to the prosecution that the defendant was a party to any duel, mutual combat, or other consensual altercation if during the course of the duel, combat, or altercation any dangerous weapon as defined in Section 76-1-601 was used or if the defendant was engaged in an ultimate fighting match as defined in Section 76-9-705.

U.C.A. 77-18-10. Petition — Expungement of records of arrest, investigation, and detention — Eligibility conditions — No filing fee.

"PLAIN TALK"

If you have had the misfortune of being convicted of a felony or other serious criminal offense, the following several sections explain how you MIGHT be able to have your criminal record wiped clean so your civil rights, including the right to bear arms, can be restored. In short, if you have been "straight" for a long time and your crimes were not too serious, a court might agree to restore your rights. "Expungement" rightfully incorporates into the law the concepts of repentance and forgiveness. The process is described in detail in sections U.C.A. 77-18-10 through 17. If you have been convicted of a capital felony, first degree felony, second degree forcible felony or any sexual act against a minor, you can forget about expungement. You MIGHT, however, be eligible for what we attorneys call a "402 Motion" (call an attorney). The concepts of expungement and 402 Motions do not apply to federal convictions.

ACTUAL TEXT

(1) A person who has been arrested with or without a warrant may petition the court in which the proceeding occurred or, if there were no court proceedings, any court in the jurisdiction where the arrest occurred, for an order expunging any and all records of arrest, investigation, and detention which may have been made in the case, subject to the following conditions:

(a) at least 30 days have passed since the arrest for which expungement is sought;

(b) there have been no intervening arrests; and

(c) one of the following occurred:

(i) the person was released without the filing of formal charges;
(ii) proceedings against the person were dismissed;
(iii) the person was discharged without a conviction and no charges were refiled within 30 days;
(iv) the person was acquitted at trial; or
(v) the record of any proceedings against the person has been sealed.

(2)(a) A person seeking expungement under Subsection (1) may petition the court for expungement before the expiration of the 30 days required by Subsection (1)(a) if he believes extraordinary circumstances exist and the court orders the division to proceed with the eligibility process.

(b) A court may, with the receipt of a certificate of eligibility, order expungement if the court finds that the petitioner is eligible for relief under this subsection and in the interest of justice the order should be issued prior to the expiration of the 30-day period required by Subsection (1)(a).

(3) As provided in Subsection 78-7-35(1)(i), there is no fee for a petition filed under Subsection (2).

(4) The petitioner shall file a certificate of eligibility issued by the division to be reviewed by the prosecuting attorney and the court prior to issuing an order granting the expungement.

(5) If the court finds that the petitioner is eligible for relief under this section, it shall issue an order granting the expungement.

(6) No filing fees or other administrative charges shall be assessed against a successful petitioner under this section.

(7) A person who has received expungement of an arrest under this section may respond to any inquiry as though the arrest did not occur, unless otherwise provided by law.

U.C.A. 77-18-11. Petition — Expungement of conviction — Certificate of eligibility — Notice — Written evaluation — Objections — Hearing.

"PLAIN TALK"

The victim of a crime, or in the case of death, the victim's family must be notified that a convicted criminal is petitioning the court for an expungement or cleansing of his record. The prosecuting attorney is also notified. This gives these people a chance to object to the expungement if they want to. If objections are received, the court sets up a hearing date. If no objections are received, the court can grant the expungement without a hearing. People who have been convicted of a capital felony, first degree felony, second degree forcible felony or sexual act against a minor may not have their records expunged. Of course, the person petitioning the court for expungement must show that he has completed all the requirements of sentencing, probation or parole.

ACTUAL TEXT

(1) A person convicted of a crime may petition the convicting court for an expungement of the record of conviction.

(2)(a)The court shall require receipt of a certificate of eligibility issued by the division under Section 77-18-12.

(b) The fee for each certificate of eligibility is $25. This fee remains in effect until changed by the division through the process under Section 63-38-3.2.

(c) Funds generated under Subsection (2)(b) shall be deposited in the General Fund as a dedicated credit by the department to cover the costs incurred in providing the information.

(3) The petition and certificate of eligibility shall be filed with the court and served upon the prosecuting attorney and the Department of Corrections.

(4) A victim shall receive notice of a petition for expungement if, prior to the entry of an expungement order, the victim or, in

the case of a minor or a person who is incapacitated or deceased, the victim's next of kin or authorized representative, submits a written and signed request for notice to the office of the Department of Corrections in the judicial district in which the crime occurred or judgment was entered.

(5) The Department of Corrections shall serve notice of the expungement request by first-class mail to the victim at the most recent address of record on file with the department. The notice shall include a copy of the petition, certificate of eligibility, and statutes and rules applicable to the petition.

(6) The court in its discretion may request a written evaluation by Adult Parole and Probation of the Department of Corrections.

  (a) The evaluation shall include a recommendation concerning the petition for expungement.

  (b) If expungement is recommended, the evaluation shall include certification that the petitioner has completed all requirements of sentencing and probation or parole and state any rationale that would support or refute consideration for expungement.

  (c) The conclusions and recommendations contained in the evaluation shall be provided to the petitioner and the prosecuting attorney.

(7) If the prosecuting attorney or a victim submits a written objection to the court concerning the petition within 30 days after service of the notice, or if the petitioner objects to the conclusions and recommendations in the evaluation within 15 days after receipt of the conclusions and recommendations, the court shall set a date for a hearing and notify the prosecuting attorney for the jurisdiction, the petitioner, and the victim of the date set for the hearing.

(8) Any person who has relevant information about the petitioner may testify at the hearing.

(9) The prosecuting attorney may respond to the court with a recommendation or objection within 30 days.

(10) If an objection is not received under Subsection (7), the expungement may be granted without a hearing.

(11) A court may not expunge a conviction of a:

(a) capital felony;

(b) first degree felony;

(c) second degree forcible felony; or

(d) any sexual act against a minor.

(e) an offense for which a certificate of eligibility may not be issued under Section 77-18-12.

U.C.A. 77-18-12. Grounds for denial of certificate of eligibility — Effect of prior convictions.

"PLAIN TALK"

Several combinations of convictions can result in a denial of a petition for expungement. Before an expungement is granted, the following time periods MUST lapse from the time the convict satisfies all conditions of incarceration, parole, probation and fines:

a. seven years in the case of a felony,

b. ten years for an alcohol related traffic offense,

c. five years for a class A misdemeanor,

d. three years for any other type of misdemeanor or infraction, and

e. fifteen years in a case of multiple class B or class C misdemeanors.

ACTUAL TEXT

(1) The division shall issue a certificate of eligibility to a petitioner seeking to obtain expungement for a criminal record unless prior to issuing a certificate of eligibility the division finds, through records of a governmental agency, including national criminal data bases that:

(a) the conviction for which expungement is sought is:

(i) a capital felony;

(ii) a first degree felony;

(iii) a second degree forcible felony;

(iv) automobile homicide;
(v) a felony violation of Section 41-6a-502;
(vi) a conviction involving a sexual act against a minor;
(vii) any registerable sex offense as defined in Subsection 77-27-21.5(1)(f); or
(viii) an attempt, solicitation, or conspiracy to commit any offense listed in Subsection 77-27-21.5(1)(f);

(b) the petitioner's record includes two or more convictions for any type of offense which would be classified as a felony under Utah law, not arising out of a single criminal episode, regardless of the jurisdiction in which the convictions occurred;

(c) the petitioner has previously obtained expungement in any jurisdiction of a crime which would be classified as a felony in Utah;

(d) the petitioner has previously obtained expungement in any jurisdiction of two or more convictions which would be classified as misdemeanors in Utah unless the convictions would be classified as class B or class C misdemeanors in Utah and 15 years have passed since these misdemeanor convictions;

(e) the petitioner was convicted in any jurisdiction, subsequent to the conviction for which expungement is sought and within the time periods as provided in Subsection (2), of a crime which would be classified in Utah as a felony, misdemeanor, or infraction;

(f) the petitioner has a combination of three or more convictions not arising out of a single criminal episode including any conviction for an offense which would be classified under Utah law as a class B or class A misdemeanor or as a felony, including any misdemeanor and felony convictions previously expunged, regardless of the jurisdiction in which the conviction or expungement occurred;

(g) a proceeding involving a crime is pending or being instituted in any jurisdiction against the petitioner; or

(h) the petitioner has not paid the full amount of court ordered restitution pursuant to Section 77-38a-302, or by the Board of Pardons pursuant to Section 77-27-6 on the conviction for which the person is seeking an expungement.

(2) A conviction may not be included for purposes of Subsection (1)(e), and a conviction may not be considered for expungement until, after the petitioner's release from incarceration, parole, or probation, whichever occurs last and all fines ordered by the court have been satisfied, at least the following period of time has elapsed:

(a) seven years in the case of a felony;

(b) ten years in the case of:

(i) a misdemeanor conviction or the equivalent of a misdemeanor conviction as defined in Subsection 41-6a-501(2); or

(ii) a felony violation of Subsection 58-37-8(2)(g);

(c) five years in the case of a class A misdemeanor;

(d) three years in the case of any other misdemeanor or infraction under Title 76, Utah Criminal Code; or

(e) 15 years in the case of multiple class B or class C misdemeanors.

(3) A petitioner who would not be eligible to receive a certificate of eligibility under Subsection (1)(d) or (f) may receive a certificate of eligibility for one additional expungement if at least 15 years have elapsed since the last of any of the following:

(a) release from incarceration, parole, or probation relating to the most recent conviction; and

(b) any other conviction which would have prevented issuance of a certificate of eligibility under Subsection (1)(e).

(4) If, after reasonable research, a disposition for an arrest on the criminal history file is unobtainable, the division may issue a special certificate giving discretion of eligibility to the court.

COMMENTARY

Because this is a book about gun law, not expungement, sections U.C.A. 77-18-13 through 17 have been omitted from this edition. You may contact a lawyer or the Bureau of Criminal Identification (BCI) for more information about the process of expungement.

U.C.A. 78-27-64. Regulation of firearms reserved to state — Lawsuits prohibited.

"PLAIN TALK"

This law prevents Utah cities and counties from bringing lawsuits against gun manufacturers like those brought by Chicago and New Orleans. Such cities have caused their own crime problems by taking guns away from the law-abiding and by encouraging generations of welfare. Rather than accept responsibility for the problems this "social engineering" has caused, the mayors of these cities are suing innocent gun manufacturers with the intent to bankrupt. Fortunately, many of these lawsuits have been dismissed.

ACTUAL TEXT

(1) As prescribed by Section 76-10-500 , all authority to regulate firearms is reserved to the state through the Legislature.

(2) A person who lawfully designs, manufactures, markets, advertises, transports, or sells firearms or ammunition to the public may not be sued by the state or any of its political subdivisions for the subsequent use, whether lawfully or unlawfully, of the firearm or ammunition, unless the suit is based on the breach of a contract or warranty for a firearm or ammunition purchased by the state or political subdivision.

STATE AND FEDERAL AMMUNITION and BLACK POWDER RESTRICTIONS

"PLAIN TALK"

Through the years gun owners have asked me if there are restrictions on the amount of ammunition or black powder a person can possess. I conducted searches in state and federal data bases and I found nothing restricting the amount of ammunition Utah gun owners can keep as part of their "food storage." This assumes you are not storing it for an imminent military coup to over-throw the government or something else that constitutes a crime in and of itself. But assuming you're hoarding ammo just so none of your friends get the impression you're letting your arsenal take on the appearances of a home - a cause of depression for most of us like-minded western males - then it's not a crime.

Although the state code below refers to 500 pounds of explosives, ammunition and reloading components are exempt from this definition. To me that indicates there is no restriction, under state law, on how much ammunition or modern gun powder you can have in your home here in Utah.

The amount of **black powder** exempted under the federal code from any kind of special license is **50 pounds** provided it is being kept for use in an antique type firearm like a pre-1898 cap and ball or flintlock (see definitions in Chapter VII) or an antique cannon. Unless you have some sort of special license or permit (which are beyond the scope of this book), you should not keep more than 50 pounds of black powder on hand.

I could not find any restrictions on ammunition or black powder in either of the Weber, Davis, Salt Lake or Utah County ordinances. I assume anyone in any of the remaining counties that doesn't have a "manly" helping of ammo or powder on hand at all times could be the subject of "Broke Back Mountain" jokes.

ACTUAL TEXT [STATE STATUTES]

U.C.A. 76-10-303. Powder houses.

Every person who builds, constructs, or uses within 300 feet of any residence or traveled county road any powder house, magazine, or building in which powder, dynamite, or other explosive is kept in quantities exceeding 500 pounds is guilty of a class B misdemeanor; provided that this section shall not apply to any magazine maintained at any mine or stone quarry.

U.C.A. 76-10-306. Explosive, chemical, or incendiary device and parts —Definitions — Persons exempted — Penalties.

. . .

(1) As used in this section [300 et. seq]:

(b) "**Explosive,** chemical, or **incendiary device" does not include** rifle, pistol, or shotgun ammunition, reloading components, or muzzleloading equipment. (Emhasis added.)

[Federal Regulations]

27 C.F.R. § 555.26 Prohibited shipment, transportation, receipt, possession, or distribution of explosive materials.

(a) General. No person, other than a licensee or permittee knowingly may transport, ship, cause to be transported, or receive any explosive materials:

Provided, That the provisions of this paragraph (a) do not apply to the lawful purchase by a nonlicensee or nonpermittee of commercially manufactured black powder **in quantities not to exceed 50 pounds, if the black powder is intended to be used solely for sporting, recreational, or cultural purposes in antique firearms as defined in 18 U.S.C. § 921(a)(16), or in antique devices as exempted from the term "destructive device" in 18 U.S.C. § 921(a)(4) [presumably antique "civil war" style cannons].** (Emphasis added.)

[The 50 pound exemption is mentioned in several federal regulations in the Code of Federal Regulations (eg. see 7 C.F.R. § 555.105 Distributions to nonlicensees, nonpermittees, and limited permittees; 27 C.F.R. § 555.108 Importation; 27 C.F.R. § 555.106 Certain prohibited distributions.)]

REGULATIONS "PROMULGATED" BY BUREAUCRATS ATTEMPTING TO REGULATE FIREARMS

The Utah Constitution gives only the Legislature the authority to regulate the use of firearms (see Chapter VI). Unless the Legislature delegates this authority by statute to another governmental entity, including the executive branch (the Governor), that entity has no authority to **regulate the possession or use of firearms**. Unfortunately, from time to time, leaders of state entities and cities and towns promulgate regulations or pass ordinances claiming to regulate firearms which conflict with state laws. THEY DON'T HAVE THE AUTHORITY! SUCH RULES AND ORDINANCES ARE INVALID! See 76-10-500 in Chapter VII again. Nevertheless, law enforcement officials still enforce some of these rules and ordinances, so if you are caught violating their terms, you may still have to hire an attorney. There are so many regulations and ordinances that they won't all fit within the cover of this book; so I left them out!

PANCHO'S LITTLE PLEASURES

- A "double tap" on a target with the two holes touching.
- A sharp knife.
- A knife sharpener that works!
- A Republican sweep in Congress.
- Explaining to a member of the Utah Symphony that you consider yourself a musician too because you "play percussion."
- A match trigger.
- Not jerking a match trigger!
- Listening to the hammer clicks of a single action pistol spell, "C-O-L-T!"
- A hand-tooled leather belt full of .45 Long Colt ammo.
- Creaky leather bandoliers sportin' of 45-70 ammo!

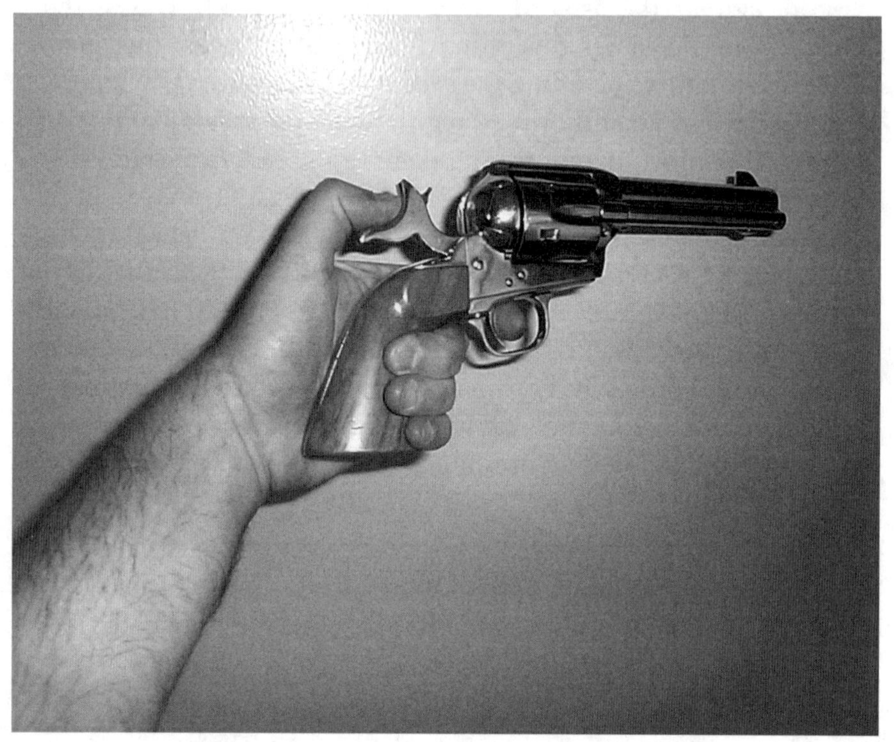

click, click, click, click, C-O-L-T

CHAPTER XIII

THE BRADY LAW and OTHER FEDERAL STATUTES

Pancho's Wisdom

ATF has NO PLACE in the Western or Southern U.S.

INTRODUCTION

The purpose of this chapter is to give the reader an overview of a few of the most important federal gun laws that affect Utahns. There is no way we could include a discussion of all federal firearms laws. We didn't feel like sticking a 500-page chapter on federal gun law, into the middle of a 300-page book about Utah gun law. We focus on laws that affect all Utah gun owners and hunters rather than laws that affect people with more specialized interests such as gun dealers, security guards and the few people who own machine guns. People involved in such enterprises generally know the rules because of their unique interests. If you have the overwhelming desire to read every federal code section relating to firearms, get *Gun Laws of America*, by Alan Korwin with Attorney Michael P. Anthony. The book can be ordered through Bloomfield Press, 12629 N. Tatum #440, Phoenix, AZ, 85032, or call (602) 996-4020 or (800) 707-4020, and also through Dillon Distributors, the reloading company that publishes "The Blue Press," Dillon Precision Products, Inc., 8009 E. Dillon's Way, Scottsdale, AZ 85260-9865, (800) 762-3845.

We find the most notorious federal gun laws in the Gun Control Act of 1968, passed largely as a result of the assassinations of

President John F. Kennedy and Senator Robert Kennedy. In the federal code it extends from 18 U.S.C [United States Code].§ 921 to 930. Title 18 deals with crime and criminal procedure. Section 922 describes what is unlawful. Section 923 applies to the licensing of gun dealers. The penalties for violating section 922 are in section 924. There is not enough space in this book permitting commentary on the whole act, but we have included the sections most relevant to Utahns. These include the Brady Act, the Lautenberg Amendment, the Assault Weapon Ban and the Gun Free School Zone Act.

Each "Plain Talk" section begins with a phrase introducing the main topic of that particular subsection, for example, "GUN DEALERS - 18 U.S.C. § 922 (a)(1)," "BUYING GUNS ACROSS STATE LINES - 18 U.S.C. § 922(a)(3)," "GUN FREE SCHOOL ZONE ACT - 18 U.S.C. § 922(q)," " THE BRADY ACT - 18 U.S.C. § 922(s),(t)," etc. These are also listed in the Table of Contents for quick reference. Also included in this edition are federal laws relating to restoring one's right to bear arms ("Relief from Disabilities") 18 U.S.C. § 925, remedies against the state and federal government for improper denial of the right to buy a gun under the Brady Act (including an award of attorney fees) 18 U.S.C. § 925A, how to transport your guns when traveling out of state, even in states that don't permit certain types of firearms, 18 U.S.C. § 926A, the effect federal law has on state law, 18 U.S.C. § 927, possession of firearms in federal facilities (including post offices), 18 U.S.C. § 930.

Congress claims it had the authority under the "Commerce Clause" to pass the Gun Control Act of 1968. But the Commerce Clause, Section 8, paragraph (3) wasn't enacted to give Congress the authority to regulate firearms. It simply states, that Congress has the authority "To regulate commerce with foreign nations, and among the several states, and with the Indian tribes." Obviously it was written to regulate TRADE between the U.S. and foreign nations, the Indian tribes and among the several states i.e. to keep these government bodies from treating each other unfairly in business deals. Neither the terms "firearms" nor "weapons" appear anywhere in the text of the clause. In fact, as late as the 1920's Congress hadn't ever regulated firearms or weapons by means of the Commerce Clause. When it tried to figure out a way to keep bootleggers from machine-gunning each other, it turned to Congress' taxing power to enact the National Firearms Act. That was pretty awkward, because the purpose of Congress' power to tax was to raise money, not to lock bootleggers up.

Hopefully, the "constitutionalists" on the Supreme Court, Justices Scalia and Thomas (Pancho prays for them nightly), will lead the charge to keep Congress from continuing to infringe on the right of American citizens to bear arms. The Supreme Court's recent decisions striking down the Gun Free School Zone Act (section 922(q) of the Gun Control Act of 1968) and the Violence Against Women Act as exceeding Congress' Commerce powers, suggest that these courageous and intellectually honest Supreme Court Justices have already begun to have a positive influence on the rest of the Court. Thank Goodness for Bush appointees Alito and Roberts. May they live forever, and maybe we get one more conservative on the Supreme Court!

One more rant before we launch into federal law la land. There is nothing expressly written in the U.S. Constitution giving Congress the power to establish a police force. There are too many cases to cite which talk about the police powers being reserved to the states. The words "police," "bureau," "investigation," "firearms," and "agency" do not appear in the Constitution. So how come we have so many federal police "agencies" and "bureaus" that no one of us can remember the names of all of them? ATF, FBI, CIA, ICE (that one gives ya warm fuzzies doesn't it?), DEA, the Secret Service . . . . which ones did I forget? If you are anything but a inert piece of wet spaghetti, you have probably violated some ridiculous federal law buried somewhere in a dusty archive and ought to be gittin' yer vittles in a federal pen cafeteria.

18 U.S.C. § 922 Unlawful acts .
GUN DEALERS - 18 U.S.C. § 922 (a)(1)

"PLAIN TALK"

If you don't have a federal firearms license (FFL), i.e. if you're not a LICENSED gun dealer, you CAN'T RUN A BUSINESS importing, manufacturing, SELLING or shipping FIREARMS in interstate or foreign commerce. The term "firearm" as used in this code section does not include most black powder and muzzleloader rifles and pistols unless they were designed to use modern ammunition, 18 U.S.C. § 921(3)(16). That is why you can still order these guns out of a catalog from out-of-state stores. If you are buying and selling guns for a profit and don't have your dealer's license, you could be charged with a federal offense. Warning: **ATF is prosecuting unsuspecting citizens who buy and sell guns at a profit for "dealing without a license!"** Even if you are just buying and selling for a hobby, I suggest you get a license so that ATF doesn't prosecute you (you'd think they 'd stay busy enough sniffing out suspected terrorists, but apparently they leave that to the FBI and go after "ruthless criminals" who would never expect that making a few hundred or thousand dollars selling guns as a hobby would put them on ATF's radar screen!) Frankly, I am not convinced ATF's enforcement of federal gun laws accomplishes ANYTHING to reduce crime. However, because there have not been any bomb attacks since the Oklahoma bombing, they MAY be having an affect on preventing such incidents. If they spend their time chasing down every dude who makes a few bucks on a gun sale, they will soon lose their effectiveness on that front also. Only one solution - Pancho for ATF director and I'll pull 'em all off firearms cases and have 'em chasin' down SERIOUS bomb threats!

Many people with clean criminal records, who could buy a gun from a dealer, prefer instead to buy from a private citizen so the gun doesn't have to be registered in their name. They are afraid that the logical result of federal gun registration will be the eventual confiscation of all firearms by the federal government. It has happened in other countries and to some extent in

California in connection with their "assault weapon ban." It is a legitimate concern for people living in a society that considers owning a gun to be politically incorrect. Therefore, you can't blame freedom loving Americans for wanting to buy modern, effective firearms without leaving any record of the purchase of that weapon. The only way to do that is to purchase from an individual who is not a federal firearms dealer. But those individuals need to WATCH OUT or BAT(f)man gonna gitcha!

ACTUAL TEXT

(a) It shall be unlawful—

(1) for any person—

(A) except a licensed importer, licensed manufacturer, or licensed dealer, to engage in the business of importing, manufacturing, or dealing in firearms, or in the course of such business to ship, transport, or receive any firearm in interstate or foreign commerce; or

(B) except a licensed importer or licensed manufacturer, to engage in the business of importing or manufacturing ammunition, or in the course of such business, to ship, transport, or receive any ammunition in interstate or foreign commerce;

18 USC 921(a) [ugly and VAGUE definitions relating to "dealing guns without a license."]

. . .

(11) The term "dealer" means

(A) any person engaged in the business of selling firearms at wholesale or retail,

(B) any person engaged in the business of repairing firearms or of making or fitting special barrels, stocks, or trigger mechanisms to firearms, or

(C) any person who is a pawnbroker. The term "licensed dealer" means any dealer who is licensed under the provisions of this chapter.

. . .

(21) The term "engaged in the business" means . . . (C) as applied to a dealer in firearms, as defined in section 921(a)(11)(A), a person who devotes time, attention, and labor to dealing in firearms as a regular course of trade or business with the principal objective of livelihood and profit through the repetitive purchase and resale of firearms, but such term shall not include a person who makes occasional sales, exchanges, or purchases of firearms for the enhancement of a personal collection or for a hobby, or who sells all or part of his personal collection of firearms;

COMMENTARY

The sheer unfairness of prosecuting otherwise law-abiding citizens for "dealing without a license" arises from the fact that there is no "bright line" for them to look at to know they are breaking the law. How much profit is too much? $1000? $100? $10? $1? It's not hard to make a profit off of guns if you keep them long enough. It's a fact of life that they are one of very few items of personal property that go up in value rather than depreciate, like your car, your furniture or your computer. And how many guns is too many to buy and then sell before the BAT(F)man wants to suck your lead- contaminated blood? 10? 5? 1 a month? How do you stay on the right side of the law when there's no line telling you where left is? This law is a CROCK and the people who passed it and vigorously enforce it would get better job satisfaction if they worked at the Kremlin!

RECEIVING GUNS FROM RESIDENT OF ANOTHER STATE - 18 U.S.C. § 922(a)(3)

"PLAIN TALK"

It's against the law to buy a gun, or receive one as a gift, from anyone living outside your state of residence without jumping through the right hoops. The "Hoops" are:

- ☻ you can INHERIT a gun from an out-of-state relative (18 U.S.C. § 922(a)(3)(A)).
- ☻ you can buy a RIFLE OR SHOTGUN from an out-of-state dealer (18 U.S.C. § 922(a)(3)(B)) if:
    - the sale is not prohibited by the state where the dealer resides
    - it's legal in the state where the purchaser resides, AND
    - the purchaser meets in person with the dealer (18 USC § 922(b)(3)(A)). [See Chapter VII for full text of 18 U.S.C. 922(b)]
- ☻ you can BORROW or RENT a gun temporarily for lawful sporting purposes, such as shooting at a target range or hunting on a game preserve (18 U.S.C. § 922(b)(3)(B)). A few years ago, I spiced up my summer vacation in Panama City, Florida by renting a Smith & Wesson 686 at a local shooting range.
- ☻ A DEALER can send firearms across state lines to other dealers (18 U.S.C. § 922(a)(2)). You can buy a handgun from an out-of-state gun store, but you will have to get an in-state dealer to fill out the "Brady" paperwork. Generally, in-state dealers charge $25 to $35 for this service. If your Uncle Mike, who lives in Idaho, wants to give you a revolver and a shotgun you have always coveted for cowboy action shooting, he will have to send them to a gun dealer in Utah. You, then, must go to the gun dealer's store and fill out the paper work before the Utah gun dealer transfers the guns to you. Uncle Mike might run across shippers who won't receive firearms from a person who is not a dealer. If that happens, he may have to pay an Idaho dealer to ship the guns to a Utah dealer.

ACTUAL TEXT

[It shall be unlawful–]

(3) for any person other than a licensed importer, licensed manufacturer, licensed dealer, or licensed collector to transport into or receive in the State where he resides (or if the person is a corporation or other business entity, the State where it maintains a place of business) any firearm purchased or otherwise obtained by such person outside that State, except that this paragraph

(A) shall not preclude any person who lawfully acquires a firearm by bequest or intestate succession in a State other than his State of residence from transporting the firearm into or receiving it in that State, if it is lawful for such person to purchase or possess such firearm in that State,

(B) shall not apply to the transportation or receipt of a firearm obtained in conformity with subsection (b)(3) of this section, and

(C) shall not apply to the transportation of any firearm acquired in any State prior to the effective date of this chapter [effective Dec. 16, 1968];

TRANSFERRING OUT OF STATE - 18 U.S.C. § 922(a)(5)

"PLAIN TALK"

This subsection is the flip side of the one above. That subsection made it unlawful to RECEIVE a firearm from out of state, this one makes it unlawful for you to GIVE OR SELL guns to someone in another state. You can't legally give your Browning "Sweet 16" shotgun to your nephew who lives in Texas. But, you can send the weapon to a dealer in Texas, who will handle the paperwork to transfer the gun to the nephew (assuming he is 18 years of age or older and the transaction does not violate the laws in the State of Texas). Aren't you glad Congress makes grandpa pay to give guns to their grandchildren so we can keep guns out of the hands of violent criminals?

ACTUAL TEXT

[It shall be unlawful–]

(5) for any person (other than a licensed importer, licensed manufacturer, licensed dealer, or licensed collector) to transfer, sell, trade, give, transport, or deliver any firearm to any person (other than a licensed importer, licensed manufacturer, licensed dealer, or licensed collector) who the transferor knows or has reasonable cause to believe does not reside in (or if the person is a corporation or other business entity, does not maintain a place of business in) the State in which the transferor resides; except that this paragraph shall not apply to

(A) the transfer, transportation, or delivery of a firearm made to carry out a bequest of a firearm to, or an acquisition by intestate succession of a firearm by, a person who is permitted to acquire or possess a firearm under the laws of the State of his residence, and

(B) the loan or rental of a firearm to any person for temporary use for lawful sporting purposes;

COMMENTARY

This section and the one above create substantial restrictions on the rights of law-abiding citizens to buy, sell or give away firearms to other citizens without criminal records. Congress passed these laws under the guise of keeping guns out of the hands of criminals. Isn't it enough that the feds have imposed heavy penalties on those who knowingly sell guns to felons (10 years) and upon felons who possess firearms (10 years) or give false information to buy them (10 years)? Why penalize a kind, old grandfather who simply wants his grandson to have his trusty old .22 to remember him by if neither the grandpa nor the grandson are felons? This is NONSENSE.

LYING TO BUY A GUN OR AMMO - 18 U.S.C. § 922(a)(6)

"PLAIN TALK"

If you lie to buy a gun or ammunition, you could be imprisoned for up to ten years (see 18 U.S.C. 924(2)). You then become ineligible to possess a firearm or ammunition under 18 U.S.C. § 922(g) (see discussion below). **Once convicted of a federal felony, you can't get it off your record short of a PRESIDENTIAL PARDON!**

ACTUAL TEXT

[It shall be unlawful–]

(6) for any person in connection with the acquisition or attempted acquisition of any firearm or ammunition from a licensed importer, licensed manufacturer, licensed dealer, or licensed collector, knowingly to make any false or fictitious oral or written statement or to furnish or exhibit any false, fictitious, or misrepresented identification, intended or likely to deceive such importer, manufacturer, dealer, or collector with respect to any fact material to the lawfulness of the sale or other disposition of such firearm or ammunition under the provisions of this chapter [18 U.S.C. 921 et seq.];

AGE RESTRICTIONS ON BUYING GUNS AND AMMO - 18 U.S.C. § 922(b)(1)

"PLAIN TALK"

This subsection of the federal Gun Control Act of 1968 prohibits gun dealers from selling handguns or handgun ammunition to persons under 21 years of age. Persons under 18 can't buy rifles, shotguns or ammunition for rifles and shotguns from gun dealers. It is interesting, however, that persons OTHER THAN GUN DEALERS may sell handguns to persons 18 or older, but younger than 21, if they are not simply acting as "middlemen" to help gun dealers get around this age restriction.

ACTUAL TEXT

(b) It shall be unlawful for any licensed importer, licensed manufacturer, licensed dealer, or licensed collector to sell or deliver—

(1) any firearm or ammunition to any individual who the licensee knows or has reasonable cause to believe is less than eighteen years of age, and, if the firearm, or ammunition is other than a shotgun or rifle, or ammunition for a shotgun or rifle, to any individual who the licensee knows or has reasonable cause to believe is less than twenty-one years of age;

18 U.S.C. § 922(b)(1)

COMMENTARY

Young adults between the ages of 18 and 21 with CLEAN CRIMINAL RECORDS are not the ones creating a problem. It's the gangsters with histories of violent crimes. Both state and federal laws already provide severe penalties for convicted felons to possess any firearm. The laws should not prevent young adults with clean records from protecting themselves with handguns. The law-abiding majority should not be held accountable for the actions of the law-breaking minority. State law prohibits anyone to sell any firearm to a minor outside the presence of his parent or guardian, U.C.A. 76-10-509.9, and this is sufficient to protect children. Unfortunately, state law could give gun dealers the impression that it is legal to sell a handgun to a minor as long as the child's parent is present. Federal law does not allow such a sale even if the parent is present. This law should be amended as follows:

(b) It shall be unlawful for any licensed importer, licensed manufacturer, licensed dealer, or licensed collector to sell or deliver—

(1) any firearm or ammunition to any individual who the licensee knows or has reasonable cause to believe is less than eighteen years of age, ~~and, if the firearm, or ammunition is other than a shotgun or rifle, or ammunition for a shotgun or rifle, to any individual who the licensee~~

~~knows or has reasonable cause to believe is less than twenty-one years of age;~~ **unless authorized by state law.**

This amendment would empower the states to pass laws more lenient than federal law if they want to. Utah legislators have decided that a dealer should be able to sell to a minor if the minor's parents are present. This amendment would allow Utah legislators to make such a decision.

SELLING OR GIVING GUNS TO PEOPLE WHO CAN'T LEGALLY BUY FROM A GUN DEALER - 18 U.S.C. § 922(d)

"PLAIN TALK"

You, AS A NON-GUN DEALER, cannot SELL or GIVE a firearm to anyone that YOU KNOW has been convicted of a felony, or a federal offense punishable by a prison term exceeding one year. The same applies to unlawful users of controlled drugs, drug addicts, fugitives from justice, illegal aliens, people with mental defects, those who have been dishonorably discharged, people who renounced their citizenship to the United States, those having a restraining order against them preventing them from threatening or attempting to injure an intimate partner or child (relating to spouse or child abuse) or to anyone who has been convicted of "domestic violence" even if it was a misdemeanor. DO NOT agree to act as a MIDDLE MAN for someone who cannot legally buy a gun from a licensed gun dealer. If you do, you are subject to imprisonment up to ten years and will lose your rights to bear arms. (18 U.S.C. § 924(2)). This is what the "Don't Lie for the Other Guy" signs mean at gun stores.

ACTUAL TEXT

(d) It shall be unlawful for any person to sell or otherwise dispose of any firearm or ammunition to any person knowing or having reasonable cause to believe that such person—

(1) is under indictment for, or has been convicted in any court of, a crime punishable by imprisonment for a term exceeding one year;

(2) is a fugitive from justice;

(3) is an unlawful user of or addicted to any controlled substance (as defined in section 102 of the Controlled Substances Act (21 U.S.C. 802));

(4) has been adjudicated as a mental defective or has been committed to any mental institution;

(5) who, being an alien, is illegally or unlawfully in the United States;

(6) who has been discharged from the Armed Forces under dishonorable conditions;

(7) who, having been a citizen of the United States, has renounced his citizenship;

(8) is subject to a court order that restrains such person from harassing, stalking, or threatening an intimate partner of such person or child of such intimate partner or person, or engaging in other conduct that would place an intimate partner in reasonable fear of bodily injury to the partner or child, except that this paragraph shall only apply to a court order that—

(A) was issued after a hearing of which such person received actual notice, and at which such person had the opportunity to participate; and

(B)(i) includes a finding that such person represents a credible threat to the physical safety of such intimate partner or child; or

(ii) by its terms explicitly prohibits the use, attempted use, or threatened use of physical force against such intimate partner or child that would reasonably be expected to cause bodily injury; or

(9) has been convicted in any court of a misdemeanor crime of domestic violence.

TAKING YOUR GUNS ON INTERSTATE (Between States) CARRIERS (Planes, Trains and Buses) - 18 U.S.C. § 922(e)

"PLAIN TALK"

If you want to take your guns with you on an airplane, you must "declare" that you have them and turn them over to the airlines. You can't take a firearm or ammunition with you on a bus or any other interstate carrier. This section also prohibits the carrier from labeling your luggage or package on the outside telling the world (and potential thieves) that the package or luggage contains firearms or ammunition. If you are going to ship a firearm or ammunition, you have to give the carrier (such as UPS) written notice.

The Code of Federal Regulations, 14 C.F.R. 108.11, spells out these procedures. We only included the paragraphs relevant to commercial passengers. The airline must require:

a. that the passenger declares in writing or orally the weapon is unloaded, and

b. pistols must be locked in the luggage, and only the passenger can retain the key or combination.

The airline has the discretion to decide what kind of container to store the firearm in during flight. Airlines that require more than this exceed the law.

WARNING: Several states including New York, New Jersey have been arresting air passengers who declare firearms and who do not have a permit to have a firearm in that particular jurisdiction. They are doing this despite the wording of the **18 U.S.C. 926A** which was intended by Congress to protect citizens traveling in interstate commerce from being prosecuted for violating local gun laws (thereby interfering with interstate commerce). Rumor has it that states such as New York and New Jersey offer $1,000 rewards for reporting anyone with a gun (to heck with the fact that you are complying with a federal law intended to keep them from doing anything as conniving as what they have been doing). Hopefully the NRA will win the lawsuit they have pending against the state of New Jersey for wrongfully arresting a Utah citizen who declared his firearm in New Jersey after his plane was diverted there through no fault of his.

ACTUAL TEXT

(e) It shall be unlawful for any person knowingly to deliver or cause to be delivered to any common or contract carrier for transportation or shipment in interstate or foreign commerce, to persons other than licensed importers, licensed manufacturers, licensed dealers, or licensed collectors, any package or other container in which there is any firearm or ammunition without written notice to the carrier that such firearm or ammunition is being transported or shipped; except that any passenger who owns or legally possesses a firearm or ammunition being transported aboard any common or contract carrier for movement with the passenger in interstate or foreign commerce may deliver said firearm or ammunition into the custody of the pilot, captain, conductor or operator of such common or contract carrier for the duration of the trip without violating any of the provisions of this chapter [18 U.S.C. § 921 et seq.]. No common or contract carrier shall require or cause any label, tag, or other written notice to be placed on the outside of any package, luggage, or other container that such package, luggage, or other container contains a firearm.

14 CFR 108.11 Carriage of weapons.

. . .

(d) No certificate holder **[airline or other interstate carrier]** may knowingly permit any person to transport, nor may any person transport or tender for transport, any unloaded firearm in checked baggage aboard an airplane unless—

 (1) The passenger declares to the certificate holder, either orally or in writing before checking the baggage, that any firearm carried in the baggage is unloaded;

 (2) The firearm is carried in a container the certificate holder considers appropriate for air transportation;

 (3) When the firearm is other than a shotgun, rifle, or other firearm normally fired from the shoulder position, the baggage in which it is carried is locked, and only the passenger checking the baggage retains the key or combination; and . . .

Pancho's Wisdom

Urban liberals are like over-crowded lemmings with a subconscious suicide wish. That's why not lettin' pilots have guns and other forms of gun control make sense to 'em.

18 U.S.C. § 922(e)

COMMENTARY

It's easier to take your guns with you on an airline (domestic flights only; not international) trip than you might think. It's part of my in-flight entertainment package to watch a busy ticket agent struggle to remember the protocol for checking a firearm ("Hmm, let's see, I remember seeing this in the instruction manual somewhere; is it procedure 649 or 496?"). Plan on checking your luggage at the ticket counter, though. You can't take your firearms into the passenger compartment of the plane, so carry-on luggage is out of the question. Sky caps at the Salt Lake Airport are not authorized to accept a Declaration of Firearms.

Let me share with you how a twisted member of the "Gun Culture" gets his jollies declaring a firearm. First, I always place my unloaded pistol or revolver in a hard gun case that fits inside my suit case. Most of the hard plastic cases have one or two small holes in the latches for placement of a luggage lock. You may want an extra one for the suitcase itself, just in case the agent interprets 14 C.F.R. 108.11(3) to mean that the suitcase must be locked. Because C.F.R. 108.11(2) gives airlines the discretion to decide what kind of case is suitable to carry a firearm, if you're not familiar with the requirements of a particular airline, you had better call in advance. This is particularly true if you are flying on more than one airline during the trip. You don't want to have an airline disapprove of your gun case when you are running late for a connecting flight and you have no one to leave your gun with.

I place my ammo, which is still in the original cardboard container, in a separate suitcase. I usually take my North American Arms mini revolver that holds five .22 Magnum rounds so that I can conceal easily in states that recognize my Utah permit. By calling the police departments in the cities in which I will be staying, I check the concealed carry laws.

I take clips (containing no ammunition of course) out of pistols and if possible, cylinders out of revolvers, to put airline agents at ease. It helps them to verify the guns are unloaded and safely stored. Some ask to see the guns, and others simply have me sign the bright orange tags declaring the guns to be unloaded. Federal law requires the tags be placed INSIDE suitcases, not OUTSIDE. If tags were attached to the outside of suitcases, they would be like miniature neon signs broadcasting to luggage handlers and fellow passengers, many of whom may be ineligible to buy guns, that you have a firearm in your suitcase.

When agents ask to see my gun, if I have my mini revolver, I tell them to brace themselves for the biggest, most repulsive looking revolver they have ever seen. When they, especially the lady ticket agents, see my tiny little "derringer," the usual response is a sigh of relief and something like, "Oh, how CUTE!" I then close and lock the gun case, zip the red Firearm Declaration Label INSIDE my suit case and hand it to the agent. To keep from having to buy cartridges in a strange city, I pack them in their original container in a SEPARATE suitcase (some airlines have added this requirement). Consistent with my policy of full disclosure, I tell the ticket agent about the bullets. If you follow these steps, you should have no trouble traveling by air with your guns UNLESS you end up checking your guns in New York, New Jersey or any other state that requires guns to be registered by you before bringing them to the state. I actually suggest you contact a "gun law" attorney in the state you intend to travel into BEFORE you go. Anything short of this may result in serious legal trouble.

PERSONS PROHIBITED FROM POSSESSING FIREARMS UNDER FEDERAL LAW - 18 U.S.C. § 922(g)

"PLAIN TALK"

It is illegal to possess or transfer a firearm or ammunition if you:

(1) have been convicted of a crime punishable by a prison term of more than one year, [like a felony];

(2) are a fugitive from justice [this is defined in 18 USC 921 (a)(15) as "any person who has fled from any State to avoid prosecution for a crime or to avoid giving testimony in any criminal proceeding];

(3) are an unlawful user of or are addicted to any controlled drug [if you get caught with illegal drugs or are proven to be addicted to a controlled drug];

(4) have been found by a court to be mentally defective or committed to a mental institution [A formal commitment of a person to a mental institution by a court, board, commission, or other lawful authority. The term includes a commitment to a mental institution involuntarily. The term includes commitment for mental defectiveness or mental illness. It also includes commitments for other reasons, such as for drug use. The term does not include a person in a mental institution for observation or a voluntary admission to a mental institution. See 27 C.F.R. § 478.11 Meaning of terms];

(5) are an illegal alien, a nonimmigrant status alien [like a tourist or here on a visa, not intending to immigrate] and don't meet certain exceptions [here for hunting or sporting purposes, on official diplomatic business etc.];

(6) have been dishonorably discharged;

(7) have renounced your citizenship;

(8) are subject to a court order [here in Utah referred to as a "permanent protective order"] preventing you from abusing an intimate partner or child of an intimate partner;

(9) or have been convicted of a misdemeanor of domestic violence. Violators could be sentenced to 10 years in prison.

ACTUAL TEXT

(g) It shall be unlawful for any person–

(1) who has been convicted in any court of, a crime punishable by imprisonment for a term exceeding one year;

(2) who is a fugitive from justice;

(3) who is an unlawful user of or addicted to any controlled substance (as defined in section 102 of the Controlled Substances Act (21 U.S.C. 802));

(4) who has been adjudicated as a mental defective or who has been committed to a mental institution;

(5) who, being an alien–

(A) is illegally or unlawfully in the United States; or

(B) except as provided in subsection (y)(2), has been admitted to the United States under a nonimmigrant visa (as that term is defined in section 101(a)(26) of the Immigration and Nationality Act (8 U.S.C. 1101(a)(26)).

(6) who has been discharged from the Armed Forces under dishonorable conditions;

(7) who, having been a citizen of the United States, has renounced his citizenship;

(8) who is subject to a court order that—

(A) was issued after a hearing of which such person received actual notice, and at which such person had an opportunity to participate;

(B) restrains such person from harassing, stalking, or threatening an intimate partner of such person or child of such intimate partner or person, or engaging in other conduct that would place an intimate partner in reasonable fear of bodily injury to the partner or child; and

(C) (i) includes a finding that such person represents a credible threat to the physical safety of such intimate partner or child; or

(ii) by its terms explicitly prohibits the use, attempted use, or threatened use of physical force against such intimate partner or child that would reasonably be expected to cause bodily injury; or

(9) who has been convicted in any court of a misdemeanor crime of domestic violence, to ship or transport in interstate or foreign commerce, or possess in or affecting commerce, any firearm or ammunition; or to receive any firearm or ammunition which has been shipped or transported in interstate or foreign commerce.

[18 U.S.C. § 921(a)(33) Definition of domestic violence as used in 18 U.S.C. § 922(g).]

(33) (A) Except as provided in subparagraph (C), the term "misdemeanor crime of domestic violence" means an offense that—

(i) is a misdemeanor under Federal or State law; and

(ii) has, as an element, the use or attempted use of physical force, or the threatened use of a deadly weapon, committed by a current or former spouse, parent, or guardian of the victim, by a person with whom the victim shares a child in common, by a person who is cohabiting with or has cohabited with the victim as a spouse, parent, or guardian, or by a person similarly situated to a spouse, parent, or guardian of the victim.

(B)(i) A person shall not be considered to have been convicted of such an offense for purposes of this chapter [18 U.S.C. § 921 et seq.], unless—

(I) the person was represented by counsel in the case, or knowingly and intelligently waived the right to counsel in the case; and

(II) in the case of a prosecution for an offense described in this paragraph for which a person was entitled to a jury trial in the jurisdiction in which the case was tried, either

(aa) the case was tried by a jury, or

(bb) the person knowingly and intelligently waived the right to have the case tried by a jury, by guilty plea or otherwise.

(ii) A person shall not be considered to have been convicted of such an offense for purposes of this chapter

[18 U.S.C. § 921 et seq.] if the conviction has been expunged or set aside, or is an offense for which the person has been pardoned or has had civil rights restored (if the law of the applicable jurisdiction provides for the loss of civil rights under such an offense) unless the pardon, expungement, or restoration of civil rights expressly provides that the person may not ship, transport, possess, or receive firearms. (**As defined in 18 U.S.C. § 921**.)

18 U.S.C. § 922(g)

COMMENTARY

Caution: Those of you involved in divorce or domestic issues beware! The definition of domestic violence is very broad under both the Utah and federal statutes. If you are charged with domestic violence ("DV") your attorney should consult with an expert in firearms law before accepting any plea. The consequences can be disastrous for a gun owner. **If you are convicted**, either by plea or by trial, **of domestic violence and possess a firearm at any time thereafter, you are a federal felon!**

Likewise, any permanent **protective order** issued against a gun owner in Utah is presumed by the Bureau of Criminal Identification to create a "firearms disability" (meaning you can't buy or even possess a gun or you are committing a federal felony). Before you agree to such an arrangement, your divorce lawyer should consult with an attorney well versed in firearms law. Protective orders and restraining orders have to be drafted VERY CAREFULLY if the parties intend to preserve the right to possess a firearm. Any mistakes in drafting could ultimately result in a felony charge or conviction for a gun owner whose attorney is unaware of the firearms issues.

Pancho's Wisdom

If judges are SERIOUS about preventing domestic violence, they'll issue a woman a Protective Order made of KEVLAR and a .38 Special!

BAN OF ASSAULT WEAPONS AND LARGE CAPACITY AMMUNITION FEEDING DEVICES - 18 U.S.C. § 922(v),(w)

"PLAIN TALK"

After 10 years of attempted tyranny by Congressional urban liberals, the infamous "Assault Weapons Ban" sunsetted [expired, sluss, vertig, gone baby!] on September 13, 2004. I wish I could've been there to see the looks on the faces of Chuck Schumer, Hilary Clinton, Sarah Brady, Diane Feinstein and Barbara Boxer! So instead of wasting space by putting in the text of a law that no longer exists, I'll let Pancho give you a few of his answers to the perplexing and age-old question, "Why does anyone NEED an Assault Rifle?" Pancho . . .

1. "Because . . . . you don't already have one!
2. "Because you don't already have FIVE of 'em!"
3. "Because you want to defend your family, your country and freedom with the BEST and MOST EFFICIENT equipment available!" (Hmmm, that's a pretty good argument for why every family member should own a machine gun as well!)
4. "Because you want your urban liberal neighbors to see you totin' them here and there and all around and EITHER move to Eastern Canada like they promised to do if President Bush was re-elected OR get so accustomed to seeing them that they no longer fear you OR them, ask to see them, then touch them, then shoot them, then become HANNITIZED ("converted to the politics of Sean Hannity") and become ONE OF US!!!!!!"

ACTUAL TEXT

[There IS no Assault Weapons Ban!]

Pancho's Wisdom

In the next few years dozens of school children, teachers and employees will die because of the foolish concept of "gun free" [free kill] zones, coupled with inadequate security. Their blood will be on the heads of politicians, school administrators and employers who institute such ineffective and foolish policies, NOT upon the heads of innocent gun manufactures, dealers or gun owners. Either protect the innocent with secured areas and heavily armed guards or let them arm themselves, if they so choose, for their own protection.

GUN FREE SCHOOL ZONE ACT - 18 U.S.C. § 922(q)

"PLAIN TALK"

This subsection prohibits carrying firearms within 1,000 feet of school property. There are several exceptions (thank goodness). If you live within the 1,000-foot zone, you can keep your weapons in your home and on your own property. You may drive through with your guns unloaded and in a locked case or gun rack. By virtue of Utah's concealed weapon law and 18 U.S.C. § 922(2)(B)(ii), those with a valid Utah concealed weapon permit, can possess a gun in a school zone. Hunters can cross these zones to get to their hunting area, if authorized by school personnel. Of course, the act prohibits the discharge of a firearm in a school zone. There are three exceptions given: (1) discharging them on private property not part of the school grounds, (2) discharging them as part of a program approved by the school (like R.O.T.C. training) and (3) by law enforcement and private security officers performing their official duties.

ACTUAL TEXT

(1) The Congress finds and declares that—

(A) crime, particularly crime involving drugs and guns, is a pervasive, nationwide problem;

(B) crime at the local level is exacerbated by the interstate movement of drugs, guns, and criminal gangs;

(C) firearms and ammunition move easily in interstate commerce and have been found in increasing numbers in and around schools, as documented in numerous hearings in both the Committee on the Judiciary of the House of Representatives and the Committee on the Judiciary of the Senate;

(D) in fact, even before the sale of a firearm, the gun, its component parts, ammunition, and the raw materials from which they are made have considerably moved in interstate commerce;

(E) while criminals freely move from State to State, ordinary citizens and foreign visitors may fear to travel to or through certain parts of the country due to concern about violent crime and gun violence, and parents may decline to send their children to school for the same reason;

(F) the occurrence of violent crime in school zones has resulted in a decline in the quality of education in our country;

(G) this decline in the quality of education has an adverse impact on interstate commerce and the foreign commerce of the United States;

(H) States, localities, and school systems find it almost impossible to handle gun-related crime by themselves—even States, localities, and school systems that have made strong efforts to prevent, detect, and punish gun-related crime find their efforts unavailing due in part to the failure or inability of other States or localities to take strong measures; and

(I) the Congress has the power, under the interstate commerce clause and other provisions of the Constitution, to enact measures to ensure the integrity and safety of the Nation's schools by enactment of this subsection.

(2)(A) It shall be unlawful for any individual knowingly to possess a firearm that has moved in or that otherwise affects interstate or foreign commerce at a place that the individual knows, or has reasonable cause to believe, is a school zone.

(B) Subparagraph (A) does not apply to the possession of a firearm—

(i) on private property not part of school grounds;

(ii) if the individual possessing the firearm is licensed to do so by the State in which the school zone is located or a political subdivision of the State, and the law of the State or political subdivision requires that, before an individual obtains such a license, the law enforcement authorities of the State or political subdivision verify that the individual is qualified under law to receive the license;

(iii) that is—

(I) not loaded; and

(II) in a locked container, or a locked firearms rack that is on a motor vehicle;

(iv) by an individual for use in a program approved by a school in the school zone;

(v) by an individual in accordance with a contract entered into between a school in the school zone and the individual or an employer of the individual;

(vi) by a law enforcement officer acting in his or her official capacity; or

(vii) that is unloaded and is possessed by an individual while traversing school premises for the purpose of gaining access to public or private lands open to hunting, if the entry on school premises is authorized by school authorities.

(3)(A) Except as provided in subparagraph (B), it shall be unlawful for any person, knowingly or with reckless disregard for the safety of another, to discharge or attempt to discharge a firearm that has moved in or that otherwise affects interstate or foreign commerce at a place that the person knows is a school zone.

(B) Subparagraph (A) does not apply to the discharge of a firearm—

(i) on private property not part of school grounds;
(ii) as part of a program approved by a school in the school zone, by an individual who is participating in the program;
(iii) by an individual in accordance with a contract entered into between a school in a school zone and the individual or an employer of the individual; or
(iv) by a law enforcement officer acting in his or her official capacity.

(4) Nothing in this subsection shall be construed as preempting or preventing a State or local government from enacting a statute establishing gun free school zones as provided in this subsection.

. . .

[Definition of School Zone, 18 U.S.C. 921(a)(25) , as used in 18 U.S.C. § 922(q).]

(25) The term "school zone" means—

(A) in, or on the grounds of, a public, parochial or private school; or

(B) within a distance of 1,000 feet from the grounds of a public, parochial or private school.

(26) The term "school" means a school which provides elementary or secondary education, as determined under State law. **(See 18 U.S.C. § 921. Definitions)**

18 U.S.C. § 922(q)

COMMENTARY

Notice a "school zone" is defined as an area 1000 feet around a school property. Virtually all schools are adjacent to roads and highways. This means that anyone WITHOUT a concealed weapon permit who drives through a school zone with a gun that is not locked in a case (e.g. hunters with UNLOADED guns in their UNLOCKED gun racks) are in violation of this law, a federal felony! In 922(q)(1) subparagraphs (A) through (I) above, Congress attempts to justify the "Gun Free School Zone Act" based on its power to regulate interstate commerce. Apparently, however, Congress had not placed this introductory language in section 922 until AFTER the Fifth Circuit Court of Appeals overturned the conviction of a Texas high school boy named Lopez, who was prosecuted for carrying a concealed weapon to school. The Fifth Circuit held that the Commerce Clause does not give Congress the authority to control activities in local schools, that control over this activity is reserved to state and local governments. As this case moved through the appeal process headed for the United States Supreme Court, Congress went back to the drawing board and inserted the language now appearing in subparagraphs (A) through (I). When the *Lopez* case finally reached the Supreme Court, the government attorney prosecuting the case tried to convince the Court that it had to accept Congress' finding that guns in the schools affect commerce. The Supreme Court in a 5 to 4 decision refused to buy the argument. It held the Gun Free School Zone Act unconstitutional stating there was not a sufficient "nexus" (connection) between the purpose of the statute and its effect on commerce. See *United States v. Lopez*, 131 L.Ed 2d 626, 115 S.Ct 1624, 95 CDOS 3074, 8 FLW Fed S 752 (1995, US). Of course, the question remains whether the subsequent amendment by Congress explaining the connection between crime in schools and interstate commerce, cures the defect. Based upon the language of the case, I don't think it does. As recently as May of 2000, the Supreme Court used the *Lopez* case as precedent to hold the federal Violence Against Women Act unconstitutional as exceeding the Commerce Clause. This sends a strong message that the Supreme Court is not going to continue to let Congress use the Commerce Clause as a ticket to control every activity in America. Some activities like regulating crime in our schools and violence against women are exclusively <u>intra</u>state, as opposed to <u>inter</u>state, activities and Congress should keep its mits off! Utah doesn't need the federal act anyway. Utah law not only prohibits students who are under 21 years of age and don't have a concealed weapon permit from bringing real guns to school, it prohibits them from bringing play guns or even objects that look like guns (U.C.A. 53A-11-904, see discussion in Chapter XII). Congress should back off and let each state handle the problem as they see fit. This whole subsection should be repealed.

What happens if someone is arrested NOW for carrying guns into school zones, AFTER Congress added paragraphs (A) through (I)? I think the language of the case is broad enough to suggest the Supreme Court will again find the Gun Free School Zone Act to be unconstitutional. But, hey, it was a 5 to 4 decision, so don't bet your favorite horse on it. If you do, make sure he's worth a million dollars so you can sell him to pay your attorneys to take the case to the Supreme Court of the U.S.

PANCHO'S WISDOM

When the Brady Act became law, ATF sent tons of paper "Brady Forms" to gun dealers. No tellin' how many trees Jim and Sarah Brady have killed. I know, let's repeal the Brady Act and save the Rain Forest!

THE BRADY ACT - 18 U.S.C. § 922(s),(t)

"PLAIN TALK"

Subsections (s) and (t) of section 922 are the "Brady Handgun Violence Prevention Act." Subsection (s) describes the Brady rules for the first five years, from November 30, 1993 until November 30, 1998. Subsection (t) explains the National Criminal Instant Check System (NICS) that took effect on November 30, 1998. From correspondence I received as a licensed gun dealer, it appears federal and state officials had to really scramble to meet the November 30, 1998 deadline. Since NICS has been up and running the computer has crashed several times. Once in the Spring of 2000 the FBI computer was down four days and no one in the country could buy a gun during that time. If the feds had kept newspapers out of circulation for four days, the media would have tried to overthrow the government.

Under Brady, the states have had the option of conducting an instant background check rather than requiring a buyer to wait 3 days before he or she could buy a handgun. Utah has been using the instant-check option for handgun purchases for several years now. Before November 30, 1998, dealers didn't have to do background checks to sell rifles and shotguns; now they do. The current procedure is set forth in U.C.A. 76-10-526 (above in Chapter VII). Until the state raises the price, the background check costs the buyer $7.50. Utah concealed weapon permit holders are exempt from the instant-check search and fee, but the Bureau of Criminal Identification still requires dealers to call BCI before selling a gun. BCI checks its CWP database to ensure that the CWP is still valid.

During the FBI computer Spring 2000 power outages, the Utah Bureau of Criminal Identification (BCI) was requiring NICS checks on CWPs although not charging the $7.50 fee. Input by the author helped convince BCI to stop this practice. Now, if the omniscient but mortal FBI computer convulses, Utah CWPs may purchase a gun from a dealer after a local background check to verify that the Utah CWP is still valid. Permit holders, please keep the mother board to Utah BCI's local computer in your nightly prayers!

As a gun dealer, I received a letter from the Bureau of Criminal Identification containing the following warning:

> You will receive one of three responses on a background check; Approved, denied or research. If you receive a research response it is unlawful for you to transfer the firearm until you receive an approval from the department. The Brady operator is required to tell you approximately how long the research period will take but there is not a mandatory time frame. *Again, it is unlawful for a dealer to transfer a firearm to a buyer unless they have received an approval from the department.* (Italics in original.)

In other words, if the computer is tied up for months, it could take you that long to get a gun! Even the Brady Act only makes buyers wait three days. If by the end of the third day, the dealer hasn't received a response prohibiting the sale, he can sell the gun to the proposed buyer, 18 U.S.C. § 922(t)(1)(B)(ii). Brady, however, doesn't seem to prohibit states from imposing longer waiting periods, 18 U.S.C. § 922(t)(2). Again we see the good guys losing out. Criminals can get machine guns overnight from gun runners; good guys may have to wait indefinitely to buy a bolt-action rifle if FBI or BCI computers are overloaded or "glitching."

Incidentally, if the state or federal government improperly deny a purchase, citizens can sue and be awarded attorney fees (see discussion of 18 U.S.C. 935A below).

ACTUAL TEXT

(s)(1) Beginning on the date that is 90 days after the date of enactment of this subsection [enacted Nov. 30, 1993] and ending on the day before the date that is 60 months after such date of enactment, it shall be unlawful for any licensed importer, licensed manufacturer, or licensed dealer to sell, deliver, or transfer a handgun (other than the return of a handgun to the person from whom it was received) to an individual who is not licensed under section 923 unless–

(A) after the most recent proposal of such transfer by the transferee—

(i) the transferor has—

(I) received from the transferee a statement of the transferee containing the information described in paragraph (3);

(II) verified the identity of the transferee by examining the identification document presented;

(III) within 1 day after the transferee furnishes the statement, provided notice of the contents of the statement to the chief law enforcement officer of the place of residence of the transferee; and

(IV) within 1 day after the transferee furnishes the statement, transmitted a copy of the statement to the chief law enforcement officer of the place of residence of the transferee; and

(ii)(I) 5 business days (meaning days on which State offices are open) have elapsed from the date the transferor furnished notice of the contents of the statement to the chief law enforcement officer, during which period the transferor has not received information from the chief law enforcement officer that receipt or possession of the handgun by the transferee would be in violation of Federal, State, or local law; or

(II) the transferor has received notice from the chief law enforcement officer that the officer has no information indicating that receipt or possession of the handgun by the transferee would violate Federal, State, or local law;

(B) the transferee has presented to the transferor a written statement, issued by the chief law enforcement officer of the place of residence of the transferee during the 10-day period ending on the date of the most recent proposal of such transfer by the transferee, stating that the transferee requires access to a handgun because of a threat to the life of the transferee or of any member of the household of the transferee;

(C)(i) the transferee has presented to the transferor a permit that—

(I) allows the transferee to possess or acquire a handgun; and

(II) was issued not more than 5 years earlier by the State in which the transfer is to take place; and

(ii) the law of the State provides that such a permit is to be issued only after an authorized government official has verified that the information available to such official does not indicate that possession of a handgun by the transferee would be in violation of the law;

(D) the law of the State requires that, before any licensed importer, licensed manufacturer, or licensed dealer completes the transfer of a handgun to an individual who is not licensed under section 923, an authorized government official verify that the information available to such official does not indicate that possession of a handgun by the transferee would be in violation of law;

(E) the Secretary has approved the transfer under section 5812 of the Internal Revenue Code of 1986 [26 USCS § 5812]; or

(F) on application of the transferor, the Secretary has certified that compliance with subparagraph (A)(i)(III) is impracticable because—

(i) the ratio of the number of law enforcement officers of the State in which the transfer is to occur to the number of square miles of land area of the State does not exceed 0.0025;

(ii) the business premises of the transferor at which the transfer is to occur are extremely remote in relation to the chief law enforcement officer; and

(iii) there is an absence of telecommunications facilities in the geographical area in which the business premises are located.

(2) A chief law enforcement officer to whom a transferor has provided notice pursuant to paragraph (1)(A)(i)(III) shall make a reasonable effort to ascertain within 5 business days whether receipt or possession would be in violation of the law, including research in whatever State and local recordkeeping systems are available and in a national system designated by the Attorney General.

(3) The statement referred to in paragraph (1)(A)(i)(I) shall contain only—

(A) the name, address, and date of birth appearing on a valid identification document (as defined in section 1028(d)(1)) of the transferee containing a photograph of the transferee and a description of the identification used;

(B) a statement that the transferee—

(i) is not under indictment for, and has not been convicted in any court of, a crime punishable by imprisonment for a term exceeding 1 year, and has not been convicted in any court of a misdemeanor crime of domestic violence;

(ii) is not a fugitive from justice;

(iii) is not an unlawful user of or addicted to any controlled substance (as defined in section 102 of the Controlled Substances Act [21 USCS § 802]);

(iv) has not been adjudicated as a mental defective or been committed to a mental institution;

(v) is not an alien who is illegally or unlawfully in the United States;

(vi) has not been discharged from the Armed Forces under dishonorable conditions; and

(vii) is not a person who, having been a citizen of the United States, has renounced such citizenship;

(C) the date the statement is made; and

(D) notice that the transferee intends to obtain a handgun from the transferor.

(4) Any transferor of a handgun who, after such transfer, receives a report from a chief law enforcement officer containing information that receipt or possession of the handgun by the transferee violates Federal, State, or local law shall, within 1 business day after receipt of such request, communicate any information related to the transfer that the transferor has about the transfer and the transferee to—

(A) the chief law enforcement officer of the place of business of the transferor; and

(B) the chief law enforcement officer of the place of residence of the transferee.

(5) Any transferor who receives information, not otherwise available to the public, in a report under this subsection shall not disclose such information except to the transferee, to law enforcement authorities, or pursuant to the direction of a court of law.

(6)(A) Any transferor who sells, delivers, or otherwise transfers a handgun to a transferee shall retain the copy of the statement of the transferee with respect to the handgun transaction, and shall retain evidence that the transferor has complied with subclauses (III) and (IV) of paragraph (1)(A)(i) with respect to the statement.

(B) Unless the chief law enforcement officer to whom a statement is transmitted under paragraph (1)(A)(i)(IV) determines that a transaction would violate Federal, State, or local law—

(i) the officer shall, within 20 business days after the date the transferee made the statement on the basis of which the notice was provided, destroy the statement, any record containing information derived from the statement, and any record created as a result of the notice required by paragraph (1)(A)(i)(III);

(ii) the information contained in the statement shall not be conveyed to any person except a person who has a need to know in order to carry out this subsection; and

(iii) the information contained in the statement shall not be used for any purpose other than to carry out this subsection.

(C) If a chief law enforcement officer determines that an individual is ineligible to receive a handgun and the individual requests the officer to provide the reason for such determination, the officer shall provide such reasons to the individual in writing within 20 business days after receipt of the request.

(7) A chief law enforcement officer or other person responsible for providing criminal history background information pursuant to this subsection shall not be liable in an action at law for damages—

(A) for failure to prevent the sale or transfer of a handgun to a person whose receipt or possession of the handgun is unlawful under this section; or

(B) for preventing such a sale or transfer to a person who may lawfully receive or possess a handgun.

(8) For purposes of this subsection, the term "chief law enforcement officer" means the chief of police, the sheriff, or an equivalent officer or the designee of any such individual.

(9) The Secretary shall take necessary actions to ensure that the provisions of this subsection are published and disseminated to licensed dealers, law enforcement officials, and the public.

(t)(1) Beginning on the date that is 30 days after the Attorney General notifies licensees under section 103(d) of the Brady Handgun Violence Prevention Act [note to this section] that the national instant criminal background check system is established, a licensed importer, licensed manufacturer, or licensed dealer shall not transfer a firearm to any other person who is not licensed under this chapter [18 U.S.C. § 921 et seq.], unless—

(A) before the completion of the transfer, the licensee contacts the national instant criminal background check system established under section 103 of that Act [note to this section];

(B)(i) the system provides the licensee with a unique identification number; or

(ii) 3 business days (meaning a day on which State offices are open) have elapsed since the licensee contacted the system, and the system has not notified the licensee that the receipt of a firearm by such other person would violate subsection (g) or (n) of this section; and

(C) the transferor has verified the identity of the transferee by examining a valid identification document (as defined in section 1028(d)(1) of this title) of the transferee containing a photograph of the transferee.

(2) If receipt of a firearm would not violate section 922 (g) or (n) or State law, the system shall—

(A) assign a unique identification number to the transfer;

(B) provide the licensee with the number; and

(C) destroy all records of the system with respect to the call (other than the identifying number and the date the number was assigned) and all records of the system relating to the person or the transfer.

(3) Paragraph (1) shall not apply to a firearm transfer between a licensee and another person if—

(A)(i) such other person has presented to the licensee a permit that—

(I) allows such other person to possess or acquire a firearm; and

(II) was issued not more than 5 years earlier by the State in which the transfer is to take place; and

(ii) the law of the State provides that such a permit is to be issued only after an authorized government official has verified that the information available to such official does not indicate that possession of a firearm by such other person would be in violation of law;

(B) the Secretary has approved the transfer under section 5812 of the Internal Revenue Code of 1986 [26 USCS § 5812]; or

(C) on application of the transferor, the Secretary has certified that compliance with paragraph (1)(A) is impracticable because—

(i) the ratio of the number of law enforcement officers of the State in which the transfer is to occur to the number of square miles of land area of the State does not exceed 0.0025;

(ii) the business premises of the licensee at which the transfer is to occur are extremely remote in relation to the chief law enforcement officer (as defined in subsection (s)(8)); and

(iii) there is an absence of telecommunications facilities in the geographical area in which the business premises are located.

(4) If the national instant criminal background check system notifies the licensee that the information available to the system does not demonstrate that the receipt of a firearm by such other person would violate subsection (g) or (n) or State law, and the licensee transfers a firearm to such other person, the licensee shall include in the record of the transfer the

unique identification number provided by the system with respect to the transfer.

(5) If the licensee knowingly transfers a firearm to such other person and knowingly fails to comply with paragraph (1) of this subsection with respect to the transfer and, at the time such other person most recently proposed the transfer, the national instant criminal background check system was operating and information was available to the system demonstrating that receipt of a firearm by such other person would violate subsection (g) or (n) of this section or State law, the Secretary may, after notice and opportunity for a hearing, suspend for not more than 6 months or revoke any license issued to the licensee under section 923, and may impose on the licensee a civil fine of not more than $ 5,000.

(6) Neither a local government nor an employee of the Federal Government or of any State or local government, responsible for providing information to the national instant criminal background check system shall be liable in an action at law for damages—

(A) for failure to prevent the sale or transfer of a firearm to a person whose receipt or possession of the firearm is unlawful under this section; or

(B) for preventing such a sale or transfer to a person who may lawfully receive or possess a firearm.

18 U.S.C. § 922(s),(t)

COMMENTARY

Printz v. United States, 138 L.Ed. 2d 914, 117 S.Ct. 2365 (1997), held, among other things, that the provision in Brady requiring the states to enforce a federal regulatory scheme at their expense, violated the sovereignty of the states, and, therefore, is UNCONSTITUTIONAL. Kind of makes you wonder why 48 states, including Utah, are still spending tons of money to enforce Brady, huh? Congress should repeal the Brady Act and federal prosecutors should begin enforcing existing laws providing enhanced penalties (including the death penalty) when felons use firearms to commit violent crimes.

The full title of the Brady Bill is "The Brady Handgun Violence Prevention Act." Anti-gun politicians are very clever choosing words to cover up their real intent, i.e., to eventually deprive all law-abiding citizens of their guns. The Brady Act was first "sold" to the public as a law that would reduce the number of "handguns" used to commit violent crimes. But this "handgun" law has now "spread and grown" to include rifles and shotguns. Is it any wonder why gun owners fear that these politicians won't stop until they take all the guns away? Can you see why sportsmen and hunters, represented by the NRA, refuse to budge an inch when new gun laws are proposed? They never regain ground once it is lost.

Pancho's Wisdom

I wonder what young David's chances against Goliath would have been if Ancient Israel had enacted a Youth Sling Violence Prevention Act?

JUVENILES AND HANDGUNS - 18 U.S.C. § 922(x)
(aka Youth Handgun Safety Act)

"PLAIN TALK"

Juveniles (anyone less than 18 years old) cannot posses handguns or handgun ammunition except to participate in the activities specifically listed in18 U.S.C. § 922(x)(3). These activities consist of farming and ranching, target practice, hunting (remember, Utahns can hunt deer with a pistol and persons as young as 12 may hunt deer), and instruction in the use of a handgun. When participating in these endeavors, a minor must transport the handgun in a locked container, unloaded, from the place where he receives possession of the handgun to the place where he uses it. It also requires the juvenile's parent or guardian to give WRITTEN CONSENT, which the juvenile must carry at all times during the activity. APPENDIX A contains a FORM parents can use to give their teenagers written consent to legally possess and shoot handguns. 18 U.S.C. § 922(x)(3)(A)(iii) requires the juvenile to have the consent form IN HAND, EVEN IF ACCOMPANIED BY THE PARENT OR GUARDIAN! So remember, anytime you take a person under 18, including your own child, to shoot pistols, make sure the person has the written consent form with him; otherwise both of you are violating 922(x), a federal crime punishable by up to one year in prison.

ACTUAL TEXT

(x)(1) It shall be unlawful for a person to sell, deliver, or otherwise transfer to a person who the transferor knows or has reasonable cause to believe is a juvenile—

(A) a handgun; or

(B) ammunition that is suitable for use only in a handgun.

(2) It shall be unlawful for any person who is a juvenile to knowingly possess–

(A) a handgun; or

(B) ammunition that is suitable for use only in a handgun.

(3) This subsection does not apply to—

(A) a temporary transfer of a handgun or ammunition to a juvenile or to the possession or use of a handgun or ammunition by a juvenile if the handgun and ammunition are possessed and used by the juvenile—

(i) in the course of employment, in the course of ranching or farming related to activities at the residence of the juvenile (or on property used for ranching or farming at which the juvenile, with the permission of the property owner or lessee, is performing activities related to the operation of the farm or ranch), target practice, hunting, or a course of instruction in the safe and lawful use of a handgun;

(ii) with the prior written consent of the juvenile's parent or guardian who is not prohibited by Federal, State, or local law from possessing a firearm, except—

(I) during transportation by the juvenile of an unloaded handgun in a locked container directly from the place of transfer to a place at which an activity described in clause (i) is to take place and transportation by the juvenile of that handgun, unloaded and in a locked container, directly from the place at which such an activity took place to the transferor; or

(II) with respect to ranching or farming activities as described in clause (i), a juvenile may possess and use a handgun or ammunition with the prior written approval of the juvenile's parent or legal guardian and at the direction of an adult who is not prohibited by Federal, State or local law from possessing a firearm;

(iii) THE JUVENILE HAS THE PRIOR WRITTEN CONSENT IN THE JUVENILE'S POSSESSION AT ALL TIMES WHEN A HANDGUN IS IN THE POSSESSION OF THE JUVENILE **[see Appendix A containing a consent form parents may use]**; and

(iv) in accordance with State and local law;

(B) a juvenile who is a member of the Armed Forces of the United States or the National Guard who possesses or is armed with a handgun in the line of duty;

(C) a transfer by inheritance of title (but not possession) of a handgun or ammunition to a juvenile; or

(D) the possession of a handgun or ammunition by a juvenile taken in defense of the juvenile or other persons against an intruder into the residence of the juvenile or a residence in which the juvenile is an invited guest.

(4) A handgun or ammunition, the possession of which is transferred to a juvenile in circumstances in which the transferor is not in violation of this subsection shall not be subject to permanent confiscation by the Government if its possession by the juvenile subsequently becomes unlawful because of the conduct of the juvenile, but shall be returned to the lawful owner when such handgun or ammunition is no longer

required by the Government for the purposes of investigation or prosecution.

(5) For purposes of this subsection, the term "juvenile" means a person who is less than 18 years of age.

(6)(A) In a prosecution of a violation of this subsection, the court shall require the presence of a juvenile defendant's parent or legal guardian at all proceedings.

(B) The court may use the contempt power to enforce subparagraph (A).

(C) The court may excuse attendance of a parent or legal guardian of a juvenile defendant at a proceeding in a prosecution of a violation of this subsection for good cause shown **(emphasis added)**.

18 U.S.C. § 925 Exceptions: Relief from disabilities

"PLAIN TALK"

This section is meaningless because Congress hasn't funded it for years. If you have been convicted of a felony under a federal statute there is no way, short of a presidential pardon, of getting your right to possess a firearm back. State felonies can be cleansed, or reduced, however. See the discussion of expungements and 402 motions in the previous chapter.

ACTUAL TEXT

. . .

(c) A person who is prohibited from possessing, shipping, transporting, or receiving firearms or ammunition may make application to the Secretary for relief from the disabilities imposed by Federal laws with respect to the acquisition, receipt, transfer, shipment, transportation, or possession of firearms, and the Secretary may grant such relief if it is established to his satisfaction that the circumstances regarding the disability, and the applicant's record and reputation, are such that the applicant will not be likely to act in a manner dangerous to public safety and that the granting of the relief would not be contrary to the public interest. Any person whose application for relief from disabilities is denied by the Secretary may file a petition with the United States district court for the district in which he resides for a judicial review of such denial. The court may in its discretion admit additional evidence where failure to do so would result in a miscarriage of justice.

18 U.S.C. § 925

COMMENTARY

Congress needs to recognize the concept of "repentance" by funding the process by which people convicted of federal felonies can cleanse their records. It's done all the time in the state court system. This is one of the problems of giving the federal government "police powers" which allegedly were to be reserved to the several states. Although Utahns believe people who have improved their lives deserve a second chance, there are eastern politicians who would do anything to disarm as many as they could for as long as possible. This permits people with different values than ours to impose their values upon our citizens.

18 U.S.C. § 925A. Remedy for erroneous denial of firearm.

"PLAIN TALK"

Governments Beware! If you improperly deny us citizens the right to purchase a firearm under the Brady Act, we can sue your sovereign back sides! The courts can make the government -federal, state or local - pay our attorney's fees.

ACTUAL TEXT

Any person denied a firearm pursuant to subsection (s) or (t) of section 922—

(1) due to the provision of erroneous information relating to the person by any State or political subdivision thereof, or by the national instant criminal background check system estab-

lished under section 103 of the Brady Handgun Violence Prevention Act [18 USC 922 note] or

(2) who was not prohibited from receipt of a firearm pursuant to subsection (g) or (n) of section 922, may bring an action against the State or political subdivision responsible for providing the erroneous information, or responsible for denying the transfer, or against the United States, as the case may be, for an order directing that the erroneous information be corrected or that the transfer be approved, as the case may be. In any action under this section, the court, in its discretion, may allow the prevailing party a reasonable attorney's fee as part of the costs.

18 U.S.C. § 926A. Interstate transportation of firearms

"PLAIN TALK"

If you lock your unloaded gun and ammo in the trunk, or if you don't have a trunk, in a locked case (but not in the glove box or console) you can drive from anywhere where it's lawful to possess a firearm (e.g Utah) to anywhere else it's lawful (e.g. Vermont) even if you drive through Washington D.C. or Chicago where the gun laws are outrageously strict. This federal law preempts (trumps) state and local laws that attempt to disarm you as you travel in interstate commerce. This statute is also referred to as the Firearm Owners Protection Act (FOPA).

Pancho's Los Pistolas Vacation - Of course, if you need your gun to protect your baby, it ain'ta gonna do ya a lotta good locked away. But the politician that passes such ridiculous laws doesn't care; he has armed body guards. Makes ya wanna spit some Beechnut in that dude's eye and holler FREEEEEEEEEDOM!!!

WARNING: Congress clearly intended to preserve the rights of citizens traveling in interstate commerce to take along a gun for personal defense (even though drawing an empty pistol out of a locked case tends to slow a gunslinger down!) Well, New York and New Jersey (and who knows how many other gun-hating states) don't care. They have been making felony arrests on gun owners relying on this federal law. The National Rifle Association has helped fund a lawsuit against such practices in New Jersey. However, until New York and New Jersey yell "uncle," I don't recommend you take a firearm into those states. Would someone please start a movement to trade states like that to Eastern Canada where they belong in return for the Western Canadian Provinces of Alberta and British Columbia?

ACTUAL TEXT

Notwithstanding any other provision of any law or any rule or regulation of a State or any political subdivision thereof, any person who is not otherwise prohibited by this chapter **[felons]** from transporting, shipping, or receiving a firearm shall be entitled to transport a firearm for any lawful purpose from any place where he may lawfully possess and carry such firearm to any other place where he may lawfully possess and carry such firearm if, during such transportation the firearm is unloaded, and neither the firearm nor any ammunition being transported is readily accessible or is directly accessible from the passenger compartment of such transporting vehicle: Provided, That in the case of a vehicle without a compartment separate from the driver's compartment the firearm or ammunition shall be contained in a locked container other than the glove compartment or console.

18 USC § 930. Possession of firearms and dangerous weapons in Federal facilities

"PLAIN TALK"

You can't take a firearm or other dangerous weapon into a federal building (presumably including a post office). If you do it's a federal misdemeanor (punishable by imprisonment for less than one year) unless the weapon was used in commission of a crime (five year felony)in a murder or attempted murder (obviously big time felonies), or the building is a federal court facility (two year federal felony). The feds want you to be disarmed when one of their employees gets sick of their bureaucratic B.S. and "goes postal."

This section requires federal facilities to post notice of the law in a conspicuous place or you can't be convicted unless you have actual knowledge of the law (if you read this before you get arrested and admit that you have, you're toast). If you carry a pocket knife with a teensy-weensy blade (less than 2 inches), it's not considered a dangerous weapon.

This section gives the courts the power to make their own rules so they can be even more strict if they want to. For example, although pocket knives with blades less than 2 inches are not dangerous weapons, the federal courts could exclude all pocket knives if they want to. Be sure to read the public notice before entering a court house, or ask the security guards.

EXCEPTIONS - Persons excepted from the general rule are described in subsection (d). Subsection (d) specifically permits federal and state police officers and employees, who carry weapons as part of their official duties, to carry a firearm. Paragraph (d)(3) is interesting because it allows carrying of firearms "incident to hunting or other lawful purposes." This leads us to a discussion of CWP holders.

CONCEALED WEAPON PERMIT HOLDERS - This section has no express exception for state concealed weapon holders (compare the federal "Gun Free School Zone Act"). Courts that have established "secured areas" are definitely off limits to CWP holders (see discussion of U.C. A. 76-10-523.5 and U.C.A. 78-7-6 in Chapter VII). With respect to courts with secured areas, federal law and state law are in harmony, they seem to prohibit everyone, including CWP holders from carrying weapons into these areas.

But what about federal buildings like post offices that have no metal detectors? Unless you have a lot of money for attorney fees to prove a point, you probably don't want to pack your piece into a post office. A zealous U.S. prosecutor might feel inclined to prosecute you despite the language of (d)(3). The Postal Service claims the authority to make its own rules including prohibiting firearms by virtue of federal code section 39 USC 410. The Postal

Service has prohibited firearms in the Code of Federal Regulations, 39 CFR S.232.1 (see additional discussion below). If a postal worker at your friendly local post office goes postal while you are getting your mail, you'll just have to die along with his or her co- workers. I found several appellate cases relating to robberies of post offices, but no cases where anyone had been prosecuted for simply possessing a firearm in a post office. So maybe you don't have to die . . . if you feel lucky . . . well punk . . . do you feel lucky ? ? ? ?

ACTUAL TEXT

(a) Except as provided in subsection (d), whoever knowingly possesses or causes to be present a firearm or other dangerous weapon in a Federal facility (other than a Federal court facility), or attempts to do so, shall be fined under this title or imprisoned not more than 1 year, or both.

(b) Whoever, with intent that a firearm or other dangerous weapon be used in the commission of a crime, knowingly possesses or causes to be present such firearm or dangerous weapon in a Federal facility, or attempts to do so, shall be fined under this title or imprisoned not more than 5 years, or both.

(c) A person who kills or attempts to kill any person in the course of a violation of subsection (a) or (b), or in the course of an attack on a Federal facility involving the use of a firearm or other dangerous weapon, shall be punished as provided in sections 1111, 1112, and 1113.

(d) Subsection (a) shall not apply to—

 (1) the lawful performance of official duties by an officer, agent, or employee of the United States, a State, or a political subdivision thereof, who is authorized by law to engage in or supervise the prevention, detection, investigation, or prosecution of any violation of law;

 (2) the possession of a firearm or other dangerous weapon by a Federal official or a member of the Armed Forces if such possession is authorized by law; or

(3) the lawful carrying of firearms or other dangerous weapons in a Federal facility incident to hunting or other lawful purposes.

(e)(1) Except as provided in paragraph (2), whoever knowingly possesses or causes to be present a firearm in a Federal court facility, or attempts to do so, shall be fined under this title, imprisoned not more than 2 years, or both.

(2) Paragraph (1) shall not apply to conduct which is described in paragraph (1) or (2) of subsection (d).

(f) Nothing in this section limits the power of a court of the United States to punish for contempt or to promulgate rules or orders regulating, restricting, or prohibiting the possession of weapons within any building housing such court or any of its proceedings, or upon any grounds appurtenant to such building.

(g) As used in this section:

(1) The term "Federal facility" means a building or part thereof owned or leased by the Federal Government, where Federal employees are regularly present for the purpose of performing their official duties.

(2) The term "dangerous weapon" means a weapon, device, instrument, material, or substance, animate or inanimate, that is used for, or is readily capable of, causing death or serious bodily injury, except that such term does not include a pocket knife with a blade of less than 2 inches in length.

(3) The term "Federal court facility" means the courtroom, judges' chambers, witness rooms, jury deliberation rooms, attorney conference rooms, prisoner holding cells, offices of the court clerks, the United States attorney, and the United States marshal, probation and parole offices, and adjoining corridors of any court of the United States.

(h) Notice of the provisions of subsections (a) and (b) shall be posted conspicuously at each public entrance to each

Federal facility, and notice of subsection (e) shall be posted conspicuously at each public entrance to each Federal court facility, and no person shall be convicted of an offense under subsection (a) or (e) with respect to a Federal facility if such notice is not so posted at such facility, unless such person had actual notice of subsection (a) or (e), as the case may be.

39 C.F.R. § 232.1 Conduct on postal property.

"PLAIN TALK"

This is the section in the Code of Federal Regulations specifically prohibiting weapons and firearms on all postal service property. Amazingly it appears to cover any real property, which arguably includes parking lots and drive ups. However, you'll notice the penalty is limited to $50 and 30 days in jail, obviously a misdemeanor. Again, I can't find any appellate cases showing that anyone has been prosecuted for simply carrying a weapon into a post office or having a one in a car in the parking lot without any evil intent. Think of it this way - if you are arrested and receive the maximum sentence, you will have plenty of time to read your mail!

ACTUAL TEXT

(a) Applicability. This section applies to all real property under the charge and control of the Postal Service, to all tenant agencies, and to all persons entering in or on such property. This section shall be posted and kept posted at a conspicuous place on all such property.

. . .

(l) Weapons and explosives. No person while on postal property may carry firearms, other dangerous or deadly weapons, or explosives, either openly or concealed, or store the same on postal property, except for official purposes.

. . .

(2) Whoever shall be found guilty of violating the rules and regulations in this section while on property under the charge and control of the Postal Service is subject to fine of not more than $50 or imprisonment of not more than 30 days, or both. Nothing contained in these rules and regulations shall be construed to abrogate any other Federal laws or regulations of any State and local laws and regulations applicable to any area in which the property is situated.

Pancho's Wisdom

Our National Park Director thinks the Second Amendment has two plausible meanings: (1) the Right of the Bears to Chew off Yer Arms Shall Not Be Infringed (2) the Right of Armed Tent Invaders to Bear Your Wife and Daughters to Their Lairs Shall Not Be Infringed!

36 CFR 2.2 and 2.4 [Firearm and Hunting Restrictions in National Parks]

"PLAIN TALK"

You are prohibited from possessing firearms or hunting in national parks unless you are specifically authorized under federal and state law. Fortunately the penalties are limited to misdemeanors (see fine print in "Commentary" section below). The term "national park" includes national monuments (see 36 C.F.R. § 8.1 (a)). 36 CFR 2.4(a)(3) says you can take your unloaded firearms through a national park in a vehicle or keep them in your tent or camper if they are in a case that prevents their "ready" use. Pancho, do you have an observation? "Hell, that'll do ya a lot of good when a camp invader or grizzly busts into your tent! But don't worry, just use your cell phone and call park rangers. If yer lucky enough to have cell phone service, they'll be there in less than four hours!"

Notice these prohibitions are REGULATIONS ("promulgated" by an appointed federal bureaucrat). They are NOT part of the United States Code (enacted by elected officials of Congress). It is one thing when Congressional leaders pass a law after they debate its virtues on the floor of the House or Senate; but it is another when they give government bureaucrats the authority to "promulgate regulations" which have the effect of law. This is why federal laws affecting the civil rights of citizens are so dangerous. Before you know it, you have a whole "truckload" of regulations that stomp on individual liberties. It's kind of like cancer cells migrating from a tumor. (For additional scathing criticism see "Commentary" below.)

ACTUAL TEXT

36 CFR 2.2 - NATIONAL PARKS

2.2 Wildlife protection.

(a) The following are prohibited:

(1) The taking of wildlife, except by authorized hunting and trapping activities conducted in accordance with paragraph (b) of this section.

(2) The feeding, touching, teasing, frightening or intentional disturbing of wildlife nesting, breeding or other activities.

(3) Possessing unlawfully taken wildlife or portions thereof.

(b) Hunting and trapping.

(1) Hunting shall be allowed in park areas where such activity is specifically mandated by Federal statutory law.

(2) Hunting may be allowed in park areas where such activity is specifically authorized as a discretionary activity under Federal statutory law if the superintendent determines that such activity is consistent with public safety and enjoyment, and sound resource management principles. Such hunting shall be allowed pursuant to special regulations.

(3) Trapping shall be allowed in park areas where such activity is specifically mandated by Federal statutory law.

(4) Where hunting or trapping or both are authorized, such activities shall be conducted in accordance with Federal law and the laws of the State within whose exterior boundaries a park area or a portion thereof is located. Non-conflicting State laws are adopted as a part of these regulations.

(c) Except in emergencies or in areas under the exclusive jurisdiction of the United States, the superintendent shall consult with appropriate State agencies before invoking the authority of 1.5 for the purpose of restricting hunting and trapping or closing park areas to the taking of wildlife where such activities are mandated or authorized by Federal statutory law.

(d) The superintendent may establish conditions and procedures for transporting lawfully taken wildlife through the park area. Violation of these conditions and procedures is prohibited.

(e) The Superintendent may designate all or portions of a park area as closed to the viewing of wildlife with an artificial light. Use of an artificial light for purposes of viewing wildlife in closed areas is prohibited.

(f) Authorized persons may check hunting and trapping licenses and permits; inspect weapons, traps and hunting and trapping gear for compliance with equipment restrictions; and inspect wildlife that has been taken for compliance with species, size and other taking restrictions.

(g) The regulations contained in this section apply, regardless of land ownership, on all lands and waters within a park area that are under the legislative jurisdiction of the United States.

AUTHORITY:
16 U.S.C. 1, 3, 9a, 462(k).

36 CFR 2.4 NATIONAL PARKS

2.4 Weapons, traps and nets.

(a)(1) Except as otherwise provided in this section and Parts 7 (special regulations) and 13 (Alaska regulations), the following are prohibited:

(i) Possessing a weapon, trap or net

(ii) Carrying a weapon, trap or net

(iii) Using a weapon, trap or net

(2) Weapons, traps or nets may be carried, possessed or used:

(i) At designated times and locations in park areas where:

(A) The taking of wildlife is authorized by law in accordance with 2.2 of this chapter;

(B) The taking of fish is authorized by law in accordance with 2.3 of this part.

(ii) When used for target practice at designated times and at facilities or locations designed and constructed specifically for this purpose and designated pursuant to special regulations.

(iii) Within a residential dwelling. For purposes of this subparagraph only, the term "residential dwelling" means a fixed housing structure which is either the principal residence of its occupants, or is occupied on a regular and recurring basis by its occupants as an alternate residence or vacation home.

(3) Traps, nets and unloaded weapons may be possessed within a temporary lodging or mechanical mode of conveyance when such implements are rendered temporarily inoperable or are packed, cased or stored in a manner that will prevent their ready use.

(b) Carrying or possessing a loaded weapon in a motor vehicle, vessel or other mode of transportation is prohibited, except that carrying or possessing a loaded weapon in a vessel is allowed when such vessel is not being propelled by machinery and is used as a shooting platform in accordance with Federal and State law.

(c) The use of a weapon, trap or net in a manner that endangers persons or property is prohibited.

(d) The superintendent may issue a permit to carry or possess a weapon, trap or net under the following circumstances:

(1) When necessary to support research activities conducted in accordance with 2.5.

(2) To carry firearms for persons in charge of pack trains or saddle horses for emergency use.

(3) For employees, agents or cooperating officials in the performance of their official duties.

(4) To provide access to otherwise inaccessible lands or waters contiguous to a park area when other means of access are otherwise impracticable or impossible.

Violation of the terms and conditions of a permit issued pursuant to this paragraph is prohibited and may result in the suspension or revocation of the permit.

(e) Authorized Federal, State and local law enforcement officers may carry firearms in the performance of their official duties.

(f) The carrying or possessing of a weapon, trap or net in violation of applicable Federal and State laws is prohibited.

(g) The regulations contained in this section apply, regardless of land ownership, on all lands and waters within a park area that are under the legislative jurisdiction of the United States.

AUTHORITY:
16 U.S.C. 1, 3, 9a, 462(k).

36 CFR 2.2

COMMENTARY

Notice at the end of both of these regulations prohibiting weapons and firearms in national parks appear the words " AUTHORITY: 16 U.S.C. 1, 3, 9a, 462(k)." This tells us that the director of the National Park Service must be able to point to a federal code section enacted by Congress from which he gets his authority to promulgate regulations. In this instance he looks to 16 U.S.C. 1, 3, 9a and 462(k) for authority to deprive a citizen of the United States of the right to protect himself and his family with a firearm in a national park. One would assume that when depriving a citizen of such an important right (a right to defend himself and his family from deadly force - indeed, a right to life itself) Congress would have stated this very plainly and carefully. But when you look up these four code sections in the United States Code, the words "weapon" and "firearm" do not appear. Certainly the Director of National Parks will argue that to carry out his responsibilities it was necessary to deprive law-abiding citizens of their Second Amendment rights; that it wasn't enough to have hundreds of federal laws prohibiting us from assaulting or harming another person with a firearm. I don't know about you, but that argument doesn't hold water with this cowboy. I'm enclosing the full text of these four code sections in this commentary so you can see the "stretch" of authority yourself.

16 USC 1 (2000) TITLE 16. CONSERVATION, CHAPTER 1. NATIONAL PARKS, MILITARY PARKS, MONUMENTS, AND SEASHORES, NATIONAL PARK SERVICE

1. Service created; director; other employees

There is created in the Department of the Interior a service to be called the National Park Service, which shall be under the charge of a director who shall be appointed by the President, by and with the advice and consent of the Senate. The Director shall have substantial experience and demonstrated competence in land management and natural or cultural resource conservation. The Director shall select two Deputy Directors. The first Deputy Director shall have responsibility for National Park Service operations, and the second Deputy Director shall have responsibility for other programs assigned to the National Park Service. There shall also be in said service such subordinate officers, clerks, and employees as may be appropriated for by Congress. The service thus established shall promote and regulate the use of the Federal areas known as national parks, monuments, and reservations hereinafter specified, except such as are under the jurisdiction of the Secretary of the Army, as provided by law, by such means and measures as conform to the fundamental purpose of the said parks, monuments, and reservations, which purpose is to conserve the scenery and the natural and historic objects and the wild life therein and to provide for the enjoyment of the same in such manner and by such means as will leave them unimpaired for the enjoyment of future generations.

16 USC 3 (2000), TITLE 16. CONSERVATION, CHAPTER 1. NATIONAL PARKS, MILITARY PARKS, MONUMENTS, AND SEASHORES, NATIONAL PARK SERVICE

3. Rules and regulations of national parks, reservations, and monuments; timber; leases

The Secretary of the Interior shall make and publish such rules and regulations as he may deem necessary or proper for the use and management of the parks, monuments, and reservations under the jurisdiction of the National Park Service, and any violation of any of the rules and regulations authorized by this Act shall be punished by a fine of not more than $ 500 or imprisonment for not exceeding six months, or both, and be adjudged to pay all costs of the proceedings. He may also, upon terms and conditions to be fixed by him, sell or dispose of timber in those cases where in his judgment the cutting of such timber is required in order to control the attacks of insects or diseases or otherwise conserve the scenery or the natural or historic objects in any such park, monument, or reservation. He may also provide in his discretion for the destruction of such animals and of such plant life as may be detrimental to the use of any of said parks, monuments, or reservations. No natural, curiosities, wonders, or objects of interest shall be leased, rented, or granted to anyone on such terms as to interfere with free access to them by the public: Provided, however, That the Secretary of the Interior may, under such rules and regulations and on such terms as he may prescribe, grant the privilege to graze livestock within any national park, monument, or reservation herein referred to when in his judgment such use is not detrimental to the primary purpose for which such park, monument, or reservation was created, except that this provision shall not apply to the Yellowstone National Park. And provided further, That the Secretary of the Interior may grant said privileges, leases, and permits and enter into contracts relating to the same with responsible persons, firms, or corporations without advertising and without securing competitive bids: And provided further, That no contract, lease, permit, or privilege granted shall be assigned or transferred by such grantees, permittees, or licensees without the approval of the Secretary of the Interior first obtained in writing.

16 USC 9a (2000), TITLE 16. CONSERVATION, CHAPTER 1. NATIONAL PARKS, MILITARY PARKS, MONUMENTS, AND SEASHORES, NATIONAL PARK SERVICE

9a. Government of parks, etc.; violation of regulations as misdemeanor

The Secretary of War [Secretary of the Army] is hereby authorized to prescribe and publish such regulations as he deems necessary for the proper government and protection of, and maintenance of good order in, national military parks, national parks, battlefield sites, national monuments, and miscellaneous memorials as are now or hereafter may be under the control of the War Department [Department of the Army]; and any person who knowingly and willfully violates any such regulation shall be deemed guilty of a misdemeanor and punishable by a fine of not more than $ 100 or by imprisonment for not more than three months, or by both such fine and imprisonment.

16 USC 462 (2000) TITLE 16. CONSERVATION, CHAPTER 1A. HISTORIC SITES, BUILDINGS, OBJECTS, AND ANTIQUITIES, GENERAL PROVISIONS

462. Administration by Secretary of the Interior; powers and duties enumerated

The Secretary of the Interior (hereinafter [in 16 USC 461—467] referred to as the Secretary), through the National Park Service, for the purpose of effectuating the policy expressed in section 1 hereof [16 USC 461], shall have the following powers and perform the following duties and functions:

. . .

(k) Perform any and all acts, and make such rules and regulations not inconsistent with this Act [16 USC 461—467] as may be necessary and proper to carry out the provisions thereof. Any person violating any of the rules and regulations authorized by this Act [16 USC 461—467] shall be punished by a fine of not more than $ 500 and be adjudged to pay all cost of the proceedings. **[So where do these statutes give bureaucrats the authority**

to take away our right to protect ourselves and our families with a firearm? Huh? Huh? Dammit you federalies, Back Off! And stop treading on our rights! Pancho V.]

36 CFR 261.10 & 261.58
[Shooting and Hunting in National Forests]

"PLAIN TALK"

Unless there is a specific order prohibiting it, it's okay to possess a firearm and hunt in Utah's national forests. You can't shoot within 150 yards of buildings, camps or people. You also can't shoot across or on forest service roads or across bodies of water adjacent to roads or into caves (you don't want to plunk a spelunker). See the Orders below prohibiting shooting on federal lands in Davis, Washington and Tooele Counties.

ACTUAL TEXT

261.10 Occupancy and use. NATIONAL FORESTS
The following are prohibited:

. . .

(d) Discharging a firearm or any other implement capable of taking human life, causing injury, or damaging property as follows:

   (1) In or within 150 yards of a residence, building, campsite, developed recreation site or occupied area, or

   (2) Across or on a Forest Development road or a body of water adjacent thereto, or in any manner or place whereby any person or property is exposed to injury or damage as a result in such discharge.

   (3) into or within any cave.

. . .

261.58 Occupancy and use. NATIONAL PARKS
When provided by an order, the following are prohibited:

. . .

(m) Discharging a firearm, air rifle, or gas gun.

. . .

(v) Hunting or fishing.

BUREAU OF RECLAMATION (hereinafter "BOR") RESTRICTIONS

43 U.S.C. § 373b. Law Enforcement Authority at Bureau of Reclamation Facilities.

"PLAIN TALK"

The purpose of my putting BOR restrictions in this book is to inform gun owners of the federal regulations prohibiting weapons on or in BOR "facilities" (see Definitions below) such as dams and power plants. Facilities are separate from lands and waterways, which are defined separately. Remember, federal laws preempt state laws, so your concealed weapon permits are not valid on or in such facilities. The following "authorizing statute" classifies violations of the weapon regulations as federal misdemeanors.

ACTUAL TEXT

(a) Public Safety Regulations — The Secretary of the Interior shall issue regulations necessary to maintain law and order and protect persons and property within Reclamation projects and on Reclamation lands.

(b) Violations; Criminal Penalties — Any person who knowingly and willfully violates any regulation issued under subsection (a) shall be fined under chapter 227, subchapter C of title 18, United States Code, imprisoned for not more than 6 months, or both. Any person charged with a violation of a regulation issued under subsection (a) may be tried and sentenced by any United States magistrate judge designated for that purpose by the court by which he was appointed, in the same manner and subject to the same conditions and limitations as provided for in section 3401 of title 18, United States Code.

43 C.F.R. § 423.2 Definitions of terms used in this part.

"PLAIN TALK"

Following are the definitions that are most relevant to the BOR regulations restricting firearms.

ACTUAL TEXT

. . .

Camping means erecting a tent or shelter; preparing a sleeping bag or other bedding material for use; parking a motor vehicle, motor home, or trailer; or mooring a vessel for the intended or apparent purpose of overnight occupancy.

. . .

Firearm means a device that expels a projectile such as a bullet, dart, or pellet by combustion, air pressure, gas pressure, or other means.

. . .

Hunting means taking or attempting to take wildlife by any means, except by trapping or fishing.

. . .

Reclamation facility means any facility constructed or acquired under Federal reclamation law that is situated on Reclamation lands and is used or occupied by Reclamation under a lease, easement, right-of-way, license, contract, or other arrangement. The term includes, but is not limited to, any of the following that are under the jurisdiction of or administered by Reclamation: Dams, powerplants, buildings, switchyards, transmission lines, recreation facilities, fish and wildlife facilities, pumping plants, and warehouses.

Reclamation lands means any real property under the jurisdiction of or administered by Reclamation, and includes, but is not limited to, all acquired and withdrawn lands and lands in which Reclamation has a lease interest, easement, or right-of-way.

Reclamation project means any water supply, water delivery, flood control, or hydropower project, together with any associated facilities for fish, wildlife, recreation, or water treatment constructed or administered by Reclamation under the

Federal reclamation laws [the Act of June 17, 1902 (32 Stat. 388, chapter 1093; 43 U.S.C. 371 et seq.), and Acts supplementary thereto and amendatory thereof].

Reclamation waterbody means any body of water situated on Reclamation lands or under Reclamation jurisdiction.

. . .

Special use area means an area at or within a Reclamation facility, or an area of Reclamation lands or waterbodies, in which special rules for public conduct apply that may differ from those established in subpart C of this part 423. A special use area must be established by an authorized official as provided in subpart E of this part 423.

43 C.F.R. § 423.30 Weapons, firearms, explosives, and fireworks.

"PLAIN TALK"

Although you can take firearms on Bureau of Reclamation land and waterways, you must still comply with all state and local laws. Furthermore, be sure not to take them into or onto BOR facilities like dams and power plants. To do so could cause you to be charged with a federal misdemeanor. You can't fire your gun unless you are using it to hunt or fish (with a gun? - don't forget, these things were written by federal bureaucrats)! Although it's not specifically mentioned, I would argue you could fire your weapon in lawful self defense, that this is contemplated by federal case law and is certainly consistent with state and local laws. But if you do use a firearm for self defense, because it's not specifically mentioned here, be half prepared to have some rigid-thinking federalie charge you with a crime.

ACTUAL TEXT

(a) You may possess firearms, ammunition, bows and arrows, crossbows, or other projectile firing devices on Reclamation lands and waterbodies, provided the firearm, ammunition, or other projectile firing device is stowed, transported, and/or carried in compliance with applicable Federal, state, and local law, with the following exceptions:

(1) You must not have a weapon in your possession when at or in a Reclamation facility.

(2) You must comply with any prohibitions or regulations applicable to weapons in a special use area established by an authorized official under subpart E of this part 423.

(b) You must not discharge or shoot a weapon unless you are:

(1) Using a firearm or other projectile firing device lawfully for hunting or fishing as allowed under § 423.32, or at an authorized shooting or archery range; and

(2) In compliance with applicable Federal, state, and local law.

(c) You must not use or possess explosives, or fireworks or pyrotechnics of any type, except as allowed by a permit issued pursuant to subpart D of this part 423, or in special use areas so designated by an authorized official under subpart E of this part 423.

FEDERAL REGULATIONS THAT OUTLAW SHOOTING ON RECREATIONAL PROPERTY IN UTAH

"PLAIN TALK"

The following three "regulations," prohibit the use of firearms in three areas of the State of Utah. The first relates to the poorly defined areas of forest service land east of Centerville in Davis County, the second to the "Red Cliffs Area" near St. George. and the third is an area south of the Oquirrh Mountains. The third area contains a few large, visible signs indicating no target shooting because of extensive OHV use. When shooting near these areas be sure to take a surveying team with you and watch for Black helicopters containing repelling ATF agents who ARE NOT your friends.

1. Davis County Closure

The Davis County closure has a penalty of up to 6 months in jail and a $5,000 fine. Copies of the maps are in Appendix G. The only way of determining exactly where the boundaries are depends upon a reading of the imprecise map contour lines. There are no signs telling people where the boundaries of the U.S. Forest Service properties are subject to this closure. Davis County shooting enthusiasts are in serious risk of huge fines and imprisonment without any reasonable notice of where they are not supposed to shoot. THIS IS A REAL PROBLEM HERE IN THE WEST WHERE AS MANY PEOPLE SHOOT AND HUNT AS PLAY GOLF!

2. Red Cliffs Closure

The "Red Cliffs closure" affects camping, fires, the use of motorized vehicles, rock climbing, the removal of wild plants and animals, and pets, but we have not included those sections because they do not relate directly to the subject matter of this book. Simply stated, this regulation outlaws shooting any weapon including modern guns, muzzle loaders and archery equipment, except during hunting season. Violators are guilty of a class A misdemeanor. Hunters and shooters can tolerate such closures if they have notice and signs on the boundaries inform them where they are not supposed to shoot.

3. Five Mile Pass, Knolls, North Oquirrh and Simpson Springs Closure - This closure prohibits **target practicing** with firearms and dangerous weapons in the closed area. It does not affect hunters who have valid hunting permits for areas that intersect with the closed area. Although the penalty is a misdemeanor (less than 12 months in federal prison), you gotta luv the potential $100,000 fine!

ACTUAL TEXT

1. Davis County Closure - Vol. 63, No. 154, SHOOTING IN THE FOOTHILLS BETWEEN WARD AND FARMINGTON CANYON ROADS SPECIAL ORDER OF FOREST SUPERVISOR

United States Department of Agriculture
Forest Service
8230 Federal Building, 125 South State Street
Salt Lake City, Utah 84138
SHOOTING IN THE FOOTHILLS BETWEEN WARD AND FARMINGTON CANYON ROADS SPECIAL ORDER OF FOREST

SUPERVISOR
WASATCH-CACHE NATIONAL FOREST
SALT LAKE RANGER DISTRICT

Pursuant to 36 CFR 261.50 (a) and (b), the following act is prohibited on all areas described below and as shown on the map. All lands affected are located on the Salt Lake Ranger District, Wasatch-Cache National Forest. This order is in effect until further notice.

1. Discharging a firearm. [36 CFR 261.58 (m)] Pursuant to 36 CFR 261.50 (e), the following acts, or persons, are exempt from this order:

1. Persons with a permit or contract authorizing the otherwise prohibited act.
2. Authorized Federal, state, or local officers, or members of an organized rescue or firefighting force in the performance of official duty, when authorized by the District Ranger.
3. Any person discharging a firearm within the boundaries of an approved public/private shooting range.
4. Any properly licensed person discharging a firearm in conjunction with legal hunting activities as provided by Utah State Code, wildlife rules or proclamations established by the Utah Wildlife board.

Area Described: All National Forest Lands along the Wasatch Front foothills located between Ward Canyon Road and Farmington Canyon Road below 5100 feet elevation (approximately the "high water" mark or "bench" for the Lake Bonneville Shoreline) as shown on the attached map.

/Bernie Weingardner/, dated 10/31/97
Forest Supervisor
Wasatch-Cache National Forest

Violation of this prohibition is punishable by fine of not more than $5,000 or imprisonment of not more than 6 months or both (16 U.S.C. 551; 18 U.S.C. 3559 and 3571 (b) (6)).

This order supercedes any previous orders/notices for the above described areas, and same said violation(s).

Order Number	04	19	90
	Region	Forest	Numeric Sequence

2. Red Cliffs Closure - Publication of Closure and Restriction Order for the Red Cliffs Desert Reserve 63 FR 42869 DATE: Tuesday, August 11, 1998

FEDERAL REGISTER,Vol. 63, No. 154, Notices, DEPARTMENT OF THE INTERIOR (DOI) , Bureau of Land Management (BLM), [UT-045-00-7122-00; 9560]

Publication of Closure and Restriction Order for the Red Cliffs Desert Reserve 63 FR 42869. DATE: Tuesday, August 11, 1998

The public land in the following described lands will be affected: **[This is great public notice if you happen to work for a title company!]**

Salt Lake Meridian, T. 41 S., R. 13 W., Sec.(s) 17 thru 19; (all) Sec.(s) 20; 21; 22; 27; 28; (all) Sec. 29, N 1/2NE 1/4, N 1/2S 1/2N , N 1/2S 1/2SW 1/4NE 1/4, SE 1/4SE 1/4SW 1/4NE 1/4, S 1/2SE 1/4NE 1/4, NE 1/4NW 1/4, N 1/2SW 1/4SW 1/4NW 1/4, NE 1/4NE 1/4SE 1/4, N 1/2NW 1/4NE 1/4SE 1/4; Sec. 30, N 1/2N , embracing that portion of land north of the Virgin River, S 1/2NE 1/4 T. 41 S., R. 14 W., Sec. 13, SE 1/4NE 1/4, S 1/2S , NE 1/4SE 1/4; Sec.(s) 15 thru 22; (all) Sec. 23, W 1/2SW 1/4, embracing that portion of land west of I-15 corridor; Sec. 24; (all) Sec. 25, Lots 1 thru 10, SW 1/4NE 1/4, NE 1/4SW 1/4NW 1/4, E 1/2SE 1/4NW 1/4, NW 1/4SE 1/4NW 1/4, E 1/2NE 1/4SW 1/4, E 1/2W 1/2NE 1/4SW 1/4, SE 1/4SW 1/4, W 1/2SE 1/4; Sec. 26, Lot 4, embracing that portion of land west of I-15 corridor; Sec. 27, embracing that portion of land west of I-15 corridor; Sec.(s) 28 thru 31; (all) Sec. 32, embracing that portion of land north and west of I-15 corridor; [*42870] Sec. 33, embracing that portion of land north and west of I-15 corridor; Sec. 34, embracing that portion of land north and west of I-15 corridor; T. 41 S., R. 15 W., Sec.(s) 13 thru 36; (all) T. 41 S., R. 16 W., Sec. 4, S ; Sec.(s) 5 thru 9; (all) Sec. 10, embracing that portion of land west of the SR-18 corridor, Lot 4; Sec.(s) 11 thru 13; (all) Sec. 14, N , NE 1/4SE 1/4; Sec. 15, embracing that portion of land west of the SR-18 corridor, E 1/2NE 1/4; Sec.(s) 16 thru 21; (all) Sec. 22, W , W 1/2E , embracing that portion of land west of the SR-18 corridor; Sec. 24, E , E 1/2W ; Sec. 25, E , E 1/2W ; Sec. 27, SW

1/4NE 1/4, NW 1/4NW 1/4, S 1/2NW 1/4, SW 1/4, W 1/2SE 1/4; Sec.(s) 28 thru 34; (all) Sec. 36; (all) T. 41 S., R. 17 W., Sec.(s) 1, 12, 13, 24; (all) T. 42 S., R. 14 W., Sec. 5, embracing that portion of land west of I-15 corridor; Sec. 6, embracing that portion of land west of I-15 corridor; T. 42 S., R. 15 W., Sec.(s) 1 thru 9; (all) Sec. 12; (all) Sec.(s) 16 thru 19; (all) Sec. 20, (all) T. 42 S., R. 16 W.,

Sec.(s) 1 thru 3; (all) Sec.(s) 11 thru 14; (all) Sec. 24, (all) EFFECTIVE DATE: August 11, 1998. This interim closure and restriction order will be superseded when the detailed recreation management plan for the Red Cliffs Desert Reserve is completed and approved by Washington County. FOR FURTHER INFORMATION CONTACT: Mark Harris, BLM Ranger, Dixie Resource Area, 345 E. Riverside Dr, St. George, UT 84790 telephone (435) 688-3371.

SUPPLEMENTARY INFORMATION: To implement decisions of the Washington County Habitat Conservation Plan which established the Red Cliffs Desert Reserve, and to protect valuable and fragile natural resources, and provide for public safety and enjoyment, and to provide consistency with regulations that have been passed by Washington County, the Utah School and Institutional Trust Land Administration, and the cities of St. George, Washington, Ivins, and Hurricane the following closures and restrictions are established for the public lands which are included in the areas described.

. . .

Weapon Use

No firearm or other weapon may be discharged except during regulated hunting within prescribed seasons. Propelling an arrow by a bow shall be considered a discharge of a weapon. Any device loaded with powder, other explosive, or any gun actuated by compressed air shall be considered a firearm.. **[This definition of "firearm" conflicts with the definition in the Gun Control Act of 1968 that excludes most** black **powder and muzzle loader rifles and pistols unless they were designed to use modern ammunition (18 U.S.C. 921(3)(16))**].

. . .

The above regulations do not apply to emergency vehicles or personnel, or vehicles owned by or persons employed by the

United States, the State of Utah, Washington County, or any municipality in Washington County when such vehicles or personnel are used or acting in the performance of official duties, or for authorized users of rights of way, or for owners of private land to access their private land.

Authority: The authority for issuing a closure and restriction order is contained in CFR Title 43 Subpart 8364.1a. A copy of these restrictions will be available in the Dixie Resource Area Office, which manages these lands. Violations are punishable as class A misdemeanors. Dated: July 31, 1998. James D. Crisp, Area Manager.

3. Fivemile Pass and Knolls Special Recreation Area Closure - Federal Register 2000

Fivemile Pass and Knolls Special Recreation Area, et al.; Emergency Closure To Discharge or Use of Firearms or Dangerous Weapons for

Purposes of Target Shooting

Volume 65, July 5, 2000

AGENCY: Bureau of Land Management, Interior.

ACTION: Closure notice and supplemental rule.

SUMMARY: Under the authority of 43 C.F.R. § 8364.1(a), notice is hereby given that an emergency closure to the discharge or use of firearms or dangerous weapons for the purposes of target shooting is in effect on public lands administered by the Salt Lake Field Office, Bureau of Land Management, as follows:

Fivemile Pass Special Recreation Management Area (SRMA)
T. 5 S., R. 3 W., SLM, Sections 33, 34;
T. 6.S., R. 3 W., SLM, Sections 3, 4, 7-11, 13-24, 26-30, 33-35;
T. 7 S., R. 3 W., SLM, Sections 1, 3-15, 17, 18, 22-27, 34, 35;
T. 8 S., R. 3 W., SLM, Section 3;
T. 6 S., R. 4 W., SLM, Sections 11-15, 22-26, 35;
T. 7 S., R. 4 W., SLM, Sections 1, 10-15.

Knolls Special Recreation Management Area:
T. 1 S., R. 12 W., SLM, Sections 19-23 south of the railroad grade, 26-31, 33-35;

T. 2 S., R. 12 W., SLM, Sections 3-11, 14, 15, 17, 18;
T. 1 S., R. 13 W., SLM, Sections 19-24 south of railroad grade, 25-31, 33-35;
T. 2 S., R. 13 W., SLM, Sections 1-15, 17, 18.

This order is put into effect to protect persons, property, and resources, located in these areas from person(s) engaged in target shooting with firearms or dangerous weapons. This emergency order does not prohibit the discharge of firearms or dangerous weapons while person(s) are engaged in bonafide hunting activities during established hunting seasons and are properly licensed for these activities.

Under the authority of 43 C.F.R. § 8365.1-6, a supplementary rule is established to prohibit the discharge or use of firearms or dangerous weapons for the purposes of target shooting on public lands administered by the Salt Lake Field Office, Bureau of Land Management, as follows:

North Oquirrh Management Area

All Existing and Future Federal Land within the following description:

T. 1 S., R. 3 W., SLM
Section 20, SW 1/4;
Sections 19, 29, 30, 31, 32;
T. 2 S., R. 3 W., SLM
Sections 5, 6, 7, 8;
Section 16, SW 1/4 SW 1/4;
Sections 17, 18, 19, 20;
Section 21, W 1/2 W 1/2;
Section 28, W 1/2, SE 1/4;
Sections 29, 30, 31, 32, 33;
Section 34, W 1/2 W 1/2;
T. 3 S., R. 3 W., SLM
Section 4, 5, 6;
Section 7, N 1/2, N 1/2 S 1/2;
Sections 8, 9;
T. 1 S., R. 4 W., SLM
Section 24, SE 1/4;
Sections 25, 36;

All lands east of the Union Pacific Railroad within:
T. 2 S., R. 4 W., SLM

Sections 1, 11, 12, 13, 14, 15, 22, 23, 24, 25, 26, 36;

T. 3 S., R. 4 W., SLM

Sections 1, 11;

Section 12, N 1/2.

Simpson Springs Campground

T. 9 S., R. 8 W., SLM

Section 17, W 1/2 NW 1/4, NW 1/4 SW 1/4;

Section 18, NE 1/4, E 1/2 NW 1/4, NE 1/4 SW 1/4, N 1/2 S.E. 1/4.

DATES: Effective July 5, 2000, this prohibition for Knolls and Fivemile Pass areas will remain in effect until revoked or replaced by supplemental rules pursuant to 43 C.F.R. § 8365.1-6. Effective July 5, 2000, this supplementary rule for North Oquirrh and Simpson Springs Campground areas will remain in effect until revoked.

FOR FURTHER INFORMATION CONTACT: Randy Griffin, BLM Ranger, Salt Lake Field Office, Bureau of Land Management, 2370 So. 2300 West, Salt Lake City, Utah, 84119; (801)-977-4300.

SUPPLEMENTARY INFORMATION: This prohibition on the discharge of firearms or dangerous weapons within the Fivemile Pass and Knolls SRMA will serve to protect the safety and health of individuals and groups visiting and utilizing the network of off highway vehicle trails located within the lands described above. In addition, this prohibition will also serve to protect the safety and health of individuals and groups visiting and hiking the network of trails in the North Oquirrh Management Area and individuals and groups camping in the Simpson Springs developed campground. Violations of this closure are punishable by a **fine up to $100,000 and/or imprisonment not to exceed 12 months** [!] as provided in 43 C.F.R.

part 8360.

Dated: June 23, 2000.

Glenn A. Carpenter,

Field Office Manager.

[FR Doc. 00-16827 Filed 7-3-00; 8:45 am]

BILLING CODE 4310-$$-P

DEPARTMENT OF THE INTERIOR

Bureau of Land Management

[NV-930-1020-JL]

Traveling through Indian Reservations

United States Code: Title 25 -Indians

"PLAIN TALK"

I couldn't find anything in Title 25 prohibiting non-Indians from taking firearms onto an Indian reservation. Furthermore, a landmark United States Supreme Court case *Oliphant v. Suquamish Tribe*, 435 U.S. 191, 212, 98 S.Ct. 1011, 1022-23, 55 L.Ed.2d 209 (1978) held that the Indian tribes had no criminal jurisdiction over non-Indians. This rule of law has been cited by many federal and state courts, some as recently as 2006. I have discussed this issue with the "Indian Law" guru at Utah's U.S. Attorney's office (unofficially) who indicated he knew of no prohibitions or prosecutions of non-Indians having firearms on tribal lands. Based upon these findings (or lack of findings), I can only conclude that if you are simply passing through Indian lands on public highways, if you otherwise comply with Utah and federal law pertaining to vehicle carry (as described in this chapter and chapters VII and VIII), you should not be harassed.

Switchblade Knives

"PLAIN TALK"

I can't count the times I've been asked about switchblades, even though I don't claim to be the Utah's "Knife Law Guru." Okay, my readers get their way. I researched it. I hope yer happy makin' Pancho crawl out of his comfort zone!

It's a five-year federal felony to introduce (sell?), transport or distribute a switchblade knife "in interstate commerce." A switchblade is defined broadly to include knives that open by gravity or inertia. That seems to exclude the knives that do not open by inertia or gravity that need to be initially opened by the use of a "thumb peg" (like most locking blade knives do nowadays). Double -edged stiletto "butter-fly" knives were held to fit the definition of "switchblade" in *Taylor v. U.S.*, 848 F.2d 715 (6th Cir. 1988). §1243 only prohibits possession in Indian territory and on the "high seas." The absence of the word "possess" in §1242 suggests that it is not illegal to possess a switchblade in your own state as long as you don't take it across state lines. However, unless you want to bless your attorney with a strongbox full of cash, you may not want to possess one of these little hot potatoes unless you are in the Armed forces in performance of your duties or a "one-armed" person (see exceptions in §1244). [Didn't a one-armed man murder Dr. Richard Kimball's wife in the movie "The Fugitive?" You'd think that would be enough for Senators from New York or California to ban the sale of switchblades to one-armed men! "If we had a law banning switchblades to one-armed men, Mrs. Kimball wouldn't have had to die!" Yes she would, you morons, it was a movie!]

ACTUAL TEXT

15 U.S.C. § 1241. Definitions As used in this chapter — (a) The term "interstate commerce" means commerce between any State, Territory, possession of the United States, or the District of Columbia, and any place outside thereof. (b) The term "switchblade knife" means any knife having a blade which opens automatically — (1) by hand pressure applied to a button or other device in the handle of the knife, or (2) by operation of inertia, gravity, or both.

15 U.S.C. § 1242. Introduction, manufacture for introduction, transportation or distribution in interstate commerce; penalty. Whoever knowingly introduces, or manufactures for introduction, into interstate commerce, or transports or distributes in interstate commerce, any switchblade knife, shall be fined not more than $2,000 or imprisoned not more than five years, or both.

15 U.S.C. § 1243. Manufacture, sale, or possession within specific jurisdictions; penalty Whoever, within any Territory or possession of the United States, within Indian country (as defined in section 1151 of title 18), or within the special maritime and territorial jurisdiction of the United States (as defined in section 7 of title 18), manufactures, sells, or possesses any switchblade knife, shall be fined not more than $2,000 or imprisoned not more than five years, or both.

15 U.S.C. § 1244. Exceptions. Sections 1242 and 1243 of this title shall not apply to —

(1) any common carrier or contract carrier, with respect to any switchblade knife shipped, transported, or delivered for shipment in interstate commerce in the ordinary course of business;

(2) the manufacture, sale, transportation, distribution, possession, or introduction into interstate commerce, of switchblade knives pursuant to contract with the Armed Forces;

(3) the Armed Forces or any member or employee thereof acting in the performance of his duty; or

(4) the possession, and transportation upon his person, of any switchblade knife with a blade three inches or less in length by any individual who has only one arm.

PANCHO'S LETTER TO SANTA

Dear Santa, I just finished my chapter on the federal gun laws and it reminded me I have been asking for years for you to bring me a machine gun; and you haven't! I don't want to appear bitter or greedy, but you can STUFF the @%*#*$*@ machinegun, er, heh, down the chimney, I mean. Instead, I hear the Air Force is trading out the F-16's for new F-22's or 35's or whatever, could you just please bring me a "used" F-16 with full armament, a Harrier for my back yard and an Apache Helicopter with all the goodies? I've been a good boy, I promise. Luv, Pancho P.S. The ATF will NEVER KNOW, 'cause its agents are too busy playin' "biker dude" at gun shows bustin' unsuspecting good guys who bought n' sold one too many guns this year fer "dealin' without a license! What? What's "one too many?" I don't know, the law's unclear to me too, even as a lawyer. I guess one less than anyone's already bought n' sold? Hey, Santa, how many have you bought and sold? Do you have a manufacturer's license? Santa . . . Santa! . . . .Remember, you have the right to remain silent; don't waste yer one phone call callin' yer elves! Call me and we'll work out the details of my FEE (this is perrrrrffffeeeect!!!!)

QUESTION: Why does anyone NEED an ASSAULT RIFLE?
PANCHO'S ANSWER: Because he doesn't already have 5 of 'em!

CHAPTER XIV

CIVIL RIGHTS LAWSUITS TO ENFORCE THE RIGHT TO BEAR ARMS

Pancho's Wisdom

The good thing about conceal carry at my age.... when people see the bulge on my side, they assume it's a colostomy pouch!

Anti-gun advocates like Sarah Brady would like the public to believe that gun owners have no enforceable civil rights. In a *Hearst Newspaper* article entitled "Guns in America, Part III," Sarah Brady is reported to have told interviewers:

> Asked about differences between her group and gun rights groups such as the National Rifle Association, Brady said, "Our objective is to cut down deaths and injury.
>
> "They [the NRA] are looking only to protect gun owners' quote — and I stress that — rights, because I DON'T BELIEVE GUN OWNERS HAVE RIGHTS . . ."

Contrary to Brady's claims, the several courts have handed down important decisions protecting the rights of gun owners. We have already discussed how the Supreme Court struck down part of the Brady law in the *Printz* case and how it found the Gun Free School Zone Act unconstitutional in the *Lopez* case (see discussion in Chapter XIII). In addition to these victories, three cases have held that gun owners can enforce their civil rights against state and local governments that try to infringe on their rights to own and possess guns, including concealed weapons.

One of the most dramatic cases was *Kellogg et. al. v. City of Gary et. al.*, 562 N.E.2d 685 (Indiana 1990). During the 1970s, the State of Indiana required a permit to possess a handgun. For years the City of Gary, Indiana had routinely given out permits (it appears residents had to obtain permits from the city in which they lived). Then on January 1, 1980, the police chief and mayor stopped handing out permits and from that time forward, Gary citizens could no longer buy a handgun. This emphasizes the danger of requiring gun owners to have a federal or state permit to possess a firearm or a handgun. What are you going to do when the bureaucrats administering the permit program decide to stop issuing permits? Sue? Did you notice how long it took this case to get to the Indiana Supreme Court [10 years]? Several citizens, including an attorney, joined to sue to enforce their rights under the federal Civil Rights Act. The Indiana Supreme Court held that Gary officials had violated the equal protection clause of the Fourteenth Amendment of the United States Constitution. The Court explained that Gary's police chief and mayor had deprived these citizens of rights that other Indiana citizens enjoyed, i.e., the right to obtain a permit to own a handgun. The justices observed that issuing the mayor's bodyguards permits while denying them to common citizens was unequal. (Does this remind you of an ex-president who committed perjury, who is still being protected by secret service agents with machine guns, and who doesn't want citizens with clean criminal records to have semiautomatic "assault weapons"?) Furthermore, the Indiana Supreme Court held that there was a "liberty" and a "property" interest created by the right to bear arms guaranteed in the Indiana State Constitution (containing language similar to Utah's), which is in turn, protected by the Fourteenth Amendment of the United States Constitution. The Court stated:

> We . . .find that this RIGHT of Indiana citizens to BEAR ARMS for their own self-defense and for the defense of the state IS AN INTEREST IN BOTH LIBERTY AND

> PROPERTY which is PROTECTED BY THE FOURTEENTH AMENDMENT to the Federal Constitution . . . by its actions, the city denied the citizens access to the state's procedural process which guaranteed them a substantive right under the Indiana Constitution (emphasis added).

562 N.E.2d at 694. The holding that gun permits are a "property right" is very relevant and important to Utah concealed weapon permit holders. Indiana's handgun permit statute was a "shall issue" statute like Utah's concealed weapon law (see analysis in Chapter VIII). The Indiana court held that when government officials must issue a permit to qualified applicants, this creates a property interest which cannot be taken away without due process of law. *Id.* at 695, 696.

A jury awarded over $800,000 in damages against the city and over $500,000 in attorney fees. Although the Supreme Court of Indiana reduced these amounts, the case stands as a warning to states, counties and cities that gun owners and concealed weapon permit holders have civil rights that can be enforced under a federal statute.

In *Miller et. al. v. Collier et. al.*, 878 P.2d 141(Colo. App. 1994) two private investigators were having a terrible time trying to get state officials to issue them concealed weapon permits. It seemed to them that police officers, former police officers and government employees could get the permits, but they (the plaintiffs) couldn't. They sued alleging they weren't being treated the same (denial of equal protection). Their complaint relied on the federal civil rights law, 42 U.S.C.1983 that states:

> Every person who, under color of any statute, ordinance, regulation, custom, or usage, of any State or Territory, subjects, or causes to be subjected, ANY CITIZEN of the United States or other person within the jurisdiction thereof to DEPRIVATION OF ANY RIGHTS, PRIVILEGES, OR IMMUNITIES SECURED BY THE CONSTITUTION AND LAWS, SHALL BE LIABLE to the party injured in an action at law, suit in equity, or

> other proper proceeding for redress (emphasis added). **[Stated simply, if a government official, acting under a state law or local ordinance, deprives a citizen of a right guaranteed by the U.S. Constitution or a federal law, the official can be sued for damages in a civil rights lawsuit]**.

The Court held that the intent of Section 1983 is to "create a civil remedy for persons who prove that one acting under the color of state law has illegally deprived them of rights guaranteed by the Federal Constitution or by Federal law." 878 P.2d at 146. The Court took special note of the fact that the Plaintiffs had alleged in their complaint:

> . . . that their applications were handled differently than those submitted by private investigators who are current or retired law enforcement officers and that defendants are, in effect, "attempting to protect the outside employment of current law enforcement officers and retired law enforcement officers to conduct private business at the expense of the plaintiffs." Plaintiffs claim there is no rational reason for this disparate treatment and that defendants are thus acting arbitrarily and capriciously.

Id. at 146. The Court of Appeals of Colorado held that these allegations were sufficient to state a claim for relief under Section 1983 of the Civil Rights Act for violation of Plaintiffs' rights to equal protection under the law.

In *Ford v. Turner*, et. al., 531 A.2d 233 (D.C. App. 1987), the District of Columbia Court of Appeals applied Section 1983 of the Civil Rights Act to spank Washington, D. C. officials for confiscating and keeping unregistered firearms without notice and a hearing. The court held a law allowing confiscation of firearms without notice and a hearing, deprived the heirs of the deceased gun owner procedural due process. The court held in assessing damages the court or jury could look to "impairment of reputation . . ., personal humiliation, and mental anguish and suffering." 531 A.2d at 240.

Utah courts should follow these legal precedents to ensure that government officials do not deprive law-abiding Utahns of the right to bear arms to protect themselves, their families, their homes and businesses. State and local agencies infringing upon such rights should be held liable for large civil damage awards, including attorney fees.

Pancho's Wisdom

In Heaven we'll have Mexican food without heartburn, shooting without hearing loss, government without liberals and country music without the Dixie Chicks!

PANCHO'S ANGELS
Badd Ash
Nikita
Coco

CHAPTER XV

CONCLUSION:

Still the Good, The Bad and the Ugly

In 1999, when I published Utah's first Gun Law Book, I subtitled it *"The Good, the Bad and the Ugly"* because it was an appropriate description of Utah's gun laws at the time. Some were good, some bad and some downright ugly, as ugly or uglier than their federal counterparts. Since then, through the tireless effort of a semi-trailer full of Utahns including government leaders, considerable positive change has been achieved. We should take enough time for a 21 gun salute to The Good before our thoughts drop into the bottomless pit of despair because of the Bad and Ugly that STILL need changin'.

THE GOOD

After my first Gun Law books were published, I began handing out copies to government leaders and encouraged readers to do the same - and they did. (Before my contemporaries and I got involved in this battle, our predecessors tirelessly stormed the "Hill," year after year, people like Attorney Woody Powell, John Spangler, Doctor Sarah Thompson, Scott Engen and many more to whom I apologize for not naming.) By the time I published *Utah Gun Law II: Pancho's Wisdom*, our current Utah Attorney General, Mark Shurtleff, had been elected and I gave him a copy of the book which targeted a beet-pile full of state and local rules and regulations that conflicted with Utah statutes. For example, former Governor Leavitt, reported giving one of his staff members a "hug" and feeling a hard bulge under the man's armpit. No, it was not a tumor; it was a Taurus! Not long afterward, the Governor convinced Human Resources to "promulgate" a regulation "banning guns in the workplace." Similarly, the Utah Division of Wildlife Resources had been prohibiting hunters with concealed weapon permits to carry their firearm on various hunts and "chases" (chasing bear and cougar to train dogs while not harvesting the animal). The state foster care agency had informed foster care parents they could not keep guns in their own homes! Most schools and universities had policies banning concealed weapon permit holders from bringing their defensive firearms to school despite state law to the contrary. A number of legislators as well as members of the Attorney General's staff also expressed their concerns to Attorney General Shurtleff. After independent research and consulting with members of his own staff, the Attorney General concluded that these restrictions conflicted with state law. Consistent with his nature, he immediately began efforts "to make things right."

Before long we began to see many positive changes. In January of 2002, the state personnel office deleted it's policy which had kept state employees with concealed weapons permits from bringing their firearms to work. Yes, finally they were again able to take their concealed weapons INTO THE WORKPLACE, THEIR DESKS, CUBICLES, AND VEHICLES! This occurred, over five years ago and guess what? Not one negative experience reported. We know that because if there had been just one, the Salt Lake Tribune and Deseret News would have both been "all over it" demanding the policy be amended "before someone gets hurt!"

The Division of Wildlife resources reversed its regulations which had unlawfully prevented permit holders from having defensive firearms on hunts and in state parks.

Although the Granite and Jordan School Districts reluctantly amended their "No Weapons" rules to comply with state law, the University of Utah was not willing to change its policy without a fight. Its attorneys sued the State and the Attorney General hoping to convince a court that they had "educational autonomy" (a warm, dark, fuzzy place where reality doesn't shine!) and should be allowed to make their own firearm policies on campus. Not unlike the disastrous policy at Virginia Tech, the University of Utah's aim was to deprive its faculty, staff and students of the means to defend their lives with a firearm and to rely instead upon campus security. After a court battle of several years, the Utah Supreme Court forced the University to recognize the rights of staff and students with permits to carry concealed weapons on campus. Raise da Roof fer Attorney General Mark Shurtleff! You da MAN! And every body say, HAAaaaahhh, HO ohohoh, for his gun-slingin' Deputy A.G., Brent Burnett, who actually slapped leather at High Noon (wrote the briefs and argued the case in the Supreme Court).

Progress has been made on the local level also. I represented a man who was charged with violating the long-standing Salt Lake county ordinance making it illegal to discharge a firearm anywhere in the county except shooting ranges. He had been target practicing with a regrettably loud .44 magnum pistol up Parley's Canyon and was complying with state law, was sufficiently distant from buildings and enclosures and otherwise conducting himself safely when the "SWAT Team" arrived. As indicated in Chapter VII, the counties have not been given authority to regulate the discharge of firearms except for spotlighting or night hunting. When I pointed this out to the county prosecutor, he was shocked. A few days later he called back and said, "You're right. We can't find anywhere in the code where counties have been given the authority to pass such an ordinance. We're dropping the charges against your client." Hopefully he passed the word on to other county attorneys at their periodic training sessions.

Not long ago I got a call from firefighters in Ogden who said the city wouldn't let firemen with concealed weapon permits carry their guns on duty. They were legitimately concerned they might be the first responders to an act of terrorism and could be shot at for putting out the fire. I called a deputy city attorney and reminded her that because of the uniformity statute (U.C.A. 76-10-500 - Chapter VII) cities could not regulate firearms without express authority from the state. After reading the code section and being aware of the holding of the University of Utah case, she called back and said they would change the rule so that their firemen with permits would be allowed to pack heat into the heat! Seems like I spend half of my time or more straightening out cities, counties and school districts that habitually feel justified stomping on gun owners' rights. I'm starting to feel like Mother Taurusa!

After just one phone call and with no contention whatsoever, Centerville City agreed to delete the phrase "No Firearms" on their city park signs. Although the St. George City Attorney was not as easy to get a commitment from, when I finally got their part-time mayor on the phone, he agreed to immediately stop prohibiting legal weapons on St. George's stunningly picturesque trail system. The trails cut through miles of almost impenetrable indigenous brush and willows reminiscent of Uncle Remus' "Briar Patch," which could easily and ironically facilitate a sexual assault near the Virgin River. The signs were changed from prohibiting all firearms to prohibiting illegal firearms. Hopefully, aspiring young rapists hiding in the bull rushes will read the signs, fantasize that all colorful women's fanny packs contain size .357 equalizers and slink away to the Socialist Republic of California where "guns don't belong on nature trails."

The acceptance of this obviously politically incorrect but brutally effective approach to public safety by state and local leaders, including prominent Democrats, may have been significantly influenced by the wonderfully brilliant idea of Representative Curt Oda (R-Clearfield) to offer concealed weapon classes to ALL government leaders. Representative Oda told lawmakers if they were going to vote on firearms issues, whether they agreed with our position or not, they should know as much about them as possible before voting. Lawmakers knew before enrolling that these classes were sponsored by the NRA. NRA lobbyist Brian Judy was available at almost every class to get to know legislators and to answer their questions. Representative Oda, premier pistol instructor Clark Aposhian and I shared time teaching the classes. These opportunities helped form lasting relationships between state lawmakers and those of us who cherish the right of self defense.

Clark Aposhian, has been a major force in bringing about positive changes in Utah's gun laws. His efforts have resulted in a significant shortening of the Concealed Weapon Application form, better communication between the states for the purpose of recognizing each other's concealed weapon permits and more open discussions between those representing the interests of gun owners and the Utah Department of Public Safety. Charles Hardy of the Gun Owners of Utah, together with Mr. Aposhian, have provided powerful and compelling presentations before the Legislature in favor of bills furthering the cause of personal defense and opposing bills which infringe on that right. An ally who has helped bridge the gap between conservatives and liberals in the battle I have described, has been David Nelson of Stonewall Shooting Sports, a pro-gun gay and lesbian organization. His group has helped promote the reality that for the victims of hate crimes, 9mm will get the job done when 911 falls short.

Indispensable contributions have been made by a host of state and local lawmakers who are too numerous to name. While I excuse myself for not naming them all, the following legislators deserve special mention: Senators Mike Waddoups, Mark Madsen, Ed Mayne, and Sheldon Kilpack, and Representatives Glenn Donnelson, Paul Ray, Roger Barrus, Carl Wimmer, Mel Brown, Aaron Tilton, Steve Urquhart, David Ure and Curt Oda. These and other astute Legislators refused to allow the University of Utah to undermine the effectiveness of concealed carry by establishing Virginia-Tech style "gun free zones."

THE BAD AND THE UGLY

Unfortunately, lobbyists representing various business-related groups such as the Human Resource Managers, Utah Restaurant Association, Kennecott Copper, and various Chambers of Commerce have convinced key figures in our Legislature that an employer's right to control his workplace is inviolate. As a result, most large Utah companies continue to get away with enforcing "No Weapons" policies. Three courageous Utahns, Luke Hansen, Paul Carlson and Jason Melling, dedicated to reversing the lunacy of such policies in employee parking lots, took on internet giant America On Line (AOL) in the internationally acclaimed case, *Hansen v. America Online, Inc.*, 2004 UT 62, 96 P.3d 950 (2004). My good friend and former partner, Bob Sykes and I were privileged to represent these bold young men in their attempt to hold AOL accountable for wrongfully terminating them for possessing guns in AOL's leased parking lot in violation of AOL's "No Weapons" policy. We put forth a vigorous case that they were wrongfully fired in violation of Utah's "clear and substantial" public policy, as evidenced by all of the powerful pro-self defense provisions in Utah's Constitution and statutes. In Utah, contractual provisions, such as AOL's "No Weapons" agreement, are voidable if they contradict clear and substantial public policy.

Unfortunately, just before oral argument in the Utah Supreme Court, the Legislature considered a bill that would prohibit employers from banning legal guns in employer parking lots, but the bill never passed. The "fickle finger of fate" took a strange twist because the bill did not pass. The Court held that because the Legislature had not been able to decide the issue, the policy must not be "clear and substantial!" Ouch! As a result of the AOL case, employers have the right to prohibit employees from bringing defensive firearms into employers'parking lots. This, in turn, disarms employees during the trip to and from work where employers have absolutely no liability for the safety of their employees. "We're sorry Widow Jones. We did everything in our power to protect Mr. Jones from 'violence in the workplace.' Gee, we just didn't expect a carjacker to murder your husband who faithfully obeyed our company 'No Weapons' policy. But look at the bright side. We prevented your husband, who had a spotless criminal record, from transforming in the blink of an eye, from a harmless, stellar employee to a raving, merciless killer because he had a gun locked in his trunk during the workday! Someone could've been killed in the resulting Wild West shootout!"

The irony of "No Weapons" policies which employers believe will prevent "violence in the workplace" is vividly illustrated in the photograph to the left. It is a picture of the "NO FIREARMS" sign in front of the Conagra plant, where a worker shot 6 helpless, disarmed employees and then shot himself. Personnel managers who encourage such foolish policies apparently believe disgruntled and usually long-previously-fired employees will give up a murder plot because they encounter a "No-Guns" sign on the way to their "Blaze of Glory."

Legislators who defend the concept of "gun free zones" keep singing the tune that "employer's property rights trump gun rights." The following analysis shows why they have it backwards.

A. Life and Liberty Interests have Priority over a Property Interests

The term "gun rights" mis-characterizes the nature of the right. The right associated with carrying a gun is not intended to preserve the gun, it's intended to preserve life and liberty. A close examination of our system of laws reveals that life and liberty interests easily outweigh property interests. This is because without life, one cannot have liberty. Without liberty, one cannot own property. Hence, when these right are mentioned together, such as in Utah's Constitution, "life" comes before "liberty" which, in turn, precedes "property." For example, the first sentence of the first article of Utah's Declaration of Rights (similar to the Bill of Rights in the federal Constitution), states:

> "**ARTICLE I DECLARATION OF RIGHTS**; Section 1. [Inherent and inalienable rights.] All men have the inherent and inalienable right to enjoy and defend their **lives** and **liberties**; to acquire, possess and protect **property** . . .

(emphasis added). The priority of life and liberty over property permeates the U.S. justice system. For example, virtually every state and federal court system has laws and rules that make it much more difficult to take an accused person's life (capital punishment) than to take a negligent person's property. This is dramatically illustrated by Section 10 of Utah's Declaration of Rights.

> **Section 10. [Trial by jury.]**
>
> In capital cases the right of trial by jury shall remain inviolate. In capital cases the jury shall consist of twelve persons, and in all other felony cases, the jury shall consist of no fewer than eight persons. In other cases, the Legislature shall establish the number of jurors by statute, but in no event shall a jury consist of fewer than four persons. In criminal cases the verdict shall be

> unanimous. In civil cases three-fourths of the jurors may find a verdict. A jury in civil cases shall be waived unless demanded.

In other words, if a court's verdict places a person's life at risk, it must insure him a jury of twelve, a unanimous verdict and the case against him must be proven "beyond a reasonable doubt." In contrast, in a civil case, where only property (money damages) is at stake, the standard is much less protective. The defendant only gets a jury of eight, three fourths of the jurors can render a verdict and the case against him need only be proven "by a preponderance of the evidence," a much lower standard than "beyond a reasonable doubt." To be deprived of life (the death penalty), a citizen must commit a horrendous crime, like pre-meditated murder. He can be deprived of his property, however, as a result of mere negligence on his part. The same priority is built into our self-defense laws. A person may kill an attacker to defend his own life or the life of another. He may, however, not use deadly force to defend his property (Chapter XI).

The principle that life interests take priority over property interests is not only evident in our criminal and civil justice systems, it is inherent in occupational, safety, fire and building codes, zoning ordinances and nuisance laws. For example, federal and state governments can force employers to install costly alarm and sprinkling systems on their property to protect the lives of their employees and customers. They can make them spend their money for scaffolding and safety harnesses. By virtue of zoning ordinances, they can prohibit property owners from building factories in or near residential areas. In virtually every aspect of our legal system, life interests trump property interests.

B. The Problem with "Gun Free Zones"

If those who create "gun free zones" watch "Animal Planet," they sure don't get it! Animal predators have teeth and claws and their prey don't. The weakest and most helpless are ALWAYS at greatest risk of being overpowered, killed and eaten.

Likewise, human predators have always preyed on the weak and the helpless. Since the beginning of time, conquerors, tyrants, pirates, rapists, robbers and terrorists have captured, dominated, defeated, sexually abused, tortured, enslaved and committed genocide against those who were not as well armed as they.

You'd think that anyone with any comprehension of past history and mortal reality would conclude that being armed and prepared is better than being disarmed and unprepared. As many times as this all has been carefully explained to gun-hating urban liberals and those who they elect, they STILLsay they don't get it! This leads me to believe one of two things: (1) They DO get it, but realize it is almost impossible to disarm a whole nation without a spectacular mass killing OR (2) they DON'T get it and should receive a Darwin Award for being on a collision course with EXTINCTION! It makes you wonder if maybe marijuana REALLY DOES cause brain damage?

Amazingly, a conservative state like Utah, with an enlightened Legislature, still has numerous gun free zones either mandated or permitted by state and federal law. These "kill-me-I-won't-fight-back zones" include many if not most workplaces (including employee parking lots), post offices, publically accessible areas of airports, private schools, national parks and monuments, and private businesses. Of course, our Legislature cannot change federal law; that is Congress' responsibility. But our Legislature can eliminate "no weapon" zones like the Governor of Texas advocated following the Virginia Tech murders:

> Gov. Rick Perry, mulling ways to stop the kind of murderous rampages that recently left 33 dead on a college campus in Virginia, said Monday there's one sure-fire solution he likes: allow Texans to take their concealed handguns anywhere. Period.
>
> Perry said he opposes any concealed gun-toting restrictions at all — whether it's in a hospital, a public school, a beer joint or even the local courthouse.
>
> "The last time I checked, putting a sign up that says 'Don't bring your weapons in here,' someone who has ill intent on their mind — they could care less," Perry told reporters. "I think it makes sense for Texans to be able to protect

themselves from deranged individuals, whether they're in church or whether on a college campus or wherever."

As reporters began clicking off a list of places where concealed permit holders face restrictions, Perry cut off the questioning and made it clear that he meant anywhere at all.

Under current law, secured airport areas, hospitals, courthouses, bars, churches and schools are among the places where weapons are or can be banned, according to the Texas Department of Public Safety.

People entering federal courts in Texas are routinely required to leave even their cell phones behind.

"Let me cover it right here," Perry said. "I think a person ought to be able to carry their weapons with them anywhere in this state if they are licensed and they have gone through the training. The idea that you're going to exempt them from a particular place is non-sense to me."

Perry: *"Allow concealed handguns anywhere,"* Star-Telegram.com (2007-4-30). Retrieved 2007-5-2.

C. The Difference between Virginia Tech and Trolley Square

Two years before the massacre of thirty two innocent students and teachers at Virginia Tech, clear-thinking Virginians tried pass a law to keep Virginia's colleges and universities from prohibiting concealed weapon permit holders from having a firearm on campus. Let's examine the words of Virginia Tech's spokesman, Larry Hincker, in opposition to the law:

I think it's fair to say that we believe guns don't belong in the classroom, . . . In an academic environment, we believe you should be free from fear. . . we think it's a common-sense policy for the protection of students, staff and faculty. . .

"Virginia Tech's ban on guns may draw legal fire," The Roanoke Times (2005-4-13). Retrieved on 2007-4/30.

After the law was defeated in January of 2006 and Virginia's colleges and universities we given free reign to establish "No Weapons" policies, Hincker joyfully thanked Virginia's legislature:

> **I'm sure the university community is appreciative of the General Assembly's actions because this will help parents, students, faculty and visitors feel safe on our campus.**

"Gun bill gets shot down by panel," The Roanoke Times (2006-1-31). Slightly over a year later, 32 students and teachers were mercilessly mowed down inside Virginia Tech's "gun free zone." So, Mr. Hincker, how "free from fear" were your students and teachers on that fateful day as they cowered under desks or jumped out of second story windows to avoid being shot? How "safe" did they feel as a result of your brainless "feel-good-but-get-killed" campus policy? What's the "common sense" of establishing restrictions which give one psychopath with a weapon the power of life and death over hundreds of disarmed students and teachers?

Which brings us to the Trolley Square Shooting of February 12, 2007. The sign on the door through which the shooter, Talovic, entered warned, "No weapons allowed on Trolley Square property." Here we go again, the notion that a sign will somehow cause a determined killer to turn around and go home. Thank goodness off-duty police officer Ken Hammond either didn't see the sign or ignored it (notice, it didn't except police officers from the prohibition). Although a SWAT team arrived in what many consider to be a phenomenally short 6 minutes after the first 911 call came in, Talovic still had enough time to kill 5 and injure 4. No one seriously disputes that the fact that Hammond, who was carrying a concealed weapon, saved countless lives by engaging the shooter for 3 minutes until the SWAT team arrived. If Ken Hammond hadn't kept the shooter busy for that amount of time, Talovic would have been able to enter crowded movie theaters and restaurants on the property containing hundreds of potential casualties. To us dyed-in-sagebrush-camo Westerners, if Hammond hadn't been there with a concealed weapon, it's a no-brainer that the casualties at Trolley would have been much higher. Of course Trolley hasn't been the only mass killing where casualties were drastically reduced because a good guy with a gun stepped in to stop the incident. It happened at Pearl, Mississippi where a school administrator dashed to his truck parked off campus and returned to stop the shooter (how many might have been saved if he had been allowed to conceal carry on campus like student and faculty permit holders can in Utah?) Similarly, law-abiding citizens with a firearm cut casualties short in school shootings in Edinboro, Pennsylvania, and at the Appalachian Law School shooting not far from Virginia Tech. Many people blame media bias for the fact that such incidents are not widely reported. Whatever the motivation of the media in failing to mention that such events have been drastically cut short by a citizen with a gun, one thing is for sure - the mass murder of 33 (eg. Virginia Tech) sells a lot more newspapers than an incident like at Pickle's Pawn Shop in Salt Lake a few years ago when two armed robbers entered the store shooting. They were immediately repelled by two armed employees shooting back. Neither of the two employees were injured, but the criminals were later caught when one of them checked into a Southern Idaho hospital with a bullet lodged in his butt (who, what, never heard about that one)?!? Hmmm, wonder why that one didn't get headlines? (For a detailed explanation as to why the media tends to "under report" such incidents read John Lott's book *The Bias Against Guns* available at *johnlott.org*).

Interestingly, instead of solving the obvious problem by doing away with "gun free zones," there has been much speculation into what makes such predators "tick." Video games? Bullies? Anti-depressant drugs? We may never know; but we DO KNOW what makes 'em NOT TICK! So if we don't get rid of "gun free zones" so innocents can make sure these creeps aren't like the Ever Ready Bunny ("keeps on ticking"), me n' Pancho are going to be TICKED (Yeah, my kids think my puns are pretty dorky too)!

A Texas politician "gets it" and the Utah Legislature "gets it." Those who don't should get the "Darwin Award" (which salutes the improvement of the human genome by honoring those who accidentally remove themselves from it... - see darwinawards.com)

It's hard to put it any more eloquently and bluntly than Ted Nugent did on CNN following the Virginia Tech tragedy:

> Zero tolerance, huh? Gun-free zones, huh? Try this on for size: Columbine gun-free zone, New York City pizza shop gun-free zone, Luby's Cafeteria gun-free zone, Amish school in Pennsylvania gun-free zone and now Virginia Tech gun-free zone.
>
> Anybody see what the evil Brady Campaign and other anti-gun cults have created? I personally have zero tolerance for evil and denial. And America had best wake up real fast that the brain-dead celebration of unarmed helplessness will get you killed every time, and I've about had enough of it.
>
> . . .
>
> Already spineless gun control advocates are squawking like chickens with their tiny-brained heads chopped off, making political hay over this most recent, devastating Virginia Tech massacre, when in fact it is their own forced gun-free zone policy that enabled the unchallenged methodical murder of 32 people..
>
> Thirty-two people dead on a U.S. college campus pursuing their American Dream, mowed-down over an extended period of time by a lone, non-American gunman in illegal possession of a firearm on campus in defiance of a zero-tolerance gun law. Feel better yet? Didn't think so.
>
> Who doesn't get this? Who has the audacity to demand unarmed helplessness? Who likes dead good guys?
>
> I'll tell you who. People who tramp on the Second Amendment, that's who. People who refuse to accept the self-evident truth that free people have the God-given right to keep and bear arms, to defend themselves and their loved ones. People who are so desperate in their drive to control others, so mindless in their denial that they pretend access to gas causes arson, Ryder trucks and fertilizer cause terrorism, water causes drowning, forks and spoons cause obesity, dialing 911 will somehow save your life, and that their greedy

clamoring to "feel good" is more important than admitting that armed citizens are much better equipped to stop evil than unarmed, helpless ones. . . . Eliminate the insanity of gun-free zones, which will never, ever be gun-free zones. They will only be good guy gun-free zones, and that is a recipe for disaster written in blood on the altar of denial [emphasis added].

Nugent, Ted, "*Gun-free zones are recipe for disaster,*" CNN.com (2007-4-20). Retrieved on 2007-4/30.

You'd think three decades of dead postal workers, meat packers, restaurant patrons, stockbrokers, school children and college students, all killed in "gun free zones" created by "No Weapons" policies, would convince normal-thinking persons that such places simply make helpless victims of the innocent and Kings of Carnage of the guilty. How come left-leaning "intellectuals" don't understand after all this evidence? It is so obvious that even a "CAVEMAN" would understand it!!!! (My apologies in advance to the two Geico cavemen - roast duck with mango salsa on me!)

Pancho's Parting Shots

America was meant to be governed by the
GOD FEARING, ARMED and COURAGEOUS,
not the GODLESS, GUNLESS and GUTLESS
(with gonorrhea and a bong)!
Pancho Vilos

CHAPTER XVI

ABOUT THE AUTHOR

James D. "Mitch" Vilos is a prominent Utah personal injury trial lawyer. He has the notable distinction of being a member of the Million Dollar Advocates Forum for having obtained numerous six and seven figure recoveries for his injured clients involving tractor-trailer accidents, car and motorcycle accidents, birth injuries, medical malpractice, products liability, on-the-job injuries and accidents involving firearms. His focus has been on brain, spinal cord, burn and other serious injuries. More information about Mitch's personal injury practice and his noteworthy cases is available on his personal injury website at www.utahinjurylaw.com.

Mitch's success as a personal injury lawyer has allowed him to delve into a unique area of the law in which he has an interest and passion - firearms law. In May of 2006 Mitch won a "NOT GUILTY" jury verdict to the charge of "brandishing" in the highly publicized case of computer industry magnate Dell Schanze ("SUPERDELL"). The details of that very interesting and important case for Utah gun owners will be forthcoming soon in his next planned book, *Utah Self Defense Law.*

Another notable victory for Mr. Vilos was his participation in the defense of premier candle company, Salt City Candle Company, which was sued for $150 Million dollars by a related company, Party Wicks and Scents, Inc. Mr. Vilos was retained by Salt City's team of attorneys as lead trial counsel in that case and was instrumental in getting the majority of the claims against Salt City Candle completely dismissed.

Mitch graduated from the prestigious J. Reuben Clark Law School at Brigham Young University in 1978. He has authored and co-authored numerous articles relating to personal injury litigation and insurance law in legal publications such as the Utah State Bar Journal and Utah Trial Lawyers Journal.

Mitch has a Federal Firearms License (FFL), is a member of the Utah Trial Lawyers Association, the National Rifle Association, and Single Action Shooting Society (Badge No. 10,586, Alias "Pancho Vilos"). He is the author of *Utah Gun Law: Good, Bad and Ugly, Utah Gun Law II: Pancho's Wisdom* and the *Utah Spotlighting and Night Hunting Manual*. He authored the article entitled, "Not Guilty But Bankrupt, Civil Liability for Negligent Self Defense," published in the American Self-Defense Institute's ASDI Oracle, 1997, Issue 2. He is a Utah State authorized concealed weapon instructor, a graduate of the Ogden Metro Swat Basic Training Course (affectionately known as "Hell Week") and Davis County Sheriff's Citizen's Academy. Mr. Vilos frequently appears on radio and television, addressing legal topics such as negligence law, medical malpractice, insurance law, representing people with traumatic brain injuries, constitutional law, self-defense law and firearms law.

Pancho's Wisdom

Pancho is an Armed, Carnivorous, Greek, Mormon, Republican, Heterosexual Male who wishes he could speak Spanish. . . any Questions?

PANCHO'S FREE LEGAL ADVICE

(worth many times the price of this book!)

You have just gone to considerable effort to protect yourself in the event of an armed confrontation. But if you think about it, you are statistically much more likely to be involved in a car wreck, probably someone else's fault. Experts estimate that 25% of all drivers have no insurance and many more have inadequate coverage.

My Pet Peeve is that although my clients may have enough LIABILITY insurance to cover them in the event THEY CAUSE an accident, they seldom have enough UNINSURED or UNDERINSURED motorists coverage if they are INJURED by an at-fault uninsured or underinsured driver. The medical bills for a serious accidental injury often range from $100,000 to $500,000. A driver is only required to have a minimum of $25,000 liability coverage. If you are seriously injured by a negligent driver, the chances are that he or she will be woefully underinsured. The only way to protect yourself is to have your own coverage that will supplement the negligent driver's inadequate liability coverage. It's called UNDERINSURED motorist coverage.

Yes, you have health insurance, but health insurance companies have a bad habit of waiting until the end of the case expecting to be paid IN FULL for what they have paid out (even though they've alredy collected your premiums for years). They call it subrogation; I call it *#^@%&*@#.

Anyway, do yourself a favor and buy as much UNINSURED (UM) and UNDERINSURED (UIM)motorists coverage as you can afford (it's really cheap - ask your agent). No, I'm not an insurance agent and I don't have stock in an insurance company! I'm just tired of seeing good, hard-working people relegated to INSTANT POVERTY through no fault of their own. Their only "fault" is not having enough UM or UIM automobile insurance coverage! Luv, Pancho

"Gun Grabbers BACK OFF!"

CHAPTER XVII

YOU JUST MIGHT BE A GUNNUT if . . .

It's just not Pancho's style to end a book on a note as somber as this edition's Conclusion. Let it ne'er be said that we gun owners are too serious to share a chuckle over our own peculiarities. So, whether you realized it or not YOU JUST MIGHT BE A GUNNUT IF . . .

1. If you have a semi-circular scar just over the eye-brow of your dominant eye.
2. If your ears ring louder than your telephone.
3. If you have a long straight dent across the hood of your truck that ends with a rifle caliber hole.
4. If, when making that dent, you discovered that yer scope and yer gun barrel ain't lookin' at the same thing at close distances.
5. If the types of bullets exceed the types of coins between the cushions of your living-room couch.
6. If you have enough faith and wisdom to kneel in prayer at your Valley Forge.
7. If a vampire ever bit you, he'd die of lead poisoning.
8. If your total PERCEPTION AND REACTION time is .15 seconds rather than 1.5 seconds.
9. If, as a result of reducing your perception and reaction time, you now have a long, deep and ugly scar down the outside of your dominant leg!
10. If you fantasize about having been the hero that saved the town in Alfred Hitchcock's movie *The Birds* as you polish your new 12 Gauge Beretta Extrema.

11. If *Thunderwear*© is your answer to your employer's "No Weapons" policy.
12. If, as a result of your answer to your employer's "No Weapons" policy, your supervisor erroneously believes you've been experimenting with male enhancement hormones.
13. If you always watched the opening scenes of *Gunsmoke* with your gun belt on.
14. If your two all-time favorite videos are *Exploding Varmints* and *Duckmen*.
15. If you get your jollies sitting on the front row at the Utah Symphony in Open Carry so you can watch the musicians sweat and miss notes!
16. If most of the shirts you've donated to DI have a large, shredded black hole in the right front flap (they call it "quick-draw from retention!")
17. If you sleep with two pistols under your pillow because one gives you a stiff neck!
18. If you would rather make one-ragged-hole than a hole-in-one.
19. If you've ever envisioned St. Peter wearing two pearl-handled Colts at the Pearly Gates.
20. If you'd rather go huntin' than go to Tahiti!
21. If you ALWAYS check your boys out of school the Friday before deer season.
22. If, when your teens come home late after you've gone to bed, they roll twice across the kitchen floor, just in case they wake you up!
23. If you think Pancho should be head of the ATF AND the EPA.
24. If *The Armed Citizen* is the first article you read when you get your monthly NRA magazine.
25. If before Christmas you give your family your calibers rather than your clothing sizes.

26. If you vehicle's GPS is programed to only take you through those states that recognize Utah's concealed weapon permit.
27. If, when you're in Vegas "pullin'" the slots, you get homesick for your Dillon 650 reloading press.
28. If you learned to use a screw driver by taking your dad's guns apart.
29. If you learned to read by reading a gun safety manual.
30. If you learned to shoot before you learned to read.
31. If you think the Second Amendment means what it says (not too many gunnut judges).
32. If your wife never washes a load of your clothes without finding at least one bullet in the washer or dryer.
33. If bullets fall into the street when you open your car door.
34. If the first item on your "trip list" is your concealed weapon.
35. If you stole your first kiss while changing targets behind the 100 yard berm as bullets whizzed over your heads at a military-style shooting range.
36. If the value of the stuff in yer gun safe exceeds the value of all the stuff in yer garage.
37. If all yer vehicles are decorated with bullet hole decals.
38. If the third person who owns your car after you do is sure to be arrested as a felon as soon as they cross the Mexican border (because no one will EVER be able to remove ALL the AMMO stuck between the cracks, under the carpet, between and under the seats after you've owned it).
39. If your friends refer to your vehicle as a CARSENAL.
40. If the heaviest piece of luggage you own is your Range Bag.
41. If you consider this book required reading.
42. If your instructions to your funeral home director include putting a pistol in your hand at your viewing.
43. If your Last Will and Testament says your most valuable personal property goes to your heirs ONLY AFTER it is "PRIED FROM YER COLD, DEAD HANDS!"

APPENDIX A

Parental Consent Form for Minor to Possess Handgun

PRIOR WRITTEN CONSENT FOR JUVENILE TO POSSESS HANDGUN AND/OR HANDGUN AMMUNITION.

I ___________________________, hereby certify I am the parent and/or guardian of ___________________________, a juvenile whose date of birth is ____________________.

I certify that I am not prohibited by Federal, State or local law from possessing a firearm. I hereby give my prior written consent for the juvenile above-named to possess a handgun and/or handgun ammunition for the following temporary use:

- ❒ A. In the course of employment, or
- ❒ B. In the course of ranching or farming at the residence of said juvenile, or
- ❒ C. On property used for ranching or farming where the juvenile has permission of the property owner or lessee to possess a handgun, or
- ❒ D. Target practice, or
- ❒ E. Hunting, or
- ❒ F. To take a course of instruction on the safe and lawful use of a handgun.

I have explained to said juvenile that the handgun must be unloaded and kept in a locked container to and from the activity described above and that this consent is temporary and only extends to, from and during the activity described above.

I have instructed said juvenile to keep this written consent in possession at all times while possessing said handgun.

Inasmuch as Federal law requires compliance with local law, in the event that said juvenile is less than 14 years of age, he/she has been instructed that he/she may not possess said handgun under any circumstances unless accompanied by a responsible adult.

DATED this _____ day of ________________, 200__.

____

Parent and/or Guardian

Note: This consent is for temporary use only. The juvenile should be instructed that once the activity described on the previous page ceases, the juvenile must return the handgun to the owner and that while traveling to and from the activity, the handgun must be unloaded and carried in a locked container.

CAUTION: There are several Utah state laws that impose additional restrictions on minors possessing firearms. Appendix F of this book shows how all of the state and federal laws interrelate. DO NOT allow a minor to possess a firearm or hunt without reviewing the law.

APPENDIX B

Order form for additional copies of *Utah Gun Law: 3rd ed.*

Order extra copies of the ***Utah Gun Law 3rd ed.*** for family, friends and legislators.

Just fill out this form and mail it to:

Attorney "Mitch" Vilos
PO Box 1148
Centerville, UT 84014

❒ Please send me copies of ***Utah Gun Law 3rd ed.***

______ Copies x $18.71 each $________

______ Copies x $3.60 (shipping & handling) $________

______ Copies x $1.22 (sales tax) $________

Total $________

(Make check or money order payable to James D. Vilos. $20.00 penalty for all returned checks. Author may hold books until personal checks clear. For immediate delivery send cashier's check or money order). Dealers call for dealer prices. Call (801) 295-3340 for details. (Toll Free: 800.530.0222.)

Where we should send your books.

Name: ______________________________

Address: ______________________________

____

____

Phone # (_____) ______________________

APPENDIX C

Order form for the
Utah Spotlighting and Night Hunting Manual

Order extra copies of the ***Utah Spotlighting and Night Hunting Manual*** for family and friends.

Just fill out this form and mail it to:
Attorney "Mitch" Vilos
PO Box 1148
Centerville, UT 84014

❒ Please send me copies of the
Utah Spotlighting and Night Hunting Manual

______ Copies x $14.95 each $________

______ Copies x $2.95 (shipping & handling) $________

______ Copies x $.97 (sales tax) $________

Total $________

(Make check or money order payable to James D. Vilos. $20.00 penalty for all returned checks. Author may hold books until personal checks clear. For immediate delivery send cashier's check or money order). Dealers call for dealer prices. Call (801) 295-3340 for details. (Toll Free: 800.530.0222.)

Where we should send your books.
Name: ________________________________
Address: ______________________________
____
____
Phone # (_____) ________________________
e-mail ________________________________

APPENDIX D

Request to be Notified of Future Changes in Utah Gun Law

Nearly every year the Utah Legislature, the Bureau of Criminal Identification (BCI), and the Division of Wildlife Resources (DWR) make changes to Utah gun law. As a shooter, hunter or perhaps a concealed weapon permit holder, you NEED TO KNOW what these changes are. If you would like to be informed of changes in the law, please fill out and mail us this form. We will place your name and address on our mailing list and will inform you if we have published a supplement or a subsequent edition of the book. We will send you an ORDER FORM for a supplement or a new edition AT THAT TIME. You may THEN DECIDE if you would like to order a supplement or updated edition. Prices of supplements will vary depending on the number of changes in Utah gun law during any given year.

I would like to be placed on your mailing list to be informed of a newly published supplement or newer edition of the book. I understand **this is NOT an order** for a supplement to your book and that **I will NOT be charged** for giving my name and address to you at this time. I also understand that after you publish a supplement or new edition, you will send me an order form and I can order at that time. I understand that the prices of the supplements, new editions and shipping and handling will vary from year to year depending upon the number of changes in Utah Gun Law. My name and address are:

Name: ________________________________
Address: ______________________________
____
____
e-mail ________________________________

Mail to: Attorney "Mitch" Vilos
PO Box 1148
Centerville, UT 84014

OR: Just email me at mitchv@firearmslaw.com and tell me you want to know of future updates.

APPENDIX E

Request to be notified of publishing of *Utah Self Defense Law*

Receive notification of the publishing of ***Utah's Laws of Self Defense*** for family, friends and legislators.

Just fill out this form and mail it to:

Attorney "Mitch" Vilos
PO Box 1148
Centerville, UT 84014

Please notify me when your new book about Utah's laws of self defense is published:

Name: ______________________________
Address: ____________________________
____
____
Phone # (____) ______________________

or:

Just email me at Mitchv@firearmslaw.com and tell me you want to be notified about my book on Self-Defense.

APPENDIX F

Youngsters, Guns and Ammo

Caution: The laws discussed below relate to age only; don't forget there are other laws that apply to purchasing or transferring a firearm, such as those that apply to transactions across state lines.

Age	≥ 21[1]	≥ 18 < 21[2]	≥ 16 < 18	≥ 14 < 16	≥ 12 < 14	< 12
Concealed Weapon Permit	Yes, if Good Character	No	No	No	No	No
Buy Handgun	Yes	No/Yes[3]	No[4]	No	No	No
Possess[5] Handgun	Yes	Yes	For limited purposes w/ parents written permission on person[6]	For limited purposes w/ parents written permission on person[7]	For limited purposes w/ parents written permission on person and accomp'd by respon-sible adult[8]	For limited purposes w/ parents written permission on person and accomp'd by respon-sible adult[9]
Buy Handgun Ammo	Yes	No/Yes[10]	No	No	No	No
Possess Handgun Ammo	Yes	Yes	For limited purposes w/ parents written permission on person[11]	For limited purposes w/ parents written permission on person	For limited purposes w/ parents written permission on person	For limited purposes w/ parents written permission on person
Buy Rifle Shotgun	Yes	Yes	Not from dealer, but from anyone else if accomp'd by parent[12]	Not from dealer, but from anyone else if accomp'd by parent	Not from dealer, but from anyone else if accomp'd by parent	Not from dealer, but from anyone else if accomp'd by parent
Possess Rifle Shotgun	Yes	Yes	Yes, but must permitted OR accomp'd by parent[13]	Yes, but must permitted OR accomp'd by parent[14]	Yes, but must be accomp'd by respon-sible adult[15]	Yes, but must be accomp'd by respon-sible adult[16]

Age	≥ 21[1]	≥ 18 < 21[2]	≥ 16 < 18	≥ 14 < 16	≥ 12 < 14	< 12
Buy Rifle Shotgun Ammo	Yes	Yes	Not from a gun dealer,[17] but from anyone else	Not from a gun dealer, but from anyone else	Not from a gun dealer, but from anyone else	Not from a gun dealer, but from anyone else
Possess Rifle Shotgun Ammo	Yes	Yes	Yes	Yes	Yes	Yes
Hunt Big Game	Yes	Yes	Yes	Yes, accomp by parent, or adult 21 and OK w/ parent[18]	Yes, accomp by parent, or adult 21 and OK w/ parent[19]	No[20]
Hunt Small Game	Yes	Yes	Yes	Yes, must be accomp'd by adult[21]	Yes, must be accomp'd by parent[22]	Yes[23]
Possess Other Dangerous Weapon	Yes	Yes	Yes, but must be permitted OR accomp'd by parent[24]	Yes, but must be permitted OR accomp'd by parent	Yes, must be accomp'd by respon-sible adult[25]	Yes, must be accomp'd by respon-sible adult
Possess Machine Gun	Yes, under certain conditions[26]	No	No[27]	No	No	No

1. Just in case you've forgotten your math symbols, this means, "greater than or equal to 21" years of age, or put another way, 21 years old or older.
2. One more translation just in case your have a mental block for math symbols. This means, "greater than or equal to 18, but less than 21" years of age, i.e., 18, 19, and 20 years of age.
3. A person at least 18, but younger than 21 cannot buy a handgun from a gun dealer, 18 U.S.C. 922(b)(1). However, 18, 19 and 20 year old people can buy a handgun from a person who is not a gun dealer, 18 U.S.C. 922(x)(1) (see Chapter XIII of this book). DO NOT BE TEMPTED TO ACT AS A "MIDDLEMAN" (also referred to as a "straw purchase") TO BUY GUNS FROM GUN DEALERS FOR PEOPLE UNDER 21! IT'S A FELONY! U.C.A. 76-10-527 (4) "A person is guilty of a felony of the third degree who purchases a handgun with the intent to: (a) resell or otherwise provide a handgun to any person who is ineligible to purchase or receive from a dealer a handgun; or (b) transport a handgun out of this state to be resold to an ineligible person." This law splits hairs. As long as the non-dealer does not have the INTENT AT THE TIME HE OR SHE PURCHASES THE GUN, to transfer it to a person under 21, it can legally be sold to a person 18 or older, but younger than 21. It's legal for grandpa, who bought his pistol 5 years ago, intending to keep it, to give or sell it, to his granddaughter who is 18; but he cannot buy it from a dealer with the intent to transfer it to his granddaughter.

4. Federal law, 18 U.S.C. § 922(x)(1), forbids anyone to sell a handgun to a person under 18 years of age. State law, U.C.A. 76-10-509.9 states, "(1) A person may not sell any firearm to a minor under 18 years of age unless the minor is accompanied by a parent or guardian. (2) Any person who violates this section is guilty of a third degree felony." Unfortunately, Utah state law suggests that a person could sell a handgun to a minor under 18 years of age if the minor was accompanied by a parent or guardian. Of course, this is illegal under federal law. Therefore, state law could mislead a person into violating federal law.
5. These handgun rules assume the person is not hunting. If a minor is hunting, he will usually need to be accompanied by someone older and with a closer relationship than if he is merely shooting, but not hunting. For example, a 13 year old who is not hunting needs only to be accompanied by a responsible adult, i.e., someone older than eighteen (U.C.A. 76-10-509(2), found in Chapter VII of this book). However, if the 13 year old is hunting, he must be accompanied either by a parent or guardian, or someone 21 or older, approved by his parent or guardian, U.C.A. 23-20-20(2), (discussed in Chapter IX).
6. Federal law requires a minor to keep a parent's written permission with him or her while possessing a handgun. 18 U.S.C. 922(x)(2),(3). Read more about this in Chapter XIII. The state law is U.C.A. 76-10-509, which says:

   "(1) A minor under 18 years of age may not possess a dangerous weapon unless he:

   (a) has the permission of his parent or guardian to have the weapon; or

   (b) is accompanied by a parent or guardian while he has the weapon in his possession."

   Notice that there is an "or" between (a) and (b) above. This means if a child is under 18 years of age and has the permission of his parent or guardian, he need not be accompanied by the parent or guardian (unless he is under 14 years of age or hunting, see applicable rules below). Therefore, if kids 14-17 years of age have written permission from their parents to possess a handgun, they do not need to be accompanied by a parent or guardian.
7. Same rule applies to kids 14 and older, but less than 16; see footnote 6 above.
8. U.C.A. 76-10-509(2) "Any minor under 14 years of age in possession of a dangerous weapon shall be accompanied by a responsible adult." (Read more about this in Chapter VII).
9. U.C.A. 76-10-509(2) "Any minor under 14 years of age in possession of a dangerous weapon shall be accompanied by a responsible adult." (Chapter VII).
10. A person at least 18, but younger than 21 cannot buy handgun ammunition from a gun dealer, 18 U.S.C. 922(b)(1), but can buy handgun ammunition from a person who is not a gun dealer, 18 U.S.C. 922(x)(1) (Chapter XIII). But see "middleman" precautions in footnote 3 above.
11. 18 U.S.C. 922(x)(2), (3), discussed in Chapter XIII.
12. A person younger than 18 cannot buy a any weapon from a gun dealer, 18 U.S.C. 922(b)(1), but there is no federal prohibition for a minor to buy a rifle or shotgun from someone who is not a gun dealer. This is left to state law and Utah has enacted U.C.A. 76-10-509.9 that states: "(1) A person may not sell any firearm to a minor under 18 years of age unless the minor is accompanied by a parent or guardian. (2) Any person who violates this section is guilty of a third degree felony." See Chapters VII and XIII.
13. U.C.A. 76-10-509(1), Chapter VII in this book.
14. U.C.A. 76-10-509(1), Chapter VII in this book.
15. U.C.A. 76-10-509(2) "Any minor under 14 years of age in possession of a dangerous weapon shall be accompanied by a responsible adult." (At first blush, this looks like it's less restrictive than for kids 14 - 17 years old; but the older kids don't need to be accompanied if they have their parents permission).
16. U.C.A. 76-10-509(2), ditto (for you Rush Limbaugh fans).
17. 18 U.S.C. 922(b)(1), the text of which is in Chapter XIII. Because federal law prohibits the sale of any ammunition to a person under 18 years of age, a person buying ammunition with the intent of "acting as a middle man" could be held criminally liable for "aiding and abetting" a gun dealer to violate federal law by selling rifle or shotgun ammunition to someone under 18. If, however, a person possesses rifle or shotgun ammunition and later decides to sell to a minor, this is probably legal.
18. U.C.A. 23-20-20(3) A person younger than 16 years old who is hunting big game with any weapon must be accompanied by:

    (a) the person's parent or legal guardian; or

    (b) a responsible person who is at least 21 years old and who is approved by the person's parent or guardian.

19. U.C.A. 23-20-20 (2) A person younger than 14 years old who is hunting with any weapon must be accompanied by:

    (a) the person's parent or legal guardian; or

    (b) a responsible person who is at least 21 years old and who is approved by the person's parent or guardian.
20. Children under 12 years of age may not hunt big game in Utah. UCA 23-19-22. Chapter IX.
21. U.C.A. 23-20-20(4)A person who is at least 14 years old but younger than 16 years old must be accompanied by a person who is at least 21 years old while hunting wildlife, other than big game, with any weapon.
22. U.C.A. 23-20-20(2) A person younger than 14 years old who is hunting with any weapon must be accompanied by:

    (a) the person's parent or legal guardian; or

    (b) a responsible person who is at least 21 years old and who is approved by the person's parent or guardian.
23. Children under 12 may now hunt wild turkeys and small game. U.C.A. 23-19-17 & 22.6 [not included in book].
24. U.C.A. 76-10-509(1), see discussion in Chapter VII.
25. U.C.A. 76-10-509(2), Chapter VII.
26. A citizen may purchase and possess a machine gun if he gets approval and pays the required fees set forth in the National Firearms Act, which is beyond the scope of this book. Contact the Bureau of Alcohol, Tobacco and Firearms. If a person possesses a machine gun illegally, the penalty is imprisonment up to 10 years, 18 U.S.C. 922(o), 18 U.S.C. 924(2). See Chapter XIII.
27. U.C.A 76-10-509.4(4) makes it a third degree felony for minors to possess a machine gun or a sawed-off shotgun or rifle. It is also a felony for an adult to let a minor have access to any of these weapons U.C.A. 76-10-509.5. See discussion in Chapter VII. It is also a federal felony for anyone, let alone a minor, to possess an unregistered machine gun or other weapon regulated by the National Firearms Act.

Pancho's Wisdom

If you're too busy to teach yer kids to shoot and hunt, you're too damned busy.

APPENDIX G

Maps of National Forest Lands in Davis County Closed to Shooting

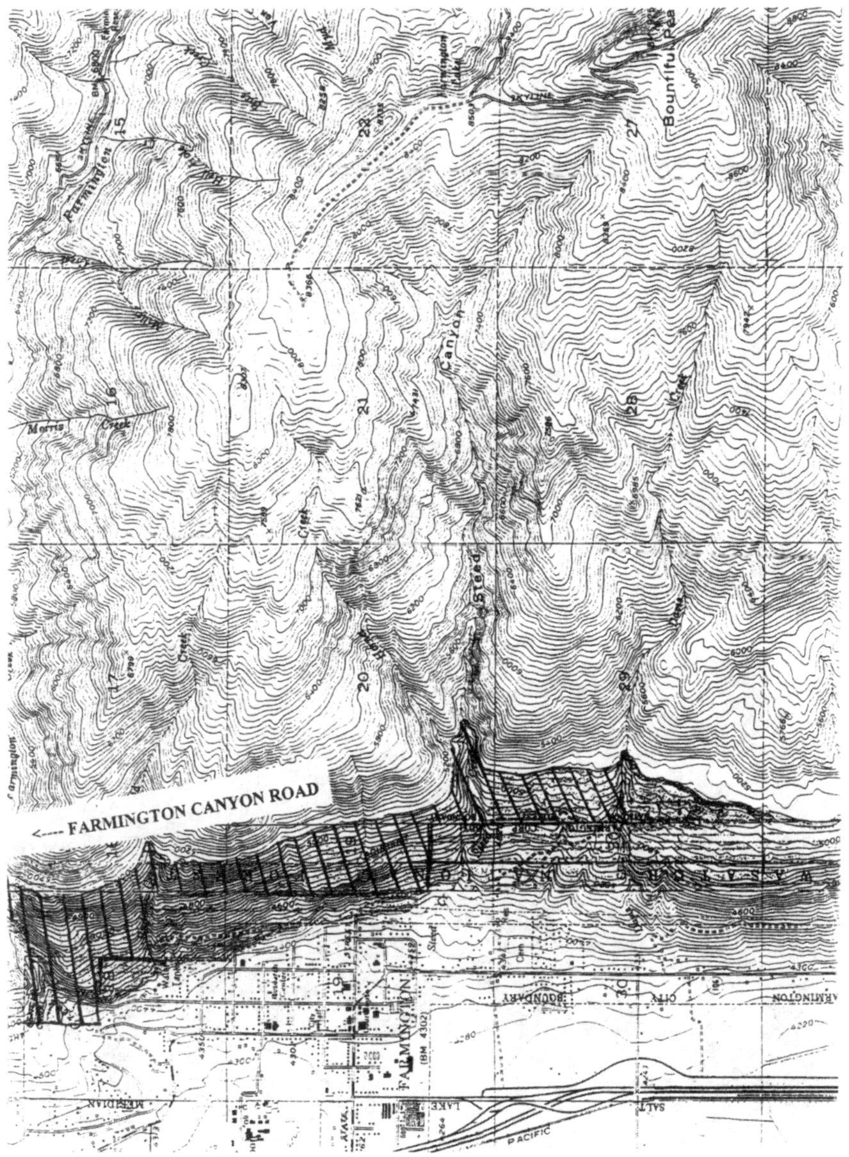

NATIONAL FOREST LANDS
CLOSED TO SHOOTING
NON-FEDERAL LANDS

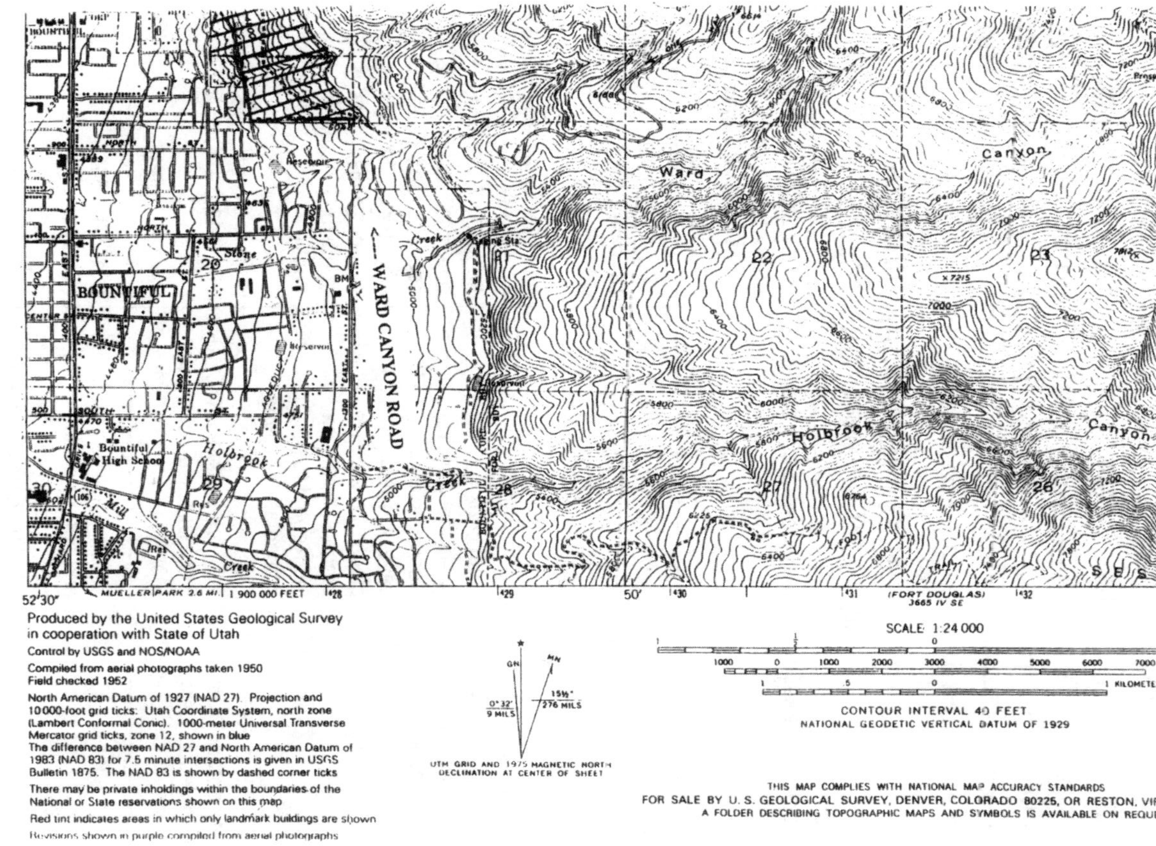
WARD CANYON ROAD
Ward
Canyon
Holbrook
Canyon
BOUNTIFUL
Bountiful High School
Holbrook
Creek
Mill
MUELLER PARK 2.6 MI.
1 900 000 FEET
52'30"
(FORT DOUGLAS)
3665 IV SE
Produced by the United States Geological Survey
in cooperation with State of Utah
Control by USGS and NOS/NOAA
Compiled from aerial photographs taken 1950
Field checked 1952
North American Datum of 1927 (NAD 27). Projection and 10 000-foot grid ticks: Utah Coordinate System, north zone (Lambert Conformal Conic). 1000-meter Universal Transverse Mercator grid ticks, zone 12, shown in blue
The difference between NAD 27 and North American Datum of 1983 (NAD 83) for 7.5 minute intersections is given in USGS Bulletin 1875. The NAD 83 is shown by dashed corner ticks
There may be private inholdings within the boundaries of the National or State reservations shown on this map
Red tint indicates areas in which only landmark buildings are shown
Revisions shown in purple compiled from aerial photographs
UTM GRID AND 1975 MAGNETIC NORTH DECLINATION AT CENTER OF SHEET
SCALE 1:24 000
CONTOUR INTERVAL 40 FEET
NATIONAL GEODETIC VERTICAL DATUM OF 1929
THIS MAP COMPLIES WITH NATIONAL MAP ACCURACY STANDARDS
FOR SALE BY U. S. GEOLOGICAL SURVEY, DENVER, COLORADO 80225, OR RESTON, VIR
A FOLDER DESCRIBING TOPOGRAPHIC MAPS AND SYMBOLS IS AVAILABLE ON REQUE

APPENDIX H
QUICK DRAW GUN LAW

The following two tables provide "simplified" rules for possessing guns in different places. Notice that Table I applies to people WITHOUT a concealed weapons permit and Table II applies to people WITH a concealed weapon permit. Consult relevant statutes (primarily found in Chapters VII, VIII and XIII) for detailed discussion.

TABLE I – POSSESSING A FIREARMWITHOUT A CONCEALED WEAPON PERMIT

Place of possession	Is Firearm permitted?	Relevant statutes(Bold indicates Federal statutes) & Book Chapter
Home	Yes - loaded (76-10-511).	U.C.A. 76-10-500 and 501 (Chapter VII)
Place of business	Yes.	U.C.A. 76-10-500 and 501 (Chapter VII)
Curtilage (place immediately around your house)	Utah code doesn't specifically address this in weapons laws but 511 says "at (as opposed to in) place of residence" which probably could be interpreted to mean immediately around.	500, 501, 511 (unless otherwise stated these sections are in Title 76, Chapter 10 -Weapons, which are discussed in depth in Chapter VII of this book)
Temporary Residence, camp	Yes - okay loaded (76-10-511). Definition of loaded (502).	501, 511 (Chapter VII)
Automobile	Yes, but not loaded (505) and not concealed (504). Not considered concealed if it is "securely encased" which means completely enclosed in container, even though not locked, or in a gun rack. However, gun cannot be placed in glove box or console (501).	501, 504, 505 (Chapter VII)

Place of possession	Is Firearm permitted?	Relevant statutes(Bold indicates Federal statutes) & Book Chapter
Open Carry	Yes, but if loaded cannot carry on public street. Caution: carrying openly could get you arrested for causing a disturbance or threatening with a deadly weapon if your intentions are misinterpreted by someone.	505 (Chapter VII)
Concealed Carry	No.	504 (Chapter VII)
Public places	Yes, but generally not loaded.	505 (Chapter VII)
State Government offices	Yes (see 502, 505), but you cannot take gun into secured area of jail, mental institution, or courthouse.	502, 505, 523.5 and 529 (Chapter VII)
Federal building (including post office)	No, if posted or you know it's illegal (now you know).	**18 USC 930 (Chapter XIII) & 39 CFR § 232.1**
Natl Park	Yes, buy only if locked away to prevent ready use, or if permitted for hunting under state law.	**36 CFR 2.4 (Chapter XIII)**
Natl Forest	Yes, unless subject to federal closure order.	**36 CFR 261.10 & 261.58** (Ch. XIII) e.g. Appendix G
State Park	Yes, in camp or tent, but watch out for regulation prohibiting firearms in state parks (this reg is probably unenforceable if you are using gun to protect a temporary dwelling).	500, 501 and 511, (Chapter VII) but see R651-612-1 (Chapter IX)

Pancho's Wisdom

Modern gunslingers no longer "slap leather;" they "palpate polymer!"

Place of possession	Is Firearm permitted?	Relevant statutes(Bold indicates Federal statutes) & Book Chapter
Schools	No.	**18 U.S.C. § 922(q)** 505.5 (Ch. VII); 53A-3-502 (Ch. VIII)
Churches, another person's private residence	Yes, unless notified orally or in writing that firearms are prohibited.	530 (Ch. VII)
In Vehicle	Yes, but not loaded (505) and not concealed (504). Okay if "securely en-cased" (501)which means completely enclosed even though not locked, or in a gun rack, but not in the glove box or console.	504, 505 (Ch. VII)
Interstate Buses & Trains	No guns allowed in passenger compartment. Weapons must be declared and locked in case in luggage compartment.	1504**, 18 U.S.C. § 922(e)** Chapters VII and XIII
Local Buses (UTA) and TRAX	No, and it's a felony if you do!	1504, Chapter VII
Airplanes	No guns allowed in passenger compartment. Weapons must be declared and placed in locked case in luggage compartment.	**18 U.S.C. § 922(e) (Chapter XIII)**
Other secured areas e.g. courts and jails	No.	523.5 and 529,(Ch. VII) U.C.A. 53-5-704 (Ch. VIII)
Interstate Transportation	Okay to transport through states and cities where firearms prohibited if not loaded and not readily accessible. Use extra caution when traveling to "gun-hating" states like NY, NJ, Cal, Wash DC whose officials refuse to comply with federal law.	**18 U.S.C. § 926A (Chapter XIII)**

TABLE II – POSSESSING A FIREARM WITH CONCEALED WEAPON PERMIT

Place of possession	Is Firearm permitted?	Relevant statutes (Bold indicates Federal statutes)
Home	Yes - loaded (76-10-511).	U.C.A. 76-10-500 and 501 (Ch. VII)
Place of business	Yes, permit is valid throughout the state without restriction.	U.C.A. 76-10-500 and 501, (Ch. VII) U.C.A. 53-5-704 (see summary at end of Ch. VIII)
Curtilage (place immediately around your house)	Utah code doesn't specifically address this in weapons laws but 511 says "at (as opposed to "in") place of residence" which probably could be interpreted to mean immediately around.	500, 501, 511 (unless otherwise stated these sections are in Title 76, Chapter 10 -Weapons and discussed in detail in Chapter VII)
Temporary Residence, camp	Yes - okay loaded (76-10-511). Definition of loaded (502).	500, 501 (Ch. VII)
Automobile	Yes, even loaded and concealed.	505, 523 (Ch. VII)
Open Carry	Yes, even loaded. Caution: carrying openly could get you arrested for causing a disturbance or threatening with a deadly weapon if your intentions are misinterpreted.	505, 523 (Ch. VII)
Concealed Carry	Yes.	U.C.A. 53-5-704 (Ch. VIII)
Public places	Yes.	U.C.A. 53-5-704 (Ch. VIII)
State government offices	Yes, but not in secured areas of jail, mental institution, or courthouse.	523.5 and 529 (Ch. VII)

Place of possession	Is Firearm permitted?	Relevant statutes (Bold indicates Federal statutes)
Federal building (including post office)	No, if posted or you know it's illegal (you know now).	**18 USC 930 and 39 CFR § 232.1 (Chapter XIII)**
Natl Park	Yes, but only if locked away to prevent ready use, or if permitted for hunting under state law.	**36 CFR 2.4 (Chapter XIII)**
Natl Forest	Yes, unless subject to federal closure order.	**36 CFR 261.10 & 261.58** (Ch. XIII) e.g. Appendix G
State Park	Yes.	500, 501 and 511, (Ch. VII) R651-612-1 (Ch. IX)
Schools	Yes.	**18 USC § 922(q)** 505.5; 53A-3-502 (Ch. VII)
Churches, another person's private residence	Yes, unless notified orally or in writing that firearms are prohibited.	530 (Ch. VII)
In Vehicle	Yes, loaded and concealed.	505, 523 (Ch. VII)
Interstate Buses and Trains	Not in passenger compartment, but okay w/ luggage if declared to bus company and locked in case in suitcase in luggage compartment.	1504**, 18 U.S.C. § 922(e)** Chapters VII and XIII
Local Buses (UTA) and TRAX	Yes.	1504 (Ch. VII)
Airplanes	Not in passenger compartment, but okay w/ luggage if declared to ticket agent and locked in case in suitcase in luggage compartment.	**18 U.S.C. § 922(e) (Chapter XIII)**

Place of possession	Is Firearm permitted?	Relevant statutes (Bold Indicates Federal statutes) & Book Chapter
Other secured areas e.g. courts and jails	No.	523.5 and 529,(Ch. VII) U.C.A. 53-5-704 (Ch. VIII)
Interstate Transportation	Yes, if just passing through and firearm is unloaded and not readily accessible. Use extra caution when traveling to "gun-hating" states like NY, NJ, Cal, Wash DC whose officials refuse to comply with federal law.	**18 U.S.C. § 926A (Chapter XIII)**

C ya in Gun Law IV… Aloha and Mahalo!